The Next Founders

The
Next
Founders

*Voices of Democracy
in the Middle East*

Joshua Muravchik

ENCOUNTER BOOKS
NEW YORK · LONDON

First American edition published in 2009 by Encounter Books, an activity of Encounter for Culture and Education, Inc., a nonprofit, tax exempt corporation.
Encounter Books website address: www.encounterbooks.com

Manufactured in the United States and printed on acid-free paper. The paper used in this publication meets the minimum requirements of ANSI/NISO Z39.48 1992 (R 1997) (Permanence of Paper).

FIRST AMERICAN EDITION

LIBRARY OF CONGRESS CATALOGING-IN-PUBLICATION DATA

Muravchik, Joshua.
    The next founders : voices of democracy in the Middle East / by Joshua Muravchik. — 1st ed.
        p.   cm.
    Includes bibliographical references.
    ISBN-13: 978-1-59403-232-5 (hardcover : alk. paper)
    ISBN-10: 1-59403-232-7 (hardcover : alk. paper)
        1.   Politicians—Middle East—Biography.   2.   Political activists—Middle East—Biography.   3.   Social reformers—Middle East—Biography.   4.   Middle East—Politics and government—1979–
5.   Democracy—Middle East.   6.   Social change—Middle East.
7.   Middle East—Biography.   I.   Title.
DS63.12.M87 2009
956.05'40922—dc22

                                                            2008053655

Contents

Introduction

Seedlings in the Desert

When I would tell people that I was writing a book about Middle Eastern democrats, the reaction was invariably the same: "That will be a short book." This jibe expressed the common knowledge that the region remains stubbornly autocratic. Roughly half of the countries are still ruled by hereditary royalty. More amazingly, those monarchies tend to be more liberal than the region's "republics" where ghastly tyranny is common, associated with names like Saddam Hussein, Hafez al-Assad, Muammar Qaddafi, Gamal Abdel Nasser, Yassir Arafat and Ayatollah Ruhollah Khomeini.

The fact that there is precious little democracy in the Middle East does not mean, however, that there are no democrats. In fact, surveys show that the vast majority say they want democracy, although it is uncertain what that term connotes to them. Perhaps more important, there are also individuals whose lives revolve around making their countries more free and democratic, and who have proven they understand well the meaning of those ideas. We know little about them because their work is peaceful and incremental, and therefore it is overshadowed by the shocking deeds and pronouncements of tyrants, terrorists, and religious fanatics.

I am about to introduce you to seven of them, six Arabs and an Iranian. Five are men; two, women. Four are Sunnis, two are Shiites, and one is mixed. Their goals are similar, but their métiers are diverse. One has reestablished a free press in Egypt. Another has won women the right to vote and run for office in Kuwait. A third has broken Iraq's fiercest taboo. A fourth may yet unseat Iran's ayatollahs whom he did much to bring to power.

Each of these individuals was raised under a highly authoritarian regime in a society hidebound in its customs.

Each belonged to a religious tradition that prized memorization over debate; each attended schools that stressed obedience and rote learning. They grew up learning that personal feelings and desires may have little effect on one's choices in life; that family connections may determine how much justice can be expected from courts; that disloyalty to those in power can consist of as little as a complaint and be punishable by as much as death; and that power is seized or retained through brutality. In such societies, obedience is the easiest way to live a long life.

How did they free their minds and become different from most around them? For some the answer lay in exposure to the West, especially in study abroad. For others, to borrow a phrase from the sixties, the personal became political. Each of the women saw her mother's life blighted by polygamy. Some of the group experienced persecution or watched their parents persecuted for being of the wrong class or religious sect. One was a free spirit who might have been content to live the life of a poet if the authorities had only made room for that. Several of the men gagged on the raw regime brutality that they witnessed up close.

And for each of these seven, to invert the slogan, the political is also highly personal. They have paid dear for their struggles. Four have been to prison, and four have had their lives threatened. Three have had their loved ones menaced or penalized. Two have recently been forced into exile, although both hope to return. One has dodged assassins and seen his children murdered. All have subordinated their material well-being to the cause for which they fight.

They share an uncommon courage. For most, that has meant the courage to face prison or even death. For all of them, it has meant the moral courage to march to their own drummer in societies that prize loyalty to family, clan and tribe—and do not hold individualism as a value. Several have had to resist pressure from family members to cease rocking the boat. Sometimes these interventions have been motivated by love and concern; other times by the selfish fear that the family will be penalized for the nonconformity of one among them. On the other hand, a few of these heroic troublemakers were quietly abetted by a parent—invariably the mother.

Their struggles are admirable in themselves and for what they are trying to do for their societies. But they also took on a special meaning for Americans after 9/11. For many years, U.S. policy toward the region was governed only by "strategic" considerations. America had promoted democracy in Eastern Europe, Latin America, and parts of East Asia. But our attitude toward Middle Eastern autocrats was, to borrow a phrase, that it was all right if they were bastards, if only they would be *our* bastards.

However, the massive terrorist attack on America prompted a reconsideration. Perhaps the internal affairs of Middle Eastern states *was* a strategic consideration for us. Terrorism had become a common tactic of Middle Eastern groups, sponsored, tolerated and condoned by the region's various governments. Public opinion polls showed that substantial minorities, if not majorities, of the citizenry supported or excused such actions. In short, terrorism found roots in the political culture of the Middle East. There, violence or the threat of violence had been the main currency of governance. The power to rule was gained and held by force. Politics was viewed as a zero-sum game, and the discourse surrounding it was chiliastic and apocalyptic, rich in extremism and conspiracy theories. It is this environment that bred so many young people willing to throw away their lives in some heroic act of mass murder.

Therefore if we wanted to see an end to Middle Eastern terrorism, it would not be sufficient to send our troops and drones and Special Forces to hunt and kill al Qaeda or arrest

Saddam Hussein. The larger challenge would be to encourage or catalyze the evolution of the region's political culture toward more peaceful ways and values, so that there will no longer be an endless supply of willing recruits to replace the terrorists we put out of action.

How might this come about? The most likely way is by democratization. Often we think of democracy as an effect rather than a cause, something that arises from other conditions. There is some truth to this. But the inverse is also true. The practice of democracy causes other effects, one of which is to socialize the people who grow up under it. They internalize habit of debating and voting, which sharpens the reason and breeds reasonableness. They learn the skills of compromise and conciliation, discouraging apocalypticism. Exposed to a free press and safe from the machinations of the secret police, they rarely fall prey to conspiracy theories. People imbued with the ways of mind of democracy generally find terrorism to be an outlandish and repugnant way to pursue a cause. Democratic countries sometimes produce homegrown terrorists, but never in large numbers.

But is democracy in the Middle East a realistic goal? In truth, no one knows. What we know is that democracy has spread to many places where it once seemed unlikely. As of the early 1970s, less than one-third of the states of the world were governed by rulers chosen in genuine elections. Thirty years later, that share had doubled to above 60 percent. In other words, under our noses, so to speak, a profound transformation has taken place in the way the world is governed. Democracy has become the norm.

However, this revolution has until now failed to reach one region, the Muslim Middle East where not a single democracy can be found. In comparison, about 70 percent of the rest of the nations of the world are democratic. No one can account for the contrast. To be sure, the dearth of democracy in the Middle East is due in part to its economic backwardness. Globally, democracy correlates strongly with wealth: most rich countries are democracies. But the correlations of this and other socioeconomic factors are not perfect. Some rich countries are not democratic. For example, Singapore enjoys a standard of living virtually equal to that of the United States, yet it has not followed the other wealthy East Asian states to democracy. Under Vladimir Putin, Russia has grown wealthier and less democratic. And the rich Arab countries are no more democratic than the poor ones. There are also exceptions of the converse kind: countries that lack the socioeconomic correlates but are democratic nonetheless. Eleven African states where the average citizen lived on less than 4 dollars a day were electoral democracies as of 2008.

Why did they turn toward democracy, however imperfect or fragile? The only apparent reason is that leaders, movements, and publics made considered choices to do so. It is doubtful that South Africa, a country of so many tears, would have metamorphosed peacefully to democracy were it not for the grace of Nelson Mandela; nor El Salvador without José Napoleón Duarte. The reverse is also true—Russia and many other countries would have had more democracy were it not for the evil genius of Lenin. Egypt and perhaps the rest of the Middle East would be more democratic today were it not for Nasser's charismatic authoritarianism.

It is not only great (or terrible) individual leaders who can make the difference. Poland led the transformation of Communist Europe thanks to a mass labor organization, *Solidarnosc*. In India, Indira Gandhi's bid to impose authoritarian rule was turned back in 1977 by a grass-roots outpouring, showing that democracy in this impoverished country divided along lines of nationality, religion and caste, rested on the cherished convictions of its citizenry. In other words, a critical requisite of democracy is democrats—people who believe in democracy and are ready to work or fight for it.

Although objective factors may help determine whether a country is ripe for democracy, subjective factors count, too, and may even trump them. Since the former seem not to work in the usual way in the Middle East, the chances for democracy depend on the latter. The power of ideas in the politics of the Middle East is amply demonstrated by the history of the last century. Apart from the advent of oil wealth, socioeconomic change has come slowly, but waves of ideology—fascist, Communist, socialist, nationalist, pan-Arab, Islamist—have swept over the region, changing regimes and sometimes even redrawing maps.

There is no reason why the democratic idea cannot have a rebirth in the Middle East, where it was popular in the early twentieth century before being upstaged by the false promises of utopian ideologies, nor that democracy itself cannot come to the region. Whether it does in our time will depend on the activists, journalists, politicians, feminists, dissidents, bloggers and other Middle Easterners who are working to advance the democratic cause in their own countries, at great sacrifice and risk. Our role as Americans is to encourage and assist them and to protect them from persecution to the extent that we can. We can begin by learning about them.

Like those who have teased me about a "short book," I did not know such people existed until I began to meet them at the rash of international conferences that broke out after 9/11. As I got to know them and to trust that they were the real thing, I grew excited and wanted to tell my countrymen about them. Hence this book.

The seven whom I have chosen to portray are very special individuals, but they are not unique. Each has co-thinkers, allies and collaborators, albeit fewer than I would wish. I make no claim that these seven are the most important ones: I would not know how to make such a judgment. But each of them is fascinating and admirable—and I am certain that each of them is having an important effect. Democracy will in all likelihood come to the Middle East within a generation, and they will be remembered as among its founders. Much more, no doubt, will be then written about them. Until then, I hope that the portraits sketched here will stand as useful first cuts.

The Protester

Saudi Arabia: Wajeha Al-Huwaider

The four-lane King Fahd Causeway stretches 26 miles across the gulf of Bahrain, linking that tiny island nation to its overshadowing mainland neighbor, Saudi Arabia, whose King Fahd commissioned and paid for the road and laid its cornerstone. Much to the disgust of Bahrainis, albeit to the great benefit of their economy, Saudi men regularly avail themselves of this fast route to their more liberal neighbor to drink alcohol and indulge in other pleasures of the flesh that are strictly forbidden and mercilessly punished in their own kingdom. The road was thus perhaps aptly named because Fahd had the reputation as the most dissolute of monarchs.

On August 4, 2006, amidst the flow of Saudi men returning home worse for the wear of a night's revelry, a far less typical traveler crossed the border. When her taxi reached the Saudi side of the manmade island that denotes the frontier, she got out and proceeded on foot. It was already hot at 6AM on a day when the temperature on the mainland would peak at 111 degrees Fahrenheit. It would have been hotter still in an abbaya, the colorless, shapeless cloak worn over other clothing, that is *de rigueur* for Saudi women. But she had determined to do without one that day. Instead she draped her body in a flowing pink Pakistani-style garment, choosing it as a reproach to the deathly black "tent" usually forced on women. Lest she be accused of immodesty, she made sure it concealed her body from wrist to neck to ankle. Her hair was covered by a scarf, but, in further daring, she allowed a few locks to peek out. As she began to walk, she pulled out a placard, holding it aloft for oncoming motorists. It read: "Give Women Their Rights."

Twenty minutes into her trek, the woman was surrounded by security officers and bundled off. They confiscated her sign, took her passport so that she could not return to Bahrain, and detained her for the rest of the day. Once a member of the religious police arrived, as required by Saudi protocol for female prisoners, she was interrogated. When they had asked their questions, the police were willing to release her, but only into the hands of a male relative. Otherwise she would have to stay in jail, as she did for several more hours until her younger brother arrived to collect her. Under Saudi rules, a woman cannot be released into her own custody but only into that of a male "guardian." This, of course, exemplified the point of her protest.

The woman was Wajeha Al-Huwaider, a forty-five-year-old divorced mother of two teenage sons. She worked as an educational specialist at Aramco, the Arab American Oil Company, although she was off that day because it was Friday, when offices in Muslim countries are closed. She had chosen the date because it was the first anniversary of the ascension of Abdullah, who had succeeded Fahd to the Saudi throne.

A year before she had greeted Abdullah's coronation with guarded optimism, urging him on in a news interview: "We need real things to happen."[1] His first year had already disappointed her, and she had begun to believe that "although King Abdullah is a sincere man with genuine heart, his brothers are not going to let him make a lot of reforms."[2]

The reason interviewers had sought her comment was that she had made a name for herself by her commentaries in newspapers and postings on the Internet, authored in her spare time. In a country where the number of political dissidents could be counted by the handfuls and the women among them perhaps on one hand, she was known as an advocate of change even before her unprecedented solo demonstration on the causeway.

Wajeha had been born into a Shiite family in 1961, three years before the inauguration of public schooling for girls in Saudi Arabia. Her birthplace was the town of Hufuf in the eastern region of Saudi Arabia called al-Hasa, which had been the seat of the tenth century Qarmatian empire, a fanatic offshoot of Ismaili Islam that pillaged Mecca and brought back the sacred Black Stone as a trophy. Today, locals boast that al-Hasa produces the world's tastiest dates. Of greater political significance, it also contains the largest share of the country's proven petroleum reserves, and it is populated largely by Shiites in an otherwise mostly Sunni country whose religious authorities place little value on pluralism.

Wajeha's mother, Salma, was native to the town, the daughter of a sometime-pearl-diver and veteran of the army of Abdel Aziz, who had subjugated the Peninsula, making himself the first king of contemporary Saudi Arabia. Wajeha's father was Hussein, four or five years younger than Salma, the scion of a family that owned a goodly portion of land in a small village nearby.

Hussein was the twelfth child born to a famous local beauty named Mariam, in the course of four marriages. Heartrendingly, all eleven of the older ones had died in birth or young childhood, making Mariam fearfully protective of Hussein. She refused to let him out of the house at all, lest he succumb to the same thing that she suspected had felled her first eleven: the evil eye. The evil eye is a fear spoken about in other faiths, too, but in Islam it has special undergirding because the Prophet was quoted as affirming its reality. It would have been normal for a boy of his economic station to go to school, at least to learn to read and write. But Mariam would not let Hussein out of her sight.

When he reached fourteen, Hussein ran away from his mother's tight grip, finding work in another part of the country. After two years, he returned to the eastern province to take a job in the burgeoning oil industry but kept his distance from his suffocating mother. He married a local girl, his cousin, but soon grew discontent with her. The wages paid by Aramco, where he now was employed, made it feasible for many of its Saudi employees to take three or four wives. So

Hussein approached a local sheikh who doubled as a match-maker and described what he had in mind. He was interested in a girl from a big city like Hufuf, in contrast to his hick of a first wife. And above all he wanted one with white skin, a great mark of beauty, in contrast to his swarthy cousin.

The sheikh found Salma, and the match was made. Although employment by a big payer like Aramco was in itself usually enough to make a prospective bride's family leap at the offer, the sheikh did not want to take chances, so he lied about Hussein's marital status, claiming he was single. Some-time after the wedding, when Salma eventually learned the truth from her new mother-in-law, she was furious. Out of pity or pride, she rebuffed Hussein's offer to divorce the first wife, but he did it anyway, and after a time, Salma forgot her pain.

She and Hussein had six children of whom Wajeha was the fourth. The day in November 1961 when she was born was the anniversary on the Islamic calendar of the birth of the Prophet's daughter, Fatimah. One of Fatimah's nicknames was Wajeha, Arabic for "perfection," and so Salma and Hussein decided to give their little girl this name.

Just after the birth of their fifth child, Ghalib, when Wajeha was five, Hussein told Salma that he was taking an additional wife. This, naturally, was even more of a blow than her discovery of his first wife. In that case, at least, she was made to feel that she was the favored one. Now, it seemed, she would play second fiddle.

Naturally, Wajeha did not understand what was going on. "My mom used to cry a lot," she recalls.[3] Worse, Salma left home several times to stay with her brother in a nearby town. She could not take the children with her because under Islamic law they belong to the father. They remained in the care of their two grandmothers, who lived with the family.

Each time, Salma would return after extracting a prom-ise from Hussein to divorce the new wife. Each time he reneged. Until his death forty-odd years later he remained married to both women. Salma had one more child by him while the other wife remained without offspring. Ordinarily in the Arab world, producing children is the measure of a woman's worth, but Hussein preferred the barren wife who doted on him with the same single-minded attention his mother had shown. In contrast, whenever he came to see Salma, she would pour out her aggrieved feelings. This was of course self-defeating: his stays grew briefer and less frequent until they ceased entirely.

Salma nursed a lifelong sense of loss and betrayal. She attempted to instill in her daughters the bitter lesson she felt she had learned: "You should not trust men. Men are all after one thing." Curiously, this warning was reinforced by Hussein, himself, who used to warn his daughters that "Men are like beasts. They will jump at you." Yet, despite these admonitions, Wajeha did not come to fear or distrust men. She did, however, absorb a poignant sense of her mother's suffering, and it helped to shape her. She says:

> I think today I am fighting for my mother more than for anybody else. Year after year, I saw her crying, I saw her in pain. She wasted her life waiting for my father to come back.... She had no income and she felt hopeless. She could not leave the house. She decided to live for us kids.

Although Salma was deeply pious and made an occupation as a *mullahya,* the female equivalent of *mullah,* qualified to perform elementary religious functions, she was not rigid in her practice. She did not believe that women's faces needed to be covered nor in other forms of extreme separation of the sexes, and she raised her children with considerable liberty. Most important to Wajeha, Salma did not object to her playing with boys. Wajeha loved hide-and-seek and other physical games that held little interest for her sister and female cousins. In short, Wajeha was a tomboy:

I remember once my sister got in trouble with a big guy. I do not know what the problem was, but I came from the house running, and he was talking to my sister harshly, and then he gave us his back. I jumped on him and knocked him down and ran away with my sister. I was defending her.

She was lucky, in a sense, that her father was rarely present because, being rural in outlook, his ways were more conservative. In villages like the one he came from, mixed play was rarely tolerated. More important, although public education for girls had been inaugurated in the kingdom by the time Wajeha reached school age, Hussein would not allow her to go, though she and her mother wanted her to. It was not a matter of money, since schools were free, except for the uniforms. It was simply that Hussein did not believe girls should be educated, and Salma's efforts to persuade him proved futile. Even though he now lived mostly with his other wife and played little part in raising Wajeha, under Saudi law, a girl cannot be enrolled without the authorization of the father.

So instead, Salma sent Wajeha, at 7, to *katatib*, a kind of ersatz school, usually in someone's home, where youngsters of both sexes were taught to read the Koran. Wajeha hated it. There were a few boys in the *katatib*, but they were from strict homes and would not play with a girl. The teacher—who had taught Salma thirty years before—had grown old, bitter and mean. Although Wajeha was obedient at home, she was defiant at *katatib*, at least more so than the other girls. One afternoon, she played hooky, unable to tear herself from a soccer game in the street with the boys. Word got back to the teacher, and the next morning she tied seven-year-old Wajeha's legs and beat her with a stick. All through the beating, she scolded Wajeha, not for missing school but for the great impropriety of mixed-sex games.

The rest of the school day, Wajeha sat at her desk and cried, forbidden to get up even for water or to use the bathroom. "It was the worst day of my life," she says.

Six months later when the old lady died and the *katatib* closed, Wajeha shed no tears. After months of cajoling, Salma persuaded Hussein at last to let Wajeha enroll in public school. Wajeha believes that what changed his mind was the discovery that the girls in his new wife's family were being sent to school. He did not want his own children to be lower than them. In any event, at age eight, Wajeha began first grade.

She found the material challenging—science, math, and other things she had not been exposed to before—but the instruction was poor. Not only did the kingdom lack school buildings for girls, it also lacked teachers, so they were imported from other Arab countries, mostly Egypt and Palestine. Their methods were not designed to cultivate critical thinking, stressing instead memorization, obedience, severe punishments and verbal belittling of students. The Egyptian and Palestinian teachers tended to look on Saudis as their backward cousins which exacerbated the disdain they showed for their charges.

Wajeha was a top student, and for the most part avoided her teachers' wrath, although she harbors a piercing memory of being slapped in front of the whole school for having gone with another girl to the roof, which was off limits. They merely had been curious to see what was up there, but the headmistress suspected that they might have been trying to look at boys.

Junior high school proved more enjoyable because it was in a new building built by Aramco, and the facilities were designed to be child-friendly, even if the teaching methods were no different than elsewhere. The school had a gym for physical education but this was barred to girls (and remains so today), in part because of fear that they may take an interest in each other's bodies and in part for fear that the exertions would cause them to lose their "virginity," that is to rupture the hymen. For like reason, Wajeha was the sole girl in her neighborhood to ride a bike.

It was also in junior high, in eighth grade, that Wajeha had to begin covering herself, not merely in an abbaya over her clothes but also in a veil completely covering her head and face. There was not even a slit for the eyes; she had to peer out through the cloth. Today, such veiling is normally required to begin as early as fourth grade, but things were less stringent then.

The years of Wajeha's childhood had been a more relaxed time in Saudi history. Rules were loose enough so that she was able to enter adolescence unveiled. Even then, this was not universally tolerated, and she recalls being rebuked by strangers while walking to or from school. Once, Salma took her children on pilgrimage to Najaf and Karbala, Iraqi cities holy to Shia. Wajeha wore just a skirt and blouse, and she remembers people shouting at her mother, "Why is your daughter walking around like that?" Salma was so embarrassed that she went to the market for fabric and sewed a makeshift abbaya for her.

The tone of the country changed after the 1979 revolution in Iran in the name of Islamic orthodoxy. "Fear of repercussions from the 'Islamic revival' touched off by [Ayatollah Ruhollah] Khomeini's victory haunted the house of Saud," reported Sandra Mackey, an American historian living in the kingdom at the time.[4]

Indeed the repercussions followed fast and furious. In November a phalanx of three to five hundred heavily armed fanatics seized the great mosque at Mecca and held it for two weeks until they were routed with the help of a few French Special Forces officers who were given instantaneous conversions to Islam since non-Muslims may not enter the holy city. Including the insurgents, hundreds died, according to official statistics, which may have understated the toll. In response, the regime wrapped the cloak of piety around itself tighter than ever, unleashing the most intolerant zealots of the religious establishment, making the 1980s and 1990s an era of reaction.

Despite harsh new restrictions on the mingling of the sexes and her parents' warnings about men—and despite, too, some unsavory experiences to which she and her sister each had been subjected by the corner grocer—Wajeha was neither afraid of boys nor averse to them, especially not to one boy in particular. His name was Amin, and he was her cousin, about three years older. He was one of several male cousins to express an interest in her, she recalls: "I picked him because he was more promising than the others. He was smarter and better looking, and he had a future. I also liked him because he was a quiet and soft person I felt I could handle."

They became involved with each other when she was about fourteen, exchanging cards and love letters and seeing each other about once a month—when their families got together. "Everyone knew about us, and it was accepted," Wajeha recalls. What, exactly, was accepted? For the pair to sit together and converse during family gatherings. This was liberal by Saudi standards. To take a walk together was unthinkable much less to go to a movie. In any case, the country's few cinemas were closing under the growing weight of conservative retrenchment.

Still, films could be seen on television, and this was consequential. "We learned how to kiss because we watched movies and saw how to do it," she recalls. Although their physical contact did not go beyond kissing, still they were daring. Wajeha remembers one time when Amin stayed the night:

> We stayed up really late. He was to sleep in the guest room, and I was with him. Then we heard my father coming to check on us. He wanted to make sure that I was not with him.

I hid in back of the door, and my father opened the door and I was standing behind it. Amin was lying down in his bed and pretending that he was sleeping. And then my father left. He did not go and check my room because usually fathers do not go to girls' rooms.

Amin's family owned a car, and sometimes his mother would have him drive her (since Saudi women are not allowed to drive) to Wajeha's house to visit her mother. Then he would drive to Wajeha's high school and pick her up. "This was really a special treat," she recalls. "I was in love."

Being older, Amin graduated ahead of her and left for college in Tucson. Wajeha wrote love letters to him in America. When she received no replies she grew heartsick. Then one day a woman who lived nearby called on her. She explained that she had just returned from visiting her husband who was studying in Tucson with Amin who had asked her to deliver a letter to Wajeha. It said that he loved her and hoped to marry her someday.

Why, then, had her letters gone unanswered? Amin had in fact written repeatedly, but sending a letter to Saudi Arabia is not easy. While streets have names, buildings do not have numbers, meaning there are no formal addresses and therefore no mail delivery to people's homes. There is, however, a system of mail delivery to businesses, and Amin had posted his missives care of his father's business. The older man, however, had failed to pass them on.

This was because the two families had had a falling out. Amin's eldest brother was supposed to marry a cousin, but chose instead a girl to whom he was not kin. This outbreeding angered the rest of the extended family, including Wajeha's parents, who stayed away from the wedding, in turn angering the groom's parents.

When she read the hand-delivered letter, she wrote back at once, vowing that they would "stay together until the families find some solution" to their estrangement. By the time he returned for summer break after his second year in the States, the rift had been healed. Amin approached Wajeha's parents and asked for her hand. Salma rebuffed him for his lack of propriety. Young men do not propose for themselves. "Bring your parents," she demanded. Amin's father, who was Salma's brother, was terribly absorbed in his business, and he asked if he could not call Wajeha's parents, and settle the matter that way. Salma was indignant. "Since when do we get marriage proposals by phone?" Finally, the proprieties were observed, and the wedding was set. It was held in August, 1981, almost the same day, Wajeha recalls fancifully, as the wedding of Prince Charles and Diana. Wajeha was nineteen, older than many Saudi brides.

She had thought of studying to become a doctor. As she recalls, "for girls there were only two options—and, by the way, it has not changed—either be a teacher or go into the medical field." These two options were open because someone had to care for female patients and, after the advent of girls' schools, someone had to teach girls. It was deemed far preferable for the providers of services to be of the same sex as the recipients. Wajeha had earned high grades in science and math, so medicine seemed the logical pursuit. But her husband was returning to his studies at Pima College in Arizona, and her role was to go with him. Two days after the wedding they boarded a flight for America, leaving behind all thoughts of medical school.

In her seat on the plane, Wajeha reached down and pulled off her abbaya, which she had come to wear without resentment. Despite her rebellious streak, by her late teens, the good girl in Wajeha had mostly taken over. She even had taken to giving lectures to younger girls about the responsibilities of Muslim womanhood, although this seems to have been motivated more by trying to find her place than by deeply felt conviction.

But she knew she was going to someplace different, and she was ready to embrace the experience. "I wanted to try this new world, to be part of it," she recalls. When they disembarked at New York's John F. Kennedy Airport:

> I felt different walking around without the abbaya. I felt like I was naked. I felt everybody was looking at me. I looked around, and nobody was looking, but that was the feeling inside. And for the first time, I saw an escalator. I did not know that stairs could move. I was really scared. I could not use it. I used the regular stairs.

That night, in a hotel near Kennedy Airport, they found themselves completely alone together for the first time, and they consummated the marriage. The main meaning, she recalls, was "just to break that barrier in your mind." They had talked of having sex even before they were married, but they had not been able to bring themselves to do it.

When they left New York for Arizona, Wajeha was in for more culture shock. Tucson in August is about as hot as it gets in the U.S. Sizzling though it is to Americans, the heat was scarcely daunting to Saudis. What was different, however, was the sartorial response to the heat. Saudi men wear long white robes, a color which deflects the sun's rays, even while making their wives and daughters wear layers of thermally absorptive black. Wajeha was shocked to see that Americans "wear nothing at all"—at least by Saudi standards.

In Tucson, she plunged into classes to improve her English, and after little more than a semester, she and Amin each passed the English proficiency exam for foreign students and were admitted to the University of Indiana at Bloomington, he to study public health, and she, math. Whereas his brother had lived with them in Tucson, two of his sisters now moved in with them in Indiana. It felt more like student housing than the cozy love nest Wajeha had envisioned. Although the disappointment was not terrible, it was compounded by Amin's insistence on maintaining his distance from her in public—never kissing or touching, or even sitting next to her. Wajeha had imagined that once outside of the restrictive environment of their homeland, Amin's gestures would match the effusive words of love he had spoken during their constrained courtship. But he avoided public displays of affection, not, she believed, out of coldness but for fear that other Saudi men would look down upon him for any demonstrativeness.

She learned something else that might have brought them closer together but instead became a source of unease. Amin revealed dark secrets of his childhood. His father, Wajeha's uncle, the most talented and successful member of her mother's family, turned out to have a sadistic streak. He had abused Amin and his siblings terribly, and this had left deep psychic scars. Neither of them knew or thought much about therapy or counseling to help him live with this past. Instead, Wajeha hoped he would be healed by pouring out his heart to her. But though he filled her ears with horrible memories, he never seemed relieved by it.

In addition to Amin's siblings, the couple had another roommate for a time, a young woman who lived a life not untypical of American college students. "Every day she had a new boyfriend," says Wajeha, "or at least every two or three months." Wajeha was jealous. It was not that she wished to be single, much less wanton. But she wished that she had had the experience as a teenager of going out with different boys. "In Saudi Arabia people are forced to grow up very fast," as far as selecting mates is concerned, she says. Despite this feeling and the frictions and disappointments in her marriage, Amin remained the love of her life.

Wajeha became exposed to politics through the Arab students' association. She had first found one in Tucson and then another in Bloomington. In each locale this group competed with a Saudi students' organization that Wajeha disdained. The latter groups were funded by the Saudi embassy.

They focused on religious activities and seemed designed to keep young Saudis from straying too far from the fold during their American sojourns. The Arab associations, in contrast, were intensely political.

Many of the members, she recalls, were Communists, and the club "was ruled by the Palestinians, so of course the Palestinian issue was the main thing." Wajeha was fully sympathetic with the Palestinian cause but also a touch jaded on the subject. Throughout her schooling, "every event was about Palestine, every poem was a poem for Palestine, and three times a year they would collect at least one rial from every student to donate to Palestine." She and her classmates were taught from first grade that "Jews are aggressive people who kill women and children and are coming to take our lands." The overload left Wajeha numb. Now she found herself more interested in the issues of "freedom and equality and human rights" and above all, "the women's issue."

Her particular goal was "to bring the Saudi students to our side, the liberal side." The fault line ran right down the middle of one Saudi marriage she observed. The husband, Abdullah, who was earning a Ph.D. in Arabic literature, "used to drink and come and sit with us," she recalls. "He was an open-minded person," so much so that he eventually was chosen to lead Wajeha's group. But his wife, Nura, studying to become an educator, was a strict Wahhabi who disapproved of all this. Periodically, Abdullah would absent himself from Wajeha's circle for a week or two at a time, apparently yielding to Nura's pressure, but then he would reappear. The couple had two young sons, "nice, cute boys," but the wife seemed stronger to Wajeha than the husband, and she feared Nura would hold the upper hand in molding the boys. The outcome was worse than she might have imagined. Some twenty years later, in 2006, she saw in the news that the two had blown themselves up, suicide "martyrs" in Iraq.

Wajeha and Amin stayed on in Bloomington after her graduation while he pursued a master's. She worked as a waitress and studied drawing. She had become sufficiently inured to American ways that rather than feeling scandalized when the instructor brought in a nude figure model, Wajeha focused on admiring the young woman's beauty. But the limits of her acculturation were exceeded a few weeks later by the appearance of a nude *male* model. If even after five years, she still could be shocked by such American doings, it was not until she returned home that she discovered how much America had reshaped her standards and expectations. "I felt I was different from the rest of the people," she recalls.

Looking back on what changed her, she observes, "Daily life in America tells you that you are a real person and you have the same rights" as men. "Teachers consider what you have to say, and women are not invisible." Having "lived for a while in the States," she says, "I felt that [in Saudi Arabia] our life was stolen from us—women, and even men."

After a year or two back home, Wajeha received a scholarship to return to the U.S. to study for a master's in reading management. In this instance, Wajeha experienced a silver lining to the cloud of the Saudi system of female subordination. Because it was unthinkable to allow a married woman to go off by herself, a scholarship was also awarded to her husband so that he might accompany her. They were supposed to begin studying in the fall of 1990, but the program was postponed for a semester thanks to the uncertainties created by Iraq's invasion of Kuwait.

Wajeha's life as a graduate student was very different from her carefree days in Bloomington. The couple's first son, Eyad, was born soon after their arrival in D.C., and a second son, Hatim, came along two years later. "I was working very hard for my degree and breastfeeding and running like crazy," she recalls. Nonetheless, the transition from college kids to young adults suited her. "I had my best years in D.C.," Wajeha says.

With her master's in hand, she was ready to return to Saudi Arabia to begin her career. Amin, however, had other thoughts. He was even more reluctant than she to return to their homeland. So he accepted a proposal from another Saudi to open a grocery store together in Canada. Amin spent a year there, and lost his investment which amounted to all their savings. She, meanwhile, returned to Dammam with the two little boys. Since she had no money, the three of them took residence with Amin's parents. Although Amin's father had treated his own children brutally, he was kind to Wajeha. In any case, she had no alternative, such as living with her mother. In Arab culture, the wife always becomes part of the husband's family, never vice versa.

Wajeha took a job as a teacher in a public school. The pay was good, the hours short, and the vacations long. But she hated it. It was not that she disliked teaching; quite the contrary. But she could not endure the prejudice she encountered as a Shiite. In Hufuf, where she had grown up, almost everyone was Shiite, so she had not experienced this. But Dammam, where Amin's family lived, was a mixed city. In all, Shiites make up perhaps ten percent of the population of the kingdom. Since the country's ruling ultra-orthodox Sunni ideology defines Shiism as a heresy, at best, Shiites are treated as second-class citizens.

This worsened when the birth of the Islamic Republic in Iran in 1979 made that country a rival for leadership of the faithful. A few months later, urged on by Iran's Ayatollah Khomeini, rioting erupted in the Saudi city of Qatif, a center of the country's Shiite population and the scene of earlier violent episodes. As a result, Shiites came to be suspected of disloyalty.

Wajeha was the sole Shiite on the staff of the school, and she felt the sting of prejudice:

> The extremists were at their highest. They were watching people, following them, attacking them, and it affected everybody.

Even people who were not extremists would try to act like them, just to be with the mainstream. So I had a really hard time. People did not talk to me; they did not want to work with me. When I touched something they did not want to touch it.

This pierced her all the more keenly having just "come from the States, enjoying freedom and the value of the individual." So she resigned.

She found a job as a reading specialist at a school for the mentally handicapped. Among her students was a particularly beautiful Bedouin girl of nine or ten years who was mute.

She was diagnosed with mental illness, but the reason she did not speak was that she was afraid because of the way her parents treated her. I got the chance to teach her and she started to talk. I cannot forget her face when she started to talk and tell me about her parents. I loved her. I taught her to read Arabic and even to write. She passed first grade, and then continued on.

The girl's name was Shough, which means "passionate." Later, when Wajeha's controversial writings forced her to disguise herself in print, she borrowed it as one of her pen names.

In 2000, Aramco was once again permitted to hire Saudi women, something which had been banned for a time due to its permissive environment. Wajeha applied successfully for a post there, giving up the joy she found in classroom teaching for a job developing curricula. Even after changing from American to Saudi management, the Aramco compound, which includes residential quarters and services, constitutes a kind of social oasis where women may drive and go about unveiled. The freer atmosphere made Wajeha feel more at ease venting her heterodox views. She had begun surfing the Internet regularly and posting her opinions on issues affecting women. Now she began to express herself more boldly and systematically.

One day in 2002 she received a call out of the blue from the editor of *Al-Watan (The Nation)*, perhaps the most prominent newspaper in the kingdom. He said that, like others, he had taken note of the heterodox opinions she was splashing across websites and asked if she would write a weekly column for the newspaper.

This offer reflected a shift in the tectonic plates of Saudi politics following the September 11, 2001, bombings. The revelation that the perpetrators of this outrage were mostly Saudi put the kingdom's reactionaries on the defensive after twenty years of holding the upper hand. In addition to being extremely autocratic, Saudi Arabia is also among the most closed societies in the world, exceeded perhaps only by North Korea. Because Al Qaeda's vicious act put Saudi Arabia to shame, weakening the position of the clerics and their political allies, *Al-Watan*'s editors felt free to add liberal content. Enlisting Wajeha was one way of doing it.

Hers was a fresh voice, and she immediately made a splash. The English language *Arab News*—itself a major paper since most of the Saudi workforce consists of foreigners whose common tongue is English—contracted to run her columns in translation. A regional newspaper, *Al Youm (The Day)*, commissioned her to write separate pieces about cultural affairs.

They all may have gotten more than they bargained for. Wajeha threw herself into this new opportunity with verve and an abandon that some thought reckless. She lambasted Saudi males:

> Arab men are incapable of helping women win anything. The fact is the men need someone else to protect them. The men here are in chains. Their muscles have been crushed and bodies weakened. A thick mustache may make them feel they are

manly. Their narcissistic nature and erroneous notions about manhood have saddled them with a burden beyond their endurance. This load breaks both their spirit and will.[5]

Having driven in this dagger, she gave it a twist in another column: "In the East, men ... have ceased expressing love for women .... [And] women feel that they find nothing in men that calls forth their love and affection and makes them enjoy their lives together."[6]

She also publicized cases of mistreatment of women. In one column she told of a normal eighteen-year-old Saudi girl who had been forced into marriage with a retarded and sometimes violent man.[7] In another she protested the widespread mistreatment of foreign workers, especially females, recounting the arrest of her own maid simply for being out on the street on her day off. So controlling are Saudis, she wrote, that most won't allow their maids out of the house on their own lest they interact with a man.[8]

In other pieces she took Arab women to task for acquiescing in their treatment. Once, she reported a poll of Egyptian women in which a majority said they approved of wife-beating. She resorted to the third person to dramatize her own agonized reaction: "She was dumbfounded; all sensation left her body and she felt as if she had been stabbed with a knife. She stood immobile, her throat dry and her eyes brining with tears."[9] In a separate article she excoriated her own: "We—particularly the women of the Gulf—are a people in need of some radical psychological surgery. Where it comes from is anyone's business. But it is the only way we can be cured of our chronic mental timidity."[10]

Male-Female issues remained at the center of her attention, but she sometimes branched out into broader areas of social and political criticism. In one column, she took aim at the rulers, writing, "Most Arab rulers utter words that underneath are nothing but lies. [They] make empty promises about reforms, change, and development."[11] In another she lamented that Arab publics do not read.[12] In her most sweeping indictment of the Arab world, she claimed that "the Ummah gave rise to pygmies afflicted with narcissism and the desire for a monopoly over power and money.... We repressed, apostasized, exiled, chased and assassinated those who didn't toe the line."[13]

As her essays attracted more attention, she wrote poignantly of the dilemma facing her and her colleagues:

> Every Arabic writer is fighting a losing battle. If he criticizes Arabs, he gains the respect of the West who call him balanced and objective, but he gets criticized by Arabs who think he is currying favor with the West. If on the other hand you criticize Western politics, you gain acceptance from your own people but in the West you are called extremist or fanatic.[14]

She did not write of another dilemma that confronted her, of a more private nature. The fame attendant on her columns generated numerous invitations to appear on television and to attend international conferences. She eagerly seized these opportunities to spread her ideas and to experience foreign peoples and places. At some women's conferences she welcomed the opportunity, rare for Saudis, to talk with Israelis. She earned the wrath of the Palestinian participants who wanted her to focus on the Israel-Palestinian conflict whereas she was more interested in exploring issues of common interest to women across the Arab-Israel divide.

Wajeha's new stature and activities, however, did not sit well with Amin. He did not object to Wajeha's mingling with men professionally. He even allowed her a passport (something no Saudi woman may have without the signature of her male "guardian"), but her travel abroad was a severe test. To have his wife spend days in distant lands interacting with strange men followed by nights in unchaperoned hotel rooms was a lot for any Saudi man to swallow. She urged him to come with her. He was reluctant, and when he tried the results were not good. Once, he and their two sons came with her to a conference in Turkey. "He did not enjoy it," she recalls. Another time he came with her to Riyadh: "He hated it."

The deeper issue for Amin beyond fear for Wajeha's fidelity was feeling diminished by her prominence. There may not be a culture anywhere in the world where men readily accept a stature beneath their wives, but if there is one, it assuredly is not to be found in Saudi Arabia. "I do not want to be your shadow," complained Amin. It was a problem Wajeha did not know how to resolve except by abandoning her new career, and this she was not willing to do.

In late spring of 2003, with the Arab world seething over the U.S. invasion of Iraq, Wajeha published a column that was extraordinarily defiant even by her bold standards. She began by citing the story of an adolescent she knew who was regularly beaten by his father "so brutally that blood is drawn." This, she went on, "is a true story that happens every day here in the Kingdom.... What is ... different ... is that the boy was born in the United States and so has the right to become a US citizen. Because of that fact, the boy has something to live for." As if this invidious comparison between the two countries was not provocative enough, she also cited a poll by *al-Jazeera* asking Arabs whether they would welcome an American invasion of their own countries. The "nos" outnumbered the "yeses" by a meager 52 to 48 percent, she said. The heart of her argument was this:

> We do not seem to pay attention to the phenomenon of our women crying out for America's help. I have met some of these women. Some of them actually think that only the US can put an end to the appalling conditions they exist under. They dream of the day the US will come to rescue them. Some

of these women are divorcees who have found justice in neither their marriages nor their divorces. Others have not been allowed to work or to complete their studies. Their guardians keep them locked up and have confiscated their passports.
Now they are waiting for George Bush's administration to free them because the institutions in their own country have failed to do so.[15]

A couple of months later, Wajeha was told by a friend that she had been "banned." She does not know if that article was the cause, because the government never told her. Indeed, it denied that she was banned. But all three newspapers for which she wrote refused to run any more articles by her. Privately, the editors confided that they had received instructions from the Ministry of Information to cease carrying her essays, but publicly were afraid to say anything.

A year later, a friend of hers started a magazine in nearby Qatar. She involved Wajeha extensively in getting it launched and they even discussed the possibility that Wajeha would become the editor. But after the first issue appeared she told Wajeha that she had received a warning that if Wajeha continued to write for the magazine, it would not be on newsstands in the Saudi kingdom. In response to this censorship, the international writers' organization, PEN, presented Wajeha with its 2004 annual Free Expression Award at a ceremony at The Hague.

There were few options left to Wajeha other than reverting to the Internet. There, she could find an audience, albeit a smaller one than read her newspaper columns. She began to contribute to various liberal pan-Arab websites, such as Middleeasttransparent.com, Aafaq.com, Elaph.com, Droob.com, and Rezgar.com. She also returned to her old method of posting comments on the sites of others. When eight Iranian women were arrested for displaying a banner demanding equal rights, Wajeha went to the website of Iranian President Mahmoud Ahmadinejad every day for three months, each time posting a demand for information about what had become of the eight.

The ban on publishing in Saudi Arabia injured Wajeha, but it also liberated her. Her Saudi editors had often pressed her to soften language. Sometimes she would even submit two entire manuscripts for a single deadline, telling them that if one was too controversial they could run the other. Now she was free of that constraint, and her anger at being banned impelled her to express herself even more provocatively.

"One of the most prominent traits of the men in this region [the Arab peninsula] is an inferiority complex ... and therefore the embarrassing malady of impotence is common among them," she wrote in 2004. "[They] are the ones who spend the most in the world on aphrodisiacs so as to achieve a sense of ... potency." It is better to be an "old maid," she counseled, than to marry one of them.[16] In an essay in 2005 she observed that "dogs and cats in the developed world have more rights than Arab women—or even Arab men."[17]

2005 was a significant year for Saudi Arabia, and an even more significant one for Wajeha. King Fahd died and was succeeded by his younger brother, Abdullah. Since the country was founded in 1932 by Abdel Aziz al Saud, it had had five monarchs, with Abdullah becoming the sixth. After Abdel Aziz, the next five were each sons of his, in descending order of age, and this process will not cease with Abdullah. He is the firstborn of Abdel Aziz's eighth wife, Fahda, making him merely the thirteenth of forty-three sons known to have been sired by the country's founder from among his countless wives.

Abdullah was reported to have already been ruling behind the scenes as crown prince, Fahd having suffered a debilitating stroke in 1995. Although now in his eighties, Abdullah was reputed to be reform-minded, and liberals hoped that, with the added authority of ruling in his own name, he would nudge the country further in the direction of modernity.

The idea that a man of his age and background would be a "reformer" sounds unlikely. But it becomes more comprehensible in context of the essential compact that holds the Saudi state together. This recognizes the political authority of the al-Saud family alongside the religious authority of the avowedly backward-looking Wahhabi clergy. Of course, in Islam these two realms are not differentiated, so there is a constant, quiet tug-of-war in which, as Lawrence Wright puts it, "the royal family [is] a conspicuously progressive force." Since 1960, it pushed through the introduction of television and education for girls and the outlawry of slavery, all against clerical resistance.[18]

This struggle reflects the defining dynamic of Saudi life: a cataclysmic collision of cultures more than a millennium apart, within the same people and within the compass of a mere two or three generations. It may have been captured best in one of the few great Saudi novels, *Cities of Salt* by Abdelrahman Munif, which depicts the uprooting of traditional life by the arrival of the Americans and the oil industry. Speaking of a fictional locale that matches Wajeha's origins in the eastern part of the country where almost all the oil is found, Munif writes:

> Al-Hadra and its surrounding areas ... had not changed since God created the earth. Since the life of the people was marked by extraordinary difficulty and harshness because of the lack of rain, the scarcity of caravans and the consequently high prices they paid for flour, sugar and cloth, they were used to it and never expected anything better. If the earth became too crowded ... it was usually death that solved that problem.[19]

Against this background, the 81-year-old Abdullah could be counted a modernizer. Wajeha had greeted his coronation with hopefulness. "The people are with him," she had said, trying to bolster his courage to make changes.[20]

Alas, the news that 2005 brought in Wajeha's personal life was calamitous. Amin announced to her that he had found a second wife. This, he suggested, was his response to her fame and independence. Although he had complained about her new life, Wajeha had never imagined such a consequence. To be sure, Amin had spoken about taking a second wife since sometime in the 1990s. But she had never taken it seriously. "Men who are going to do it, do not say it. Rather, they go and find one," she explains. "I had a friend, a colleague. She discovered it because she found a gold necklace, and her husband never gave her anything. When she asked him about it, he confessed he had gotten married." On the other hand, "When men start to threaten to get married again, most likely they will not do it. It is a cultural thing. I thought it was just a joke; his brother was saying the same to his wife."

Wajeha reacted to Amin's announcement by saying, "Go ahead, marry her." That, of course, was not what she was truly feeling, but she would not beg him to stay. "I wanted to keep my dignity," she recalls.

Through the balance of 2005, Wajeha and Amin quarreled about his plans. He protested that in the past when he had spoken about taking another wife, she had always told him she would not mind. She explained that she always thought he was kidding—and so was she. In early 2006, Amin went ahead with the second marriage. Wajeha was crushed, but she did not bow. She demanded an immediate divorce. Amin tried to talk her out of it. Wajeha recalls: "He tried to convince me that she is only a friend. He said, 'I only married her because I needed someone to talk to and you were busy with your writing.' He even tried to convince me that they had no sexual relationship." But she was adamant. "You want a friend, a sister, a cousin, whatever," she said. "It is not my problem anymore. It is yours."

Her unyielding stand was not because she had developed any ambivalence toward the marriage. Quite the contrary, she was heartbroken. "I had a very good life with him," she reflects. "My kids were the happiest kids in the [extended] family. . . . And he helped me a lot to be what I am now." She even told him, "If I were to live again, I have made many mistakes in my life, but one thing that I would not change is to be your wife." Nonetheless, despite her anguish, she would not accept being part of a harem.

He agreed to grant the divorce, and she told him how she wanted it done:

> I asked him to go to the Sunni court because it is fast. Usually they do not even ask the woman if she wants to get divorced or not. They will get the paper in a week, or maybe less if you have connections. But the Shiites, the husband has to bring the wife, and I did not want to go through this. I wanted something to be quick and easy. So now I am legally divorced.

This was not the end of the formalities, however. It still remained for Amin to file papers releasing her from his "guardianship," as every Saudi female must have a male guardian. In theory it could be either of her two teen sons, but the older was in boarding school in the United States, and the younger was soon to join him there, which made it impractical, so another male relative would have to be found. Any of her brothers would do, but two years after the divorce—which Wajeha bitterly notes came through on Valentine's Day of 2006—Amin was still her "guardian." Perhaps he dragged his feet out of reluctance to let go of her. Perhaps she neglected to push him for like reasons. She says that he spoke to her of reconciliation, but that she told him that "the Wajeha you knew and helped to create has died."

Fiercely as she defended her dignity, Wajeha felt destroyed. From the time he announced his serious intent to take the other woman, Wajeha ceased to write. "I could not read, I could not write, I could not sleep," she recalls. At the beginning of 2006, she managed to produce a single piece, not about political issues but on the theme that "when people die, you cannot bring them back."

Around the time the divorce came through, Wajeha regained her authorial voice. Her polemics about women's rights grew ever sharper, perhaps honed by her personal pain, but they lost none of their cogency. "In Arab countries, and particularly in the Gulf countries, the cycle of discrimination against the woman begins when she is a fetus in her mother's womb, ... and goes on until her death," she wrote for one of the websites, detailing how this works in each phase of life.[21]

She invoked the image of Guantanamo, a *cause célèbre* in the Arab world because it allegedly proves that America is hypocritical in its espousal of human rights and that Arabs are victims. Wajeha, however, gave this a reverse twist. "Arab women are worse off than the prisoners in Guantanamo," she wrote in May 2006. To show that this was not merely rhetoric, she enumerated half a dozen ways in which the situations of Guantanamo prisoners and Arab women were alike. But, she said, there were also differences, among them:

> a prisoner in Guantanamo [can] see the sun, feel its rays and enjoy the caress of fresh air on his face, even when he is physically in chains, whereas the women in some Arab states are shackled [both] physically and spiritually.... The minute the girl enters her teens, she no longer sees the light of day, and she cannot breathe fresh air except through a veil, since she is covered from head to toe in black garments.

Moreover, she went on, "The plight of the Guantanamo prisoners is temporary.... Arab women, on the other hand, will remain prisoners until the day they die." And "Finally, the female Arab[s] have never been warriors or suicide [bombers]. They never joined any terrorist organization and have never harmed anyone, but they nevertheless live as prisoners all their lives."[22]

Despite her grief at having lost her husband, Wajeha recalls, she "felt free, with nobody to answer to." But this proved to be an illusion. She got a call from one of her brothers, a businessman, who complained that he had lost a contract with the Ministry of the Interior (responsible for the security services) because she was in bad odor with the authorities. Why should I suffer on your account, he asked. Wajeha resented his pressure, but yielded to it, thereafter issuing some of her writing under pseudonyms. She used Rosa Parks—the American civil rights heroine—and also the name, Shough, borrowed from the mute little Bedouin girl whom she had coaxed into speaking.

Still, she did not allow her brother's pressure to deter her when, a few months later, she decided to commemorate the first anniversary of Abdullah's rule with her one-woman march on the causeway. "I wanted to do something to shake the system," she says. With war raging between Israel and Hizbullah in southern Lebanon, Saudi Shiites were staging demonstrations in support of Hizbullah, and this provoked her:

> I felt that was really stupid. These people have nothing and they were going out to demonstrate for causes far from home, like Palestine or Danish cartoons. They should be demonstrating because most of their young men and women are jobless, and over other issues that affect us in our daily life.

Prime among these issues in Wajeha's mind was the plight of females. "The King has promised us that he will improve the situation of Saudi women. He asked us to have patience. A year has passed and our situations did not change much," she explained after the police released her in her younger brother's custody.[23]

Her boldness won plaudits from her small network of sister feminists, but also a hint of jealousy. Why had she done it
alone? This inspired her at once to lay plans for a "mass"
protest of fifteen women. She hoped to get five each in the
cities of Khobar, Riyadh, and Jeddah to stand with signs on
September 23, Saudi National Day. She secured the collaboration of Fouziah al-Ouni, a friend of hers and the wife of Ali
al-Dumaini, one of the country's few well-known dissidents.

In January of 2003, he and a few colleagues had
launched a petition calling for a transition to a constitutional
monarchy with an elected parliament. Slowly over the next
year the petition accrued signatures. In March 2004, police
arrested 13 men who were circulating the petition and
charged them with "issuing statements," "gathering signatures," and "using Western terminology." After a few weeks,
ten of the thirteen were released upon promising to desist
from petitioning. But Dumaini and two others refused to
recant, and they were put on trial. They were represented by a
famous constitutional jurist, Abdul Rahman al-Lahim, but in
November he was arrested for making statements in defense
of his clients and was incarcerated until after their sentencing,
six months later. Dumaini was sentenced to nine years for
"criticism of the people charged with authority in the Islamic
regime" in a manner "contrary to the principle of mutual
advice with the ruler." In August 2005, upon his accession to
the throne, King Abdullah pardoned the three convicts and
their lawyer. After that, Dumaini kept a low profile but
encouraged his wife's efforts on behalf of women's rights.

Wajeha and Fouziah worked the phones, but as the date
for the protest drew near, all of the other women got cold feet.
Wajeha and Fouziah planned to proceed anyway. A two-
woman demonstration would still be an increase of one hundred percent over Wajeha's August march. But the authorities
were not going to risk such a show of dissent. Either because
one of the invited women snitched or through electronic

eavesdropping, the security forces knew of the plans and thwarted them by arresting Wajeha three days before the event. She was held for six hours and released only on pledge not to go through with it, and her passport was confiscated. That was a particular hardship because she was living in Bahrain with her younger son, Hatim, and commuting back and forth across the causeway each day to her job at Aramco. Now, she was in effect imprisoned in her own country, unable to travel to her home and child. Fortunately, the authorities relented after a couple of weeks and returned the document. Perhaps she got off this lightly because of her fame and the vigorous protests raised by PEN, Human Rights Watch, and other international organizations.

If this put an end to Wajeha's venture into the practice of street protest, her rhetorical sallies against the regime and the system only grew more daring. She continued to do a part of her writing under pen names, but despite her brother's unease, she maintained a public profile as well. In an appearance on al-Hurra television in 2007 she declared:

> Saudi society is based on masters and slaves, or, to be more precise, masters and maids, because the masters are the men, and the slaves are the women. . . . The ownership of a woman is passed from one man to another . . . from the father or the brother to . . . the husband. The woman is merely a piece of merchandise, [to] her guardian.[24]

While the treatment of women remained her dominant concern, in some of her writings she began to articulate a sweeping critique of Arab society. It was no less searing than her feminist polemics. In February 2007, she contributed this remarkable "ode" to the liberal Arab website, Aafaq.com:

- When you cannot find a single garden in your city, but there is a mosque on every corner—you know that you are in an Arab country. . .

- When you see people living in the past with all the trappings of modernity—do not be surprised, you are in an Arab country...
- When religion has control over science—you can be sure that you are in an Arab country...
- When clerics are referred to as scholars—don't be astonished, you are in an Arab country...
- When you see the ruler transformed into a demigod who never dies or relinquishes his power, and whom nobody is permitted to criticize—do not be too upset, you are in an Arab country...
- When you find that the large majority of people oppose freedom and find joy in slavery—do not be too distressed, you are in an Arab country...
- When you hear the clerics saying that democracy is heresy, but see them seizing every opportunity provided by democracy to grab high positions in the government—do not be surprised, you are in an Arab country...
- When monarchies turn into theocracies, and republics into hybrids of monarchy and republic—do not be taken aback, you are in an Arab country...
- When you find that the members of parliament are nominated by the ruler, or else that half of them are nominated and the other half have bought their seats through bribery... you are in an Arab country...
- When you discover that a woman is worth half of what a man is worth, or less—do not be surprised, you are in an Arab country...
- When you see that the authorities chop off a man's hand for stealing a loaf of bread or a penny, but praise and glorify those who steal billions—do not be too surprised, you are in an Arab country...
- When you are forced to worship the Creator in school and your teachers grade you for it—you can be sure that you are in an Arab country...

- When young women students are publicly flogged merely for exposing their eyes—you are in an Arab country. . .
- When a boy learns about menstruation and childbirth but not about his own body and the changes it undergoes in puberty—roll out your prayer mat and beseech Allah to help you deal with your crisis, for you are in an Arab country. . .
- When land is more important than human beings—you are in an Arab country. . .
- When covering the woman's head is more important than financial and administrative corruption, embezzlement, and betrayal of the homeland—do not be astonished, you are in an Arab country. . .
- When minorities are persecuted and oppressed, and if they demand their rights, are accused of being a fifth column or a Trojan horse—be upset, you are in an Arab country. . .
- When women are seen as house ornaments which can be replaced at any time—bemoan your fate, you are in an Arab country. . .
- When birth control and family planning are perceived as a Western plot—place your trust in Allah, you are in an Arab country. . .
- When at any time, there can be a knock on your door and you will be dragged off and buried in a dark prison— you are in an Arab country. . .
- When fear constantly lives in the eyes of the people— you can be certain that you are in an Arab country.[25]

While her broadsides thus at times covered a gamut of issues, she decided nonetheless to focus her activism on a single narrow and concrete one, the right to drive. When automobiles were introduced into the Kingdom, there had been no restriction on who could drive them, since there is nothing in *shariah* about motor vehicles. But in 1957, King

Saud decreed a prohibition on women driving. The reason had nothing to do with road safety but rather, like so much else in Saudi Arabia, with sexual taboos. It was feared that the freedom of women to move about on their own might lead to all kinds of temptations.

The issue was at the center of the constraints put on women, and it also affected Wajeha very personally. In 2004, when she was still together with Amin, they had taken residence in Bahrain, where she was allowed to drive. Still, for her daily commute to her job at Aramco inside Saudi Arabia, she needed to be driven. At first it was no problem, since Amin worked there, too. After her divorce, she relied on rides from co-workers, but this became too cumbersome, so she moved back to Saudi Arabia. In September 2007, together with Fouziah, she launched an Internet petition on the subject, quickly garnering 1,100 signatures that were submitted to King Abdullah on Saudi National Day, exactly a year after their aborted demonstration.

For her next salvo, Wajeha posted an appeal on the Internet for international help. It was addressed to "all car makers and car dealers around the world." It read:

> Women in Saudi Arabia need you to help them in order to buy your cars. . . . Women in Saudi Arabia are willing to buy your cars. But you need first to support the campaign to allow women to drive cars. Write to your government officials; make the Non-Governmental Organizations aware, inform the parliament members in your countries about the status of women in Saudi Arabia. . . . Help women in Saudi Arabia to buy your cars.[26]

None of this drew any official response, but a few weeks later, in February 2008, *Arab News*, the same leading English language daily that had run Wajeha's columns before she was banned, quoted two senior religious figures suggesting a modification of the driving prohibition. A member of the Council of Senior Islamic Scholars said, "In principle women driving is permitted in Islam." The other cleric spoke of a "package" of measures that would provide proper safeguards to go along with such a change. The newspaper added that it had polled 125 men, and that an overwhelming majority favored allowing women to drive, mostly with various conditions. It also reported that some women surveyed spoke of concerns about driving safety, a quite understandable issue given the number of young men in the kingdom who, owning cars easily replaced by oil wealth and enjoying ready access to few other adolescent thrills, careen wildly through congested streets and highways.[27]

Meanwhile, Wajeha and Fouziah and a couple of colleagues had resumed circulating their petition, gathering another roughly two thousand signatures. This time they conveyed it to Prince Nayef, minister of the interior, who was known as a stalwart conservative. They did this on International Women's Day in March 2008 and punctuated it by posting a two-and-a-half minute video on YouTube.com. The video showed Wajeha driving. It was shot from the passenger seat next to her, and as she drove, keeping her eyes on the road, she delivered this soliloquy:

> Today is International Women's Day. First, I'd like to congratulate all the women who have achieved their rights. I hope that all the women still fighting for their rights will achieve them soon. Obviously, I am currently driving my car in a remote area. Only in remote areas in Saudi Arabia are women allowed to drive, I'm sad to say. In cities – where they really need to drive – it is still forbidden. On the occasion of International Women's Day, let me express my hope that His Highness Prince Nayef bin Abd Al-'Aziz, the minister of the interior, will soon allow us to drive. All the women who signed the petition we sent him today have driving licenses, and we are capable of driving in our cities. In addition, many of us

are willing to help the country instruct women, so that they can get their driving licenses.... I hope that by the International Women's Day next year, this restriction will have been lifted.[28]

Ten days later, the Saudi-owned satellite television network, al-Arabiya, published a report on its website that the Saudi Shura Council had passed on to the monarch a recommendation that women be allowed to drive, albeit with a long list of conditions, for example that they be modestly dressed, carry cell phones so that they need not interact directly with any man in case of a road emergency, and that this privilege be restricted to the hours of 7AM to 8PM and not include Thursdays or Fridays, the Saudi weekend.[29]

The Shura Council is an appointed body whose role is purely advisory and whose deliberations need not be public. In this case, its action was reported in the form of a leak that was not echoed in other news outlets and that was soon withdrawn from the al-Arabiya website. Thus the authenticity of the report, not to mention the monarch's likelihood to follow any such advice, remained uncertain. Nonetheless, it was clearly a straw in the wind, pointing to an ultimate victory for Wajeha's crusade—or, more exactly, one battle in her crusade.

The Politician

Iraq: Mithal al-Alusi

Mithal Jamal Hussain al-Alusi sat alone in the coffee shop, sipping cup after cup of Turkish coffee and smoking successive bowls of *shisha*, the flavored tobacco used in a hookah. He was wrestling with a portentous choice. He had come as far as Istanbul, and the question now was whether to complete the journey to Israel. He had not made a final decision before starting out, had not told those who invited him that he was coming. His destination was only an hour-and-a-half's flight time away, but it may as well have been the moon before Neil Armstrong got there. No Iraqi political figure had ever set foot there before.

He had received an invitation to speak at a conference on terrorism at an academic center in Herzliya, but this was only a pretext for the trip. His reason for wanting to go was not primarily to make a speech, although he often orated against terrorism. Rather, he wanted to break a barrier that separated his country from the future he envisioned for it. For this reason he had told an intermediary that he would be willing to attend, but when the invitation had arrived, he had not replied, and now the fateful moment was upon him. Just like the astronauts, he knew that the trip would be perilous, but he did not know exactly what form those perils would take or the odds that he could survive them.

Mithal, the scion of a line of Sunni religious scholars from Anbar province near Fallujah, was tall, broad-shouldered, vigorous. His handsome face was adorned with the straight dark mustache that is favored by Arab men. He was a man of contradictions, a physical man with an intellectual bent, a liberal with all the fiery conviction that usually drives illiberal ideologies. And although he was passionately Iraqi, he had lived half his life abroad. Most of this time in exile, he had resided in Hamburg, and there Mithal experienced ways very different from those he had known in Iraq or the other Arab countries where he had taken refuge before coming to Germany—individual liberty, democratic governance, and the prosperity that can come from market economics. This became his ideal for Iraq, and he believed that he could help guide his country to its fulfillment. Breaking the impenetrable barrier separating Iraq from Israel was a step in bringing his country into the Western world.

Mithal was born in 1953 in the village of Alus. His father, Jamal Hussein al-Alusi, had been orphaned at age three, but had flourished thanks to the unflagging devotion of a grandmother. He not only finished secondary school, but went on to university and then into teaching. Eventually, he completed graduate studies, becoming a professor of education, highly respected in his field. Although his grandmother was devout and traditional, Jamal, like many young thinkers of his generation, turned his back on faith and embraced Communism.

He married a cousin, Wahabia Jaralla, who came from the town of Dayr as Zahr, across the border in Syria, an isolated spot where in 2007 Israel was to bomb an apparent nuclear facility. With his help, Wahabia completed enough schooling to become a teacher, herself, and the couple had six children, of whom Mithal was the oldest.

Following in his father's footsteps, Mithal read avidly as a child. With both parents being teachers, books were readily available, and Mithal especially loved the encyclopedia. It was not only intrinsically interesting, but it enabled him to learn things his peers didn't know so he could show off his knowledge. As a teen, he turned to Western philosophers: Rousseau and Montesquieu made special impressions. Not that he was all seriousness. His favorite pastimes, he says, were "hunting of both kinds." In the country he would hunt animals, and in the city he and his buddies "hunted" for girls.[1]

Mithal was an impressionable fourteen when the whole Arab world was rocked by the terrible humiliation of defeat at the hands of Israel in the Six Day War. He experienced these events as a rite of passage:

> I brought a small radio to school with me and listened. The broadcasters made many clear statements, "Our Iraqi fighters have attacked Israel." I was sitting, and I was crying. It was something totally new: war and fighting. But I was not crying because I was afraid. No. I do not know why. Something touched me greatly. From there, we received big propaganda about pan-Arabism, Israel, socialism, America. I was trying to be part of this fight, of this important, big thing.

Within the next few years the emergence of Palestinian guerrillas restored a modicum of Arab pride. The moribund Palestine Liberation Organization was upstaged and then taken over by Yassir Arafat's Fatah, which carried out more attacks against Israel. To his parents' dismay, Mithal went to the Fatah office in Baghdad, and signed up to become a *fedayee* to fight in Palestine. This meant dropping out of high school for full-time training at a military base in Baghdad.

After two to three months, Mithal grew disillusioned. Noticing that none of the recruits got sent into action, he concluded that it was all an elaborate show. The people in charge were garnering prestige and income—since Arab governments and charities lavished funds on the cause of liberating Palestine. But he doubted that any of his cohort of Iraqis would ever get there.

Jamal was able to get Mithal readmitted to high school, but his newfound interest in politics did not fade, and he became active in the Baath youth organization. The Baath Party was then quite small, comprising perhaps a few hundred core members. But it was one of two that had captured the imagination of the most active body of young intellectuals, officers and students. The other was the Communist Party, and these two waged a bitter struggle for dominance of the country. Although a miscellany of other politicians and soldiers also jockeyed for power, the Baathists and Communists were the most cohesive blocs.

When the Baathists seized power for the first time in 1963, they had conducted wholesale arrests of Communists. Even though Jamal al-Alusi had left the Communist Party in 1959, the Baathists had arrested him and held him for two months in a prison where Mithal brought him breakfast and lunch each day. Mithal, then ten years old, had hated the people who imprisoned his father. But by his mid teens he had put this behind him and embraced Baathism's pan-Arab ideology, a choice that came as "a big shock" for his father.

The party seemed to embody the deep sense of power and belonging that had welled up within him as he listened on his transistor radio to false reports of Arab victories in the 1967 war. By the time he enrolled it had seized power for a second time, following a brief ouster. The party was still quite small, but several of Mithal's friends and cousins shared his sense that it represented the country's future. "We were new," he recalls. "This was the strong point of the Baath regime, we were totally new. Saddam was a young man. All of the leaders were in their twenties or at most early thirties. We were a young party."

Mithal rose quickly through the ranks. By the time he was 19, he was appointed one of the top administrators of a secret school to train party cadres. The director of the school was a Syrian. Baathism had been founded in Syria, and for a long time the Syrians continued to play the part of ideological elders to their Iraqi comrades. The Iraqi official to whom Mithal reported was Abdel Khaliq Al-Samarrai, the leader of the party's left wing, someone Mithal still regards as having been a Baathist true-believer amidst many opportunists.

This position brought Mithal perks that most men his age could only fantasize about: a car and driver and his own bodyguards, as well as access to the highest reaches of the party and government. Within a year, however, this would lead him to observe things that destroyed his faith in the party.

The first blow came when a Shiite friend and fellow Baathist sought Mithal's help. The man's wife was Sunni, and her cousin found it intolerable that she had married a Shiite. The cousin happened to be the chief of the presidential bodyguard, a position so powerful that the couple felt endangered by him.

Mithal was taken aback. "My God, what are they talking about?" he wondered. "What does this mean, Sunni and Shia? We did not know such categories. And who cares if someone is married to someone else?" Such sensitivities flew in the face of cardinal principles of Baathism, which was secular and whose core idea was pan-Arabism. How was it possible to preach Arab unity while drawing lines between sects? Mithal approached President Ahmed Hassan al-Bakr, whom he knew personally since the Baathist party was a tight circle, to tell the man what mischief his bodyguard was making. The president listened to him without sympathy and then admonished: "Do not get involved in this case." Could it be, Mithal wondered, that the leaders of his party did not believe their own ideology?

Other incidents were to shock Mithal more. Around this time, he received a call from Shibley al-Aysami, deputy general secretary of the party who also was seeking Mithal's help. Two brothers, neighbors of his, had been arrested, he explained, and they were being held in a dreaded prison called *Castle Nihaya,* meaning roughly, "the last stop." Aysami believed the two were guilty of nothing, and he wanted Mithal to help get them released.

Aysami outranked Mithal, but Mithal had a crucial contact. *Castle Nihaya* came under the authority of a protégé of Saddam Hussein's named Nazim Kazzar. Kazzar, by then about 35, had been the head of the Baath youth organization. He was described thus by historians:

Even when judged by the fairly undemanding standards set by most of his colleagues and contemporaries in the Ba'ath leadership, Nazim Kazzar's reputation as a sadistic torturer and murderer is particularly unsavoury [although his] influence rose high because he eliminated elements considered dangerous to the party.[2]

Despite his rank, Aysami was helpless to intervene in the affairs of that prison, but Mithal was known to be especially close friends with Hassan al-Mutayri, a deputy to Nazim Kazzar who was personally in charge of *Castle Nihaya*. Short and wiry, Hassan al-Mutayri was a few years Mithal's senior, but they had worked together in the Baath youth movement and had become something of a pair, spending many spare hours together. Hassan often hung out at Mithal's home, enjoying his mother's cooking.

So on Aysami's behalf Mithal headed off to *Castle Nihaya*. He knew its deadly reputation, but this in itself had not alarmed him. They were revolutionaries, and as Stalin said, you cannot make an omelet without breaking eggs. "I thought that it was a necessary part of the system, that those held there were agents working against Iraq or the Arab nation."

After exchanging greetings with characteristic friendliness, Mithal told Hassan that he had come to seek the release of two prisoners. "Who are they?" asked Hassan, and Mithal named the brothers. Hassan responded with a gesture of wiping his hands.

Not understanding, Mithal persisted. Hassan replied airily: "Take some others. I'll give you any two you want."

"What do you mean?" asked Mithal. "I came for those two." And Hassan repeated his gesture and, to make sure his meaning was not missed, said, "They are finished." Mithal protested that they had been arrested only two or three days before. "When were they investigated? When did you hang them? What is going on here?"

Hassan bristled at Mithal's tone and warned him: "Be careful. I am in charge here, and I make the decisions." Mithal responded with a defiant epithet, and Hassan pressed a button on his desk, and quickly guards appeared. Mithal describes the scene that ensued:

> "Arrest him," said Hassan. And the guard said to me: "Sir, would you like to come with me, please?" I said: "What?" And the guard warned: "I said 'sir' because I know you." And then Hassan dismissed the guards and said to me: "Get out. Don't look back. Be careful."

Hassan had been bluffing, but Mithal got the message. "I left understanding what kind of mafia and killing machinery we had here," he says.

There was still one more portentous encounter between the two old friends. When the anger of this moment passed, Hassan made Mithal a proposition: "Why don't you join me and be my assistant?" Mithal replied, "Because I am not a killer." And Hassan looked at him very hard and said: "Mithal, don't ever say that to me again."

Ironically, Mithal's determination not to take part in killing probably saved his own life. Within a year of these incidents, Hassan's patron, Nazim Kazzar, fell out with Saddam Hussein. The historians Marion Farouk-Sluglett and Peter Sluglett give this account:

> Kazzar devised a plan . . . to dispose of all his rivals . . . simultaneously. Taking advantage of one of al-Bakr's relatively rare visits abroad, and realising that protocol would demand that most of the party leadership would be on hand at Baghdad Airport to greet the president on his return . . . Kazzar invited the . . . Minister of Defence, and . . . the Minister of Interior . . . to a 'banquet'. . . . On their arrival, the two ministers were bundled down to the cellars, while a special detachment of Kaz-

zar's own men was dispatched to the airport to assassinate both the president and his reception committee.[3]

However, the plot went awry when the plane was delayed, and Kazzar made an unsuccessful dash for the border, shooting his hostages en route. A week later, the government announced that Kazzar and 35 followers had been tried, convicted and executed. Hassan al-Mutayri was among the 35. Had Mithal accepted the position of Hassan's deputy, there is no way he could have avoided taking part in the coup, and he would surely have been the thirty-sixth victim of Saddam's retribution.

One other Baath leader barely escaped with his life from this episode. During the course of his flight, Kazzar had offered to negotiate directly with President al-Bakr over the two high ranking hostages still in his grip. He proposed they meet at the home of Abdel Khaliq Al-Samarrai, Mithal's old boss at the party cadre school. This was enough to cast suspicion on Al-Samarrai, who was also sentenced to death, which was commuted to life imprisonment in response to a direct appeal from Michel Aflaq, the Syrian who had founded the Baath movement.[4]

The arrest of Al-Samarrai in 1973 and the flight of the cadre school's Syrian director amidst growing tensions between the Iraqi and Syrian wings of the Baath, left Mithal in charge of the institution. A new curriculum had been developed by Al-Samarrai, and staff members turned to Mithal to decide whether to put it into effect. He ordered them to proceed and soon received a summons from Saddam Hussein. As everyone in the small Baath core knew each other, the two had met before but this was their first one-on-one encounter as superior and underling. Mithal recalls the meeting, which offers a fascinating glimpse into Saddam's style of wielding power even before he had become the undisputed ruler of Iraq:

I thought I was going to lose my head. I went there, and this was the first time that I called him "sir."

He asked, "How is everything in the school?"

I said, "Very good."

"What are you going to do with the new curriculum?"

I said, "We are giving the order to print."

He asked me, "Even the parts by Abdel Khaliq Al-Samarrai?"

I said, "Yes."

"Did he include anything of his own, or is it the party ideology?"

I said, "No, this is the party ideology. That is why I gave the order."

He said, "Good, continue. If you need anything, contact me."

I said, "Yes, sir." And I left. I had been afraid I would be killed, but nothing happened.

1973, the year he turned twenty, became a momentous year in Mithal's life, not only because he survived the party's internecine broils. One day, while he was visiting a cousin, the fellow's wife arrived accompanied by her sister. The sister was 16 or 17, and her name was Elham. Mithal found her beautiful and determined to marry her.

He did not communicate this to her. Instead he went to his father. As he explains: "My family is traditional family even if it is very liberal." He told his father that he was ready to marry. His father was pleased with the news and understood that it meant that someone had caught Mithal's eye. "It is the daughter of uncle Tofi," said Mithal, using the colloquial title that Arabs apply widely to older male friends. Jamal objected, "Her father is a good man, has never done something bad in his life, and I know you. You will make troubles for him just as for me." Although Jamal's words were to prove prophetic, he meant them only tongue-in-cheek. So Mithal's parents approached Elham's parents and proposed the union. Only after it was agreed by the families did the young couple spend any time together. Within a few months, they were wed.

Meanwhile, Mithal's escape from his face-to-face with Saddam did not quell his sense of vulnerability. At the cadre school, a Baathist from Saddam's home town of Tikrit replaced the Syrian as director. Rumors reached Mithal that added to his worries. He recalls:

> I was always afraid because in 1973, we began to hear big stories that there is a Mafia killing people, killing politicians, attacking diplomats, killing good Iraqi citizens. I thought, and I still believe, it was not a Mafia. It was Saddam, doing this circus to control Baghdad and to control the party, and to control the army. I was so afraid, really, very afraid.

Mithal decided he would be safer from the internecine intrigues if he left the cadre school. So he resigned and arranged to do military service in Baghdad and to take classes at the 750-year-old Mustansiriya University, once a great center of Islamic learning. But, out of sight was not out of mind. Saddam got word of Mithal's departure from the cadre school and apparently was unhappy with it. After some months—it was now 1974—Mithal was summoned to his commander's office and found him in the company of a civilian official. "Saddam wants to see you," said the commander.

On being ushered into Saddam's office, Mithal saluted briskly, and Saddam got to the point quickly. "How many people like you do we have in the army?" he asked, meaning experienced Baathists. "Who gave you permission to join?" Military service was mandatory, but students were officially exempt, not to mention that well-connected Baathists could find other exemptions. Mithal had declined to exercise his exemption.

Despite Mithal's insistence that he was a soldier, Saddam summarily reassigned him, and the new job could scarcely have been less appealing. He was to serve Saddam's uncle, Hadji Ferallah Hairallah Tilfa, as an aide, in effect as a babysitter. "Be careful. People are trying to use him, so keep your eyes and ears open, and stay close to him," Mithal recalls Saddam instructing.

Not only did this assignment promise to be a crashing bore but the task was hopeless.

Uncle Ferallah was something of a wild man, exploiting his proximity to power to engage in all kinds of rackets. "He was a really big criminal," says Mithal. For the better part of a year, a nervous Mithal stayed as close to Uncle Ferallah as he could, observing more than his fill of felonies. He felt trapped. To try to intervene to stop his boss would have been as good as his life. He could report the goings-on to Saddam, but he was certain that Saddam knew all about them. On the other hand to acquiesce would make him an accomplice.

Finally, one morning, he tossed caution aside, and instead of showing up at Uncle Ferallah's he reported to his military unit. But when the unit's commander learned of his presence, he summoned Mithal to his office. "Please don't come here without Hadji Ferallah's permission," he said in an embarrassed, almost pleading, tone.

Mithal went home and asked his father, "What would you say if I were killed?" Then before Jamal could answer, Mithal posed an alternative. "What would you say if I were disgraced as corrupt and a criminal?" Presenting his father with this devil's dilemma was an elliptical way of appealing for help. Mithal foresaw that Uncle Ferallah's criminal exploits would catch up with him, and then he would share the disgrace. "It will end in my own arrest," lamented Mithal. So Jamal took his son and paid a call on Hadji Ferallah, bringing along an influential friend. They won his consent for Mithal to leave his service and return to his army unit.

Mithal was out of the frying pan, but there was fire all

around. With various Baath factions jostling for position, and the ruthless Saddam climbing steadily to the top of the heap, Iraq was a dangerous place to play politics. It did not take much to kindle Saddam's distrust or paranoia, and Mithal already sported a couple of red flags: his association with Al-Samarrai at the cadre school and his withdrawal from the service of Saddam's uncle.

To make Mithal all the more sensate to the perils, he was by now the head of a family, Elham having given birth to their first child in 1975, a son they named Ayman. Then, because Mithal was serving in the army, he was offered the opportunity to study flight engineering in Cairo. He seized this opportunity for escape, taking Elham and Ayman with him.

The schooling in Egypt was in English in which Mithal was weak. But feeling his responsibility as head of a family, he threw himself into his lessons with a diligence he had never exerted before. Nonetheless, his newfound conscientiousness did not extend to keeping his head down politically. On the contrary, away from Baghdad, he felt freer to vent the disillusionment with his country's ruling elite that had welled up over the previous two years.

He committed these thoughts to paper and circulated them to some of his fellow Iraqis in Cairo. The distribution was limited, to be sure, but the Baathists had many informers, and word of his apostasy found its way to Iraqi authorities. One day in 1976 when Mithal went to the Iraqi embassy to collect his government stipend, security officers were waiting for him. They confiscated his passport, and told him he was to return to Baghdad that same day. Although only 23, he "understood that this was the end."

Desperate, Mithal tried a brazen gambit. Feigning indifference to the summons to Baghdad, he waxed indignant at the demand that someone of his stature should be asked to travel in such haste. He turned on the officers:

Are you crazy? You order me to go back to Baghdad? Fine. It is my Baghdad and my leaders. I will go back and when we are there I will teach you how to talk to me. I will go now out. I have things I need to do, and packing. Tomorrow I will go to Baghdad, and you will see what I will do there.

The officers wavered in the face of his display of self-assurance. If Mithal was not bluffing, it could cost them dear. So they gave him a day to arrange his affairs, confident that he could not escape. Mithal, however, had seen more than enough from his old friend Hassan and his months at the side of Hadji Ferallah to know that his chances of eluding a *mukhabarat* dragnet in Cairo, however slim, were better than his chances of surviving a return to Baghdad. By chance, Elham had taken Ayman to Baghdad to visit her family. This was a stroke of luck. Had they been in Cairo with him, it would have been all but impossible for the three of them to flee together. On the other hand, if he left them behind, Elham would have been subject to rough treatment when the *mukhabarat* came looking for him at their Cairo flat. That she and Ayman were in the home of her family in Baghdad, and not on the scene when he fled, worked to their advantage, at least for the time being.

But where to hide? Mithal believed that one of his fellow students, Talal al-Haj, was watched less closely than the others, due to his family's circumstances. Although they were not close, Mithal knew that Talal disliked the Iraqi regime and distrusted the embassy. So he appealed for Talal's help. It was an "all-in" bet. Mithal's classmates were sure to be interrogated, and Talal could betray him. Instead, Talal proved to be a man of compassion and courage. "Talal hid me in his house and even gave me some money," says Mithal. "He was taking a huge risk. If they knew it, they would have killed him."

In addition to Talal, two other friends gave Mithal shelter. He shaved his mustache, and he ventured out only in jeans or other clothing different from his accustomed garb. But after two months he said to Talal, "This can't continue; one of these days they'll find me."

He realized he must flee Egypt, but his passport had been confiscated, so he needed help. He calculated that the one foreign government so bitterly at odds with Baghdad that it would shelter him was the Baathist government of Syria. The Syrian and Iraqi wings of Baathism had split in 1960, and the division had widened to the point that now, in 1976, each of these two brother parties viewed the other as its most dangerous enemy, spying on it assiduously. Mithal felt confident that Syrian intelligence would know that he was an up-and-comer in the Iraqi Baath because of his time near the helm of the cadre school. He was sure, too, that they would value his first-hand knowledge of the Iraqi leadership.

Talal mounted his motorcycle with Mithal in back, and drove to the Syrian embassy which was guarded by Egyptian officers. Talal screeched to a stop in front of them and jumped off the bike to create a distraction while Mithal ran inside the grounds to the front door. A Syrian diplomat came to the door and told him that the embassy was closed. Mithal replied: "There is an arrest order against me in Syria, and I am coming to turn myself in." This got Mithal in the door where the ambassador took him in hand and quickly ascertained his potential importance.

The next day he was handed a new passport and other identity papers. These documents said that his name was Samir Khaled al-Ahmed, a Syrian born in Dayr as-Zawr (his mother's real home town), who was passing through Cairo on his way home from Libya. He was ticketed on a flight to Damascus accompanied by two Syrian intelligence officers who told him to hold their hands all the way.

After his departure, the faithful Talal did him one more dangerous service. As a stratagem, Iraqi security had told Mithal's father, Jamal, that his son had died in Cairo. They knew he would travel to Cairo to bring the body home. They planned to trail Jamal as he searched for it, in the hope he would lead them to Mithal. When they met, Talal told Jamal of Mithal's flight to Syria and enjoined him to continue his search in Cairo so as to mislead the spies.

When Mithal's flight landed in Damascus, his two escorts left him in the hands of a greeting party of fellow Iraqis. Various of the losers in the faction fights within the Iraqi Baath had taken refuge in Syria and maintained a small group there which the Syrians naturally used for their own purposes. They had notified these Iraqis of Mithal's imminent arrival and told them to play host.

They put him up for the night, and the next day a leader of the group came to see him. As someone who had once ranked high in the Iraqi Baath, Mithal was a big fish who was expected to assume a prominent role in their group. They assured him that he would be given his own flat and other necessities. But this role held little appeal for him. He knew that they were dependent on Syrian intelligence, thus under its control. Having refused to join Iraq's security service when Hassan had invited him, why would he want to join Syria's?

From the balcony of the flat where they took him, he spotted a small tobacco shop across the street and told his hosts that he wanted to go down for cigarettes. Inside the shop, he offered the clerk the 100 Lira (about twenty-five dollars) in pocket money he had been given and asked him to put through a phone call for him. The loyalty of extended families is one of the glories of Arab culture, and Mithal calculated that he could tap into it. He had Syrian relatives on his mother's side, and he succeeded in getting a cousin on the phone. Within a few hours several carloads of his kin arrived to collect him.

At first, the Syrian *mukhabarat* was content to let him stay with his relatives while it worked to enlist his services by means of inducements and threats. The family meanwhile used its resources to try to get him off the hook. "My uncle is a rich man," recalls Mithal. "He was really trying everything he could: giving gifts, petitioning through connections. Nothing helped."

Finally, in the beginning of 1977, Mithal was arrested and taken to an old prison in Damascus where he was interrogated in the manner of the region—with lots of beatings—over the course of several months. But he was not willing to go to work for them and had little else to offer. Finally he was told he was to be sent back to Iraq. "Let them kill you. Why should we have to do it?" said one of his jailers. But one colonel intervened, arguing that Mithal was too important in the Iraqi Baath to give up on so easily. Instead, he was transferred to another prison where the beatings and interrogation resumed.

The colonel who intervened had, in truth, been bribed by the family. No doubt for further emoluments, he got Mithal out of jail and furnished him with Syrian papers, in the name of Naji Aboud al Khombar. Relatives arranged to drive Naji Aboud across an unguarded part of the Syrian-Lebanese border to a flat in Beirut.

After a short stay there, his uncle arrived with the valid Syrian passport of one of Mithal's cousins. Mithal carefully removed his cousin's photo from the document and replaced it with his own. Then he booked a flight from Beirut to Budapest, a natural destination for a Syrian in those days of close ties between Syria and the Warsaw Pact. From there he traveled by ground to East Berlin and that same day by bus from East to West Berlin.

He made his way to Hamburg where he hoped that the knowledge gained during his incomplete training as a flight engineer might help him find work in an airplane factory, despite his lack of German. Language, however, was only the first obstacle. More daunting, he was in the country illegally, having entered on a forged passport bearing a false name. He decided to turn himself in and serve whatever sentence was imposed. Then, he imagined, he could regularize his situation, use his real name, and get on with life. He had already known prison in Syria, and he figured that it would be less difficult in Germany.

Still, before relinquishing his freedom, he wanted to taste some of the novel pleasures he saw around him. Hamburg had an amusement park, and he wanted to experience the roller coaster and other rides. In the evenings he went to nightclubs and discotheques. This self-indulgence lasted a few days; then he went to the police station and surrendered.

"This is not my passport and not my name," he said to the officer on duty, displaying his false documents. The response stunned him. The officer, and others around the squad room, burst into laughter. Then they told him that this was not their problem, and that if he wanted to confess, he had to go to the *auslander polizei,* the external police. But they recommended that he first see a lawyer. Mithal felt a sense of irony: he had fled a country where it was hard to stay on the right side of the law to one where it was hard to run afoul of it.

This feeling redoubled when he informed the *auslander polizei* of his illegitimate circumstances. They listened to his confession, then, instead of locking him up, they offered him housing and a document entitling him to a monthly stipend. This was a far cry from dealing with the *mukhabarat.* Mithal made a decision to settle in Germany, learn the language and bring his family.

However, before Elham and Ayman joined him in Hamburg, her family made a naïve effort to bring Mithal home. Some of its members arranged for Elham to have a private audience with Saddam Hussein. Elham pleaded on Mithal's behalf, and Saddam was forthcoming, commenting that Mithal had been "one of our good people." Then he made her a magnanimous offer: "Because of his young son, if he writes me a letter, I will forgive everything." Elham left happy, and she sent a message through intermediaries for Mithal to call her at her family's home. When he reached her she told him about Saddam's offer. Knowing Saddam as he did, Mithal was furious at Elham for her gullibility, fearing she was endangering herself by getting lured into these machinations. "You stupid woman, go home and lock the door," he ordered.[5]

In Hamburg, Mithal got a part-time job, off the books, refinishing furniture, and he rented a small flat that he shared with a Russian immigrant colleague. The hours he was not working he spent mostly riding trains. He learned he could buy a local commuter pass that allowed unlimited usage, and that was how he studied German. He would find a seat next to an old person, since they were often lonely and ready to chat with strangers, and he would strike up conversation, as best he could.

Happily, his fears that Elham would get caught in the wheels of Saddam's vengeance were not realized, and, securing travel documents through family connections, she joined Mithal in Hamburg. Elham felt out of her element in Germany, and she tried to persuade Mithal to return to Iraq and accept Saddam's offer of absolution. "He likes you," she insisted, recalling her interview with the charming ruler. But Mithal would not think of it and drew a line in the sand: "You may go back or you may stay here with me, which is what I wish." She stayed.

After the arrival of his family, he succeeded in landing a fulltime job in one of the airplane factories. But it was not his calling, and he lost a finger in an industrial accident.

That prompted him to go into business, variously in export-import, textiles, and clothing, but he was never very successful. "I have no idea how to run a business," he says. "So I always had troubles, and if I made some money, it was just because I was lucky, not because I'm a businessman."

Still, the family got by, and it was augmented by the arrival of a second son, Jamal, named after Mithal's father, born in 1982. His indifferent success at business did not distress Mithal much since he was concerned less with money than with the upbringing of his sons and the politics of his native country.

"We gave everything that we had to our sons," says Mithal. "We put them in good schools. We followed their education very seriously. We taught them whatever they wanted: karate, basketball, surfing, or even flying. Gave them everything what we could." In addition, he recalls, during school holidays, "we took many trips—to the U.S., to England, to Italy, to France, many countries. If I had small money, we did it. If we had big money, we did it. The difference was which hotel or whether by airplane or car or which restaurants we were looking for. But we always did it."

The boys attended local schools and grew up fluent in German, which Mithal and Elham gradually mastered, and the family adopted German citizenship. Mithal felt himself change under the impact of the surrounding culture. "I started to think in a free way," he says. Particularly striking to him were his encounters with Jews, which came as a novelty. Early in the twentieth century, Baghdad had been an ethnic mosaic in which Jews constituted one of the largest groups. But almost the entire community had fled when the state of Israel was born, and the Arab states, including Iraq, declared war. Of the tiny remnant that remained, a dozen were publicly hanged as "spies" after Israel's victory in the 1967 Six Day War, prompting the rest to flee. As a result, Mithal had never met a Jew.

He discovered that the neighbor boy with whom Jamal went to kindergarten was Jewish, and there were a couple of other German Jews living on the street. He was cordial with them, but remote. Then some friends introduced him to a mother and son of Iraqi background. Mithal was impressed with her fluent "Iraqi," which she had been taught by her immigrant father, much as he was teaching it to his own sons.

He was stunned when she revealed that she had been born in neither Iraq nor Germany but in Israel. Then he met another Iraqi Jew who shared his longing for their homeland. He recalls:

> He knows he is not welcome in Iraq, but this crazy man, he wants when he dies to be buried in Iraq. Well, this is something new. And here is a young lady, she has a child. She speaks Iraqi, clear Iraqi, then she say, "I have been born Israeli. I'm Israeli." And then, it started you know, always I was thinking about this issue. What is going on? How should we deal with it?

The impact of this experience reflected a contradiction deep within Mithal. On the one hand, he was beginning to adopt Western ideas, as exemplified by opening his heart to Jews. On the other hand, a big part of what attracted him to these particular Jews was that they were *Iraqis,* and despite their German naturalization, Mithal and Elham never ceased yearning for home. "There was no week—I cannot say no day—when we did not say in our house, 'maybe next week we will be able to go back,'" he recalls.

The family, thus, lived between two worlds. Mithal insisted that only "Iraqi" be spoken in their home:

> I was always telling my sons Iraqi stories. Telling them about their grandfather, how beautiful our village, how beautiful Baghdad, and how great the Iraqi is and what are Iraqi values. Telling them many stories about my family, and how I was as a child. Both of us, my wife and I were trying to put them always in an Iraqi atmosphere. The house was an Iraqi house, totally Iraqi in our way.

Although Mithal did not join Elham in growing religious in exile, he often took his sons to Friday prayers at various mosques in Hamburg. Occasionally, they attended one of the smaller ones, the al Quds mosque, that turned out to be the hub of the 9/11 terrorists. Mithal believes he must have encountered some of them, but he has no specific memory of it.

He knew well, however, one young man who was apparently an important accomplice, Mohamed Haider Zammar. Haider, as he was called by Mithal, was the son of a Syrian immigrant who was one of Mithal's close friends in Hamburg. Mithal had watched him grow up, and always viewed him as "naïve, primitive, stupid." Then as a teen, Haider went off to fight in Afghanistan. Sometime after his return, and not long before 9/11, he and Mithal had a disconcerting encounter. Upon greeting, Haider noticed Mithal's hand and said: "Uncle, you are not allowed to wear a gold ring." "Why not?" asked Mithal. "Because Allah will send you to hell," came the answer. "Haider, get out" yelled Mithal.

After 9/11, the 300-pound Haider was identified as a key jihadist operative in Hamburg. According to the *New York Times,* he was "believed to have helped recruit [Mohammed] Atta and other cell members to receive terrorist training from Al Qaeda in Afghanistan."[6] A month after the attacks on the United States, Zammar boarded a flight for Casablanca, but according to news accounts, Moroccan authorities, alerted by U.S. intelligence, refused him entry, placing him on a flight to Syria where he was arrested.[7]

Mithal's attachment to his native land found voice not only in the manner of raising his children but also in political activity aimed at changing the Iraqi regime. He composed anti-Saddam flyers and circulated these among the Iraqi exile community in Hamburg and other European cities. But he knew full well that these distant scribblings could make little dent on Iraq's well fortified regime. He felt deeply frustrated at the meager weapons available to him.

Then, in 1982, the possibility of more effective action arose unexpectedly when he met a Libyan in Hamburg who was affiliated with the Libyan Islamic Movement, or Da'wa (not to be confused with the Iraqi party of the same name). A fierce rivalry had developed between Saddam Hussein and Libya's dictator, Muammar Qaddafi, as these two narcissists competed for leadership of the radical Arab camp. When Saddam Hussein launched war on Iran in 1980, Qaddafi quickly declared: "It is our Islamic duty to align ourselves with the Muslims of Iran, instead of fighting them on America's behalf."[8]

Saddam returned the insult and upped it. Not only was Qaddafi "up to his ears in interaction with America," declared the Baath Party's newspaper, but, worse, "both [Iran's Ayatollah Ruhollah] Khomeini and Qaddafi are racing . . . to serve Zionism."[9]

The man Mithal met was Abdul Basit Abdul Samad al-Qaddafi, who claimed to be a cousin of the Libyan ruler. After a few conversations, he introduced Mithal to the Libyan ambassador, and then Mithal received an invitation to attend the Libyan General People's Congress which passes for a parliament in Qaddafi's jury-rigged political system.

For this, however, Mithal needed a travel document, so he applied to the *auslander polizei* which denied the request. He then asked his lawyer to file an appeal, and the lawyer reported that the judge had told him unofficially that he would grant the request. But the judge reversed himself at the last moment, apparently in response to an off-the-record intervention. Mithal inferred that West German intelligence was watching and did not wish him to deepen his Libyan connections.

Mithal, however, was not easily deterred. He and the Libyans arranged an alternative itinerary. He traveled to West Berlin where he was picked up by a car bearing diplomatic plates. In the car, he was handed a new passport, identifying him as a Libyan diplomat. They drove through Checkpoint Charlie to East Berlin, where he spent the night as a guest of the Libyan ambassador to East Germany before being put on a flight to Tripoli.

After a few days in Libya, one of the officials hosting him, a man named Mohammed, told him that they had been invited to a wedding which would be an opportunity for him to observe Libyan customs. When the wedding banquet was served, Mohammed discouraged Mithal from partaking: "We're going to dine elsewhere, my friend."

About an hour later, Mohammed told Mithal that it was time to go to the other dinner: "Someone is waiting for you." They drove to a building and were shown into a waiting room where they were served some juice. Shortly, Mohammed's phone rang. Smiling, he turned to Mithal and said, "*Al Qaid* [The Leader] is waiting for you," and they were ushered into Qaddafi's presence.

After some pleasantries and picture-taking, Qaddafi turned serious and asked what Iraqis thought of him. Mithal recalls that he answered by saying, "Sir, they think you have stabbed them in the back." In the face of Qaddafi's stony silence, he hastened to explain that Iraqis wanted Qaddafi's support against Saddam but not by backing Iran. To Mithal's relief, the Libyan relaxed and asked what kind of support. Mithal replied that he wanted weapons, military training and a radio transmitter to up a guerrilla base in northern Iraq.

Qaddafi promised him the equipment, and they planned for its delivery to Mithal in Ankara, Turkey, where it could be transported across the border into Iraq. Mithal says that Qaddafi tried to recruit him for a terrorist act in Europe, and he put him off. When Mithal got the word that the promised shipment was ready, he traveled to Ankara but was arrested before he could collect it, never learning who had betrayed him. Although he was held only ten days, his dream of creating an anti-Saddam guerrilla base was dashed.

Mithal returned to writing leaflets, and by the 1990s, he had developed a circle of followers in Hamburg and a few other European cities. They numbered a few dozen, mostly men younger than Mithal who was now in his forties. They remained apart from the two umbrella organizations of exiles, the Iraqi National Congress of Ahmed Chalabi, and the Iraqi National Accord of Ayad Allawi, that the CIA helped organize. Mithal says he regarded these as "an American project," and he was not convinced that "the Americans really wanted to get rid of Saddam Hussein."

For years, he was limited to writing and talking, trying to keep hope alive among his band. Then came 9/11. He was appalled by the attack but also saw that it created new opportunities. He concluded that America might at last turn seriously against Saddam Hussein. So he concocted a plan to push the Americans along.

The plan was to "liberate" Iraqi embassies in Berlin, Amsterdam and Vienna "in order to make an international demonstration that the Iraqi citizens reject Saddam and his party." How could Mithal reconcile seizing an embassy with the liberal values he imbibed in Germany? "We did not have the right to punish people, to kill people, to cause damage, and we have not done that," he said. "But any nation has the right of resistance, the right to exist and be safe. And do not forget, this [embassy] is an Iraqi house." Moreover, as he told his followers, the embassy was a base for the *mukhabarat* which not only spied on exiles, but sometimes murdered them.

Mithal turned to Ali Furaji, a trusted follower active in their Berlin group. Furaji, 37, had fled Iraq nine years earlier after scrawling anti-Saddam slogans on the walls of Mustansiriya University where he was studying mathematics. Ali had taken refuge in Jordan, Syria and Tunisia, making phone contact with Mithal whose reputation he knew. Mithal urged him to come to Germany so as to be safer from the Iraqi *mukhabarat* which operated with considerable impunity in the Arab states. Finding asylum in Germany, Furaji received shelter and a refugee stipend from the state while devoting himself, under Mithal's leadership, to agitation among fellow Iraqi exiles.

Ali understood that the mission for which Mithal now chose him would be dangerous, but he did not think twice. "For me and my friends, afraid or not, when Mr. Mithal Al-Alusi asks you, you answer."[10]

Although Mithal instructed him to select four others, Ali showed up with five. Mithal's plan was very precise, and he did not want an extra. The obvious choice for dismissal from the team was the oldest of the men, a physician, but the man was adamant. "Saddam killed my father," he told Mithal. "You have no right to send me back." So Mithal discharged one of the others.

On August 19, 2002, while diplomats around the world were debating what should be done about Saddam's defiance of UN weapons inspections, Mithal alerted his team that the operation would be the next day. He wanted to avoid lethal force, so he equipped them with only one fire arm, as well as pepper spray, an ax, and a second pistol that did not fire bullets. Some news reports described it as a tear gas gun. Mithal says it was more like a starter's pistol.

The embassy was surrounded by a fence. While three of the team concealed themselves in a bus stop enclosure next to the gate, two others rang the outer bell. Mithal and one other colleague watched the action from cars parked across the street, armed and prepared to enter the fray if the operation went awry.

When a guard opened the gate, the five rushed him, firing the starter's pistol for effect, and he fled. The team was now on the embassy grounds. The sequence that ensued is attributed by Mithal and his colleagues to the perfection of their plan; but it may as well have been due to the Keystone Kops response of the embassy guards, or to sheer luck. The guards inside, realizing there were attackers on the embassy grounds, responded by locking the front door, readying their arms, then proceeding to the basement and out a back door to surprise the attackers. But Mithal's team forced the front door before the guards could circle around to stop them. They then bolted both doors, leaving the guards stranded outside, while they seized the two diplomats present, binding them with duct tape. Two embassy personnel received minor injuries in the takeover, one from pepper spray, the other from shock. Once they were firmly in control, Faruji and his team allowed those two to leave together with the few women and children who were there, family of the diplomats.

The captors proceeded to hang Iraqi flags emblazened with "Death to Saddam" from the windows. A statement faxed to news agencies read: "We declare that the liberation of Iraqi soil begins on this day." It was signed in the name of the Democratic Iraqi Opposition of Germany. Among themselves, however, Mithal's followers called their group the Enemies of Saddam.

In addition to making a display, the captors ransacked drawers, files and computers, aiming to uncover and expose *mukhabarat* activities. They say they found machine guns and pistols—weapons less suitable for use by embassy guards than by hit men or terrorists—and a document ordering the assassination of nine Iraqi exiles in Europe. They claim they discovered a classified message instructing the embassy to funnel money to the reelection of Social Democratic Chancellor Gerhard Schroeder, who was campaigning on a platform of opposition to any military "adventure" against Saddam's regime.

After five hours, German commandos stormed the embassy to end the siege. Mithal had instructed his team not to resist, and they greeted the commandos with their hands in the air. At the success of their operation, Faruji says, he was "very, very, very, very happy," except for worrying that Saddam would retaliate against his family in Iraq.

Mithal also felt delight, but this was tempered by one harsh disappointment. The action was disowned by other Iraqi exile groups. He felt especially bitter toward Ayad

Allawi. Mithal claims that he and Allawi, who had known each other for years, had discussed the operation, indeed collaborated on the planning. But when the event unfolded, Allawi denied all knowledge and denounced it. Ahmed Chalabi's public response was similar, but Mithal did not resent it. They did not know each other, and Chalabi was unaware of Mithal's plans. During the takeover, Chalabi had phoned Mithal, asked if there were any way that he could give private succor to his group, even as he informed Mithal that he would speak publicly against the action. This he did, but he also added a sympathetic note, telling the press that Mithal and his followers "had been talking to the German government for a long time [about Iraqi *mukhabarat* operations in Germany] without getting any support for their position."[11] Mithal saw Chalabi's response as more honorable than Allawi's.

In any event, the general disavowal of his action by other exile groups impelled Mithal to cancel plans for similar takeovers in Amsterdam and Vienna that he had other teams ready to execute in the next days. Instead, he went home, packed a few items to take to prison, and waited for the police to arrive.

Any state is embarrassed when foreign missions under its protection are violated, but in this instance the German government experienced an extra embarrassment. In addition to Mithal's claims of having found evidence that Saddam was trying to boost Schroeder's reelection, the dramatic acts and words of these Iraqi exiles lent authenticity to American claims about the horrors of Saddam's regime. Berlin threw the book at them.

Mithal and the team of five were tried together. They remained defiant. Mithal readily acknowledged directing the plot, and called his five co-defendents "heroes." Citing the weapons and orders to attack Iraqi exiles that they found within the building, he declared, "The Iraqi embassy is a terrorist cell." Pointing out that they had harmed neither their hostages nor anyone else, he argued that the action "was about saving our lives and those of numerous other people."[12]

They were sentenced to three years each—except Mithal who was given an extra three months—in Berlin's historic Moabit prison, where the Nazis first held Pastor Martin Niemoller, where the Communist *Stasi* tortured its prisoners, and where East German boss Erich Honecker was in turn held for trial after the collapse of the Communist state.

Mithal and his comrades arrived there at a fortuitous moment, just as America and its allies launched their invasion of Iraq. Mithal followed events on television and via short wave radio. He was elated at the "liberation," as he insisted on calling it, correcting anyone who used a different term. But he was burning with frustration at not being home to be part of it.

The ouster of Saddam put a new twist on the status of Mithal and his co-conspirators. No doubt they had committed a serious crime, but German courts are not deaf to diplomatic pressures. The state of Iraq had been the principal victim of the seizure of its territory by Mithal's team. Suddenly, in the eyes of Iraq they were exemplars rather than "terrorist mercenaries" and "agents of the CIA and Mossad," as Saddam's regime had characterized them.[13] In September, after the group had served thirteen months, the court released them, pending an appeal.

Soon after release, Mithal made his way to Iraq with Elham who was overjoyed to be going home. They had succeeded so well in imbuing their sons with Iraqi identity that the two young men hardly thought twice before deciding that their futures lay in Iraq, despite the fact that Ayman had left that land at the age of three, and Jamal had never set foot in it. For Ayman, it meant uprooting his Iraqi exile wife and their three young children. Nonetheless, the two sons left for Baghdad even before Mithal was able to get there. When he arrived and launched into political activity, they became his closest aides and advisors.

None of the team of Mithal's followers who had been imprisoned and paroled with him held German passports. Given their refugee status, they needed special documents to travel. These they could not get while on probation. From Baghdad, Mithal lobbied for them to be allowed to join him in Iraq. In fact, he did more than lobby. Embedding himself at once in the embryonic political structures of post-Saddam Iraq, he pressed for discrimination against German business interests. This infuriated German authorities who put out a warrant for his arrest, apparently for violating his own parole. In the end, nonetheless, his colleagues were allowed to depart. They boarded a plane in Mainz for Amman and then traveled by land to the Iraqi border where Mithal and a few others gave them a hero's welcome before caravanning back to Baghdad.

In November 2003, less than two months after his return, Mithal held several meetings with Ahmed Chalabi. Although he had remained aloof of Chalabi's Iraqi National Congress (INC) while in exile, the situation was now quite different. Chalabi, a favorite of some American officials, was a prominent member of the Governing Council that the invaders had appointed and was in the thick of Iraq's reviving politics. The INC was, moreover, secular, as was Mithal. So he agreed to merge his band of followers into the INC. And Chalabi agreed that Mithal would assume a senior position within the INC leadership. Indeed, in the ensuing months, Mithal served often as Chalabi's spokesman.

The Governing Council appointed Chalabi chairman of the DeBaathification Commission (Nouri al-Maliki, who later became prime minister, was the vice-chairman), and Chalabi hired Mithal as one of five directors general. It was not a position from which to win friends. Mithal was already a sworn enemy of the Baath, but he believed that reviving the country

required clearing skilled professionals to return to their jobs—
so long as they had been ordinary party members and not
enforcers. As he told an interviewer: "The main point, they
are human being. The main point, they are Iraqi. And the
main point, we are going to have a new Iraq. From this reason
we need every Iraqi man, if he is not killer."[14] This earned him
enmity from the other direction—those who felt that Baathists
should not be forgiven. If these weren't enemies enough,
Mithal also ran afoul of Paul Bremer, chief of the American
occupation, apparently over differences over how to handle
members of the old Iraqi army. Mithal reacted with characteristic steeliness: "I am not afraid of Mr. Bremer. [He] is an
American and I am an Iraqi, and I will stay in Iraq, and he
has to leave."[15]

But Mithal was not prepared for the change in his rela-
tions with Chalabi that unfolded over the course of 2004. In
May, U.S. authorities accused Chalabi of passing secrets to
Iran and of misuse of funds that America had given the INC.
At the same time an Iraqi judge charged him with responsibility for a shakedown racket connected to the Ministry of
Finance, which was under his influence, and with other mis-
feasance. Then, in August, an Iraqi court indicted him for
counterfeiting on the complaint of the Iraqi central bank. As
Mithal explains, Chalabi had put himself in a compromising
situation. To shore up the national currency, a new dinar was
issued. Holders of old dinars could exchange them for new,
and the old ones were incinerated. The whole operation was
largely under Chalabi's authority as a member of the cabinet,
and the site for burning the old currency was located not far
from Chalabi's home in a neighborhood over which Chalabi's
forces maintained control. According to some accusers, Chalabi's minions recycled some of the old dinars rather than tossing them in the flames.

Chalabi was on a visit to Iran when the indictment was
handed down, and Mithal largely took things into his own

hands. He concluded that some INC leaders were in fact corrupt, and he moved to freeze them out. But he believed that Chalabi himself was innocent, and he rallied to his defense. He organized a street demonstration of two thousand people in support of the INC leader, and he fired Chalabi's defense attorneys, finding a new one who succeeded in getting the charges dismissed. This role, however, brought Mithal very close to the case, and despite initially having championed Chalabi, he came away doubting his innocence even though he had gotten off.

Soon, the two men had a more profound falling out. It began in May 2004 as Mithal discussed his fear and loathing of terrorism over dinner with a Western expert. The man mentioned that an international conference on the subject was to be held that summer at the International Institute for Counter-Terrorism, a part of the Herzliya Interdisciplinary Center in Israel. He asked Mithal if he would be willing to attend if invited, and Mithal said yes.

A few months later, the invitation arrived by e-mail. Mithal consulted the circle of close followers whom he had led into the INC, most of whom were supportive of his going, but he did not consult others in the INC, including Chalabi. He did not respond to the invitation, delaying a final decision. In early September, some days before the conference, he packed his bag and his German passport and traveled to Turkey, stopping in Istanbul. There he sat for a few days, downing coffee and smoking shisha, and turning it over in his mind. He believed that opening a door between his country and Israel was the right thing to do. He knew, too, that he would pay a heavy price, but he was not sure in what coin. Ostracism? Expulsion from the INC? Death? All were possible. Nonetheless, after three days he boarded a flight for Tel Aviv.

Why did he do it? Mithal offers several reasons. First, he says,

Israel is our enemy. Well, good. We got two or three wars. But what is the end? How many wars should we start? Our responsibility as politicians is not to start war and war and war, and we know there is no result [except] more damage to the economy, more damage to the society, and for nothing.

Nothing for the Arab populace, that is. "There is only one beneficiary: the regimes: the Syrian regime, the Nasser regime, Arafat regime, only they benefit. They are cheating their people in the name of [fighting] Zionism." He continues, "If I cannot find a solution after 60 years through this mechanism, is it not time for a change?"

Second, he sounds a note of compassion for the Jews, seeming especially moved by the memory of Iraq's once-thriving Jewish community. He points out that Jews were active in the first Iraqi state of 1920. "Some of them were ministers," he points out. "One of the best Iraqi finance ministers was an Iraqi Jew." Then he asks rhetorically of the Arab nationalists: "if you do not accept them to come back and you want to throw them [from Israel] into the sea, where they should go? Why give yourself the right to exist and not accept that the other human being has the same right?"

Third, Mithal sees common interests and values between Israel and Iraq or at least the Iraq he hopes to erect. "If we want to have a democratic system, the first democratic country in the Middle East, whether we like it or not, is Israel." He adds, "We have the same interests because we have the same problems. We are suffering here from the terrorists. The same people who are attacking [Israeli] society are attacking my society."

The common interest Mithal sees is rooted in his vision of the future of Iraq, which in turn owes a great deal to his years in Germany. The irony of Mithal is that he remained fiercely Iraqi throughout that long exile but drank deeply of Western ways. He did not for a moment wish to become a westerner; instead he developed the goal of westernizing Iraq.

He wants his country "just to be normal. For 30, 40, 50, 60 years the Iraqi people did not get the chance to be normal, to dream normal. Now is the chance to do it."

Mithal is not alone in describing Western culture as "normal." Mikhail Gorbachev did, too.[16] One explanation for such terminology is that Western artifacts dominate global commerce and communication, establishing a "norm" by the overwhelming weight of their presence. Another explanation, put by Francis Fukuyama, is that democracy and capitalism fulfill innate, therefore universal, human strivings.[17] Mithal's views are similar.

When Mithal arrived in Israel, Chalabi got word of his presence and sent a message, asking him not to make any public statement while he was there. Mithal chose to ignore this. In the midst of his five days, he gave a long interview to one of the pan-Arab satellite networks that made immediate headlines in Iraq. A spokesman for the INC announced at once that Mithal had been summarily expelled from the party.

He was also quoted in the Israeli press advocating peace between Iraq and Israel. "There is a need to be far away from fanatical ideas," he said, "and it is time for Iraq to have politics based on reality.... The reality is that Israel is a fact, and I cannot accept Iraqi politics based on Palestinian or Syrian interests."[18]

At the end of his visit, Mithal flew back to Turkey. There, he received various messages from Chalabi the thrust of which was: do not return to Baghdad. Chalabi's spokesman had focused on Mithal's failure to consult with the party before going to Israel, but the issue was not procedural. Chalabi was embarrassed politically by Mithal's trip. He urged Mithal to go settle in London for a long while or perhaps permanently. When Mithal insisted on returning to Iraq, Chalabi suggested that he retire to Suleimaniya in Kurdistan, far from Arab Iraqi politics—and Mithal says that Chalabi offered help with housing and living expenses.

Mithal asked for some time to mull this proposal, but he was dissembling. He made a decision to head straight for home. His violation of the barrier against contact with Israel had created a political scandal in Iraq. Even Prime Minister Allawi, although close to the Americans, had denounced it. Mithal knew that there would be attempts on his life, and he was particularly vulnerable while traveling. So his ploy was to get back to the security of his home while people believed he was still in Turkey.

He made phone contact with close supporters who met him at the border and escorted him back to Baghdad. They were armed, and he expected to be attacked en route, but his stratagem worked, and he reached home unmolested. "I was so happy to see my people waiting for me in my house with machine guns and saying, 'we are not leaving you alone.'"

Mithal did have a circle of devoted followers who were prepared to risk their lives for him. This, however, was but a small shield against the torrent of troubles he had brought down on himself by the cardinal sin of setting foot in "the Zionist entity." An Iraqi official declared that, "Al-Alusi committed a crime by visiting the enemy, Zionist state," making it necessary "to protect the Islamic and Arab identity of Iraq."[19]

A few weeks after his return, Mithal received a visit from the brother of Iraq's chief investigative judge, bearing a warning:

> There is an arrest order from a very high level in the government. They will arrest you under the spying article because you went to Israel, and this means the death penalty. My brother sent me to you to tell you he will sign it Saturday, and you will be arrested. So you have now two days. Please leave the country.

Would an Iraqi government dependent on U.S. support execute someone for visiting America's ally, Israel? The question was beside the point, explains Adil al-Jaboory, a former top security aide of Chalabi's who broke with him to join

Mithal: "They would have killed him in prison."[20] But Mithal did not run. Instead, he got in his car and drove to the studio of an Iraqi television station that he knew would like the story. He was soon on camera describing the pending arrest order and declaring his defiance, saying he would go nowhere.

The warrant was never issued, but this was far from the end of Mithal's woes. Not content with expelling him from the INC, Chalabi also fired Mithal from his post as director general of the de-Baathification commission, although this was a government body and not the fiefdom of Chalabi or his party. Mithal's dismissal entailed the loss of lifesaving perquisites: bodyguards, government-issued vehicles, weapons and ID that facilitated entry into the Green Zone and authorized carrying powerful weapons. Al-Jaboory, who was still in the INC at the time, says he asked Chalabi to detail bodyguards and equipment to protect Mithal against the obvious danger that flowed from his notorious travels as well as his role in de-Baathification. But these entreaties fell on deaf ears.

Mithal, although Sunni, lived with his family in the poorer Shiite part of Baghdad called Sadr City. Aside from himself and his two sons, the only men capable of bearing arms to aid in his protection were a few political followers. He says that he asked American authorities for permission to move with his family into the Green Zone but did not receive it. Mithal believes that, like Chalabi, the Americans working in Iraq shunned him for fear of being linked to Israel.

In the ensuing months, Mithal escaped two assassination attempts. He was unbowed. "I will not give in to the Baathists or the Islamists. I made a choice to visit a country in the region, and I stand by that choice." In December 2004, he founded the Democratic Party of the Iraqi Nation to take his vision of Iraq's future to the Iraqi people. Elections for the transitional national assembly were held one month later, which was much too soon for the party to make much of a showing, but it did appear on the ballot, fielding a list of twenty-four candidates. His sons, who worked with him at building the new party, mirrored his steadfastness. The younger, twenty-two-year-old Jamal who inherited his father's charisma, told a reporter, "It is true that we are in danger, but if this is the price for democracy and peace, it is a very low price."[21]

On the morning of February 8, Mithal was scheduled to attend an event at the Baghdad Convention Center which had become the seat of the Iraqi parliament. When he received notice that the meeting was postponed until later in the day, Ayman and Jamal decided to take the car and go over to the party office. They were accompanied by a "third son," a devotee of Mithal's, their age, who had been serving as a volunteer bodyguard and living in the house with them.

When the car had traveled about one hundred meters from the house, Mithal heard a tremendous burst of gunfire. He realized by reflex what it signified. He grabbed his automatic weapon and went running toward the car his "three sons" had taken, firing at vehicles that were fleeing the scene. He struggled to pull his boys from the car, but he was too late. Medics soon arrived, but there was nothing they could do except comfort Mithal. One embraced him and said, "We are all your sons." It had been a massive ambush, leaving the car riddled with bullets. Knowing that he was the intended target intensified Mithal's anguish.

Mithal had thought he was willing to pay any price to build the Iraq he envisioned: obloquy, banishment, jail, even his life. But his children's lives? This was a sacrifice for which he had not been prepared. Who could be? Nonetheless, he managed to tell Radio Free Europe later that day:

> Again, the ghosts of death are going out. They are ready to kill a person, ready to kill the peace, ready to kill the victory of Iraqis and their right to life. Again, henchmen of the Ba'ath

[party] and dirty terrorist gangs, al-Qaeda and others, are going out convinced that they can determine life and death as they desire. Iraq will not die. My children, three people [in all]—one of my bodyguards and two of my children—died as heroes, no differently from other people who find their heroic deaths. But we will not, [I swear] by God, hand Iraq over to murderers and terrorists.[22]

A day or two after the sons' deaths, Mithal sat and received condolences, a traditional Arab ritual, from family and friends and many other Iraqis he had never met who had heard the news and were stricken by it. Gunmen attacked the ceremony, and Mithal and a few colleagues, who were armed themselves, fought them off. This led to yet another bitter moment in the deteriorating relations between Mithal and his former comrade, Chalabi. In exchanging fire with the attackers, Mithal exhausted his ammunition, and he and his team had no ready supply. He called al-Jaboory, still a security aide to Chalabi, to ask for some bullets. Al-Jaboory says he relayed the request to Chalabi who failed to act on it. Fortunately, the gunmen did not return. Belatedly, U.S. authorities gave Mithal permission to move to a house inside the Green Zone.

His defense of his actions and defiance of his critics only intensified. In an interview on Iraqi TV, he said he would accept assistance even from the Mossad—the greatest bogeyman in the Arab world—if it would help defeat the terrorists in Iraq. A month after the assassinations, he traveled to Washington for meetings with members of Congress, hoping "to make it clear to everybody that the Iranian and Syrian governments are against liberalization in Iraq."[23] Later that year, he returned to Israel to address the same annual anti-terrorism conference that he had attended the year before. This time he went beyond calling for peace between Iraq and Israel. He told the gathering:

We need to have an alliance against terrorism.... Iraq is not in a position to fight alone against terrorism. Also United

States of America cannot do it alone, Israel cannot do it alone. It will be safer for our societies, the free societies, if we are making a political decision for dialogue and peace and reform. . . . Through a real strategic alliance, we can make our world safe, and save our children and families from those bad killers, the terrorists.[24]

With a dignity and self-restraint almost painful to behold, he did not allude to the fact that it was too late to save his own family.

In addition to its heterodox position on Israel, Mithal's Democratic Party of the Iraqi Nation is aggressively secular. Although Mithal is Sunni, most of the other members and leaders are Shiite. The party's weekly newspaper always features a centerfold of photos of attractive young women clothed none too modestly. "It is not a joke," says Mithal. "We do that to show them, 'look, how beautiful. Be teenagers, be young, enjoy your age. Be normal.'" Also, Mithal flaunts his opposition to Islamist parties. "We said here first—and not Mr. Bush in America—that they are Islamic fascists," he says. If they can, he says, the Islamists "will stop the democratic process as Hitler did in Germany."

The election of a permanent national assembly followed in December 2005 by which time the Democratic Party of the Iraqi Nation was a year old. It could not compete with the main sectarian or ethnic parties. Nonetheless, it polled enough votes to win a single seat—for Mithal—while many prominent Iraqis won nothing. Among those who failed to win any representation at all was Chalabi and his INC.

Although holding only one seat out of 270, Mithal won the respect of most colleagues. His name surfaced more than once in speculation about cabinet positions. In 2007, when the parliament created a special committee to investigate a violent clash between rival Shiite militias in Karbala, it selected Mithal as the chairman. In the summer of 2007, as criticism of Nouri al-Maliki's performance as prime minister crescendoed, *TIME* ran a list of eight possible successors. One of them was Mithal whom it described thus:

> One of the most unusual figures in Iraqi politics .... He is Sunni—a major handicap in the Prime Ministerial stakes—but is widely viewed as secular and independent.... His Democratic Party of the Iraqi Nation is tiny, but Alusi has a high profile because of his frequent appearance on TV news shows, where he rails against sectarianism and government corruption. This has earned him the respect of many Iraqis, and his personal popularity could make him a compromise candidate for Maliki's job.[25]

Mithal also received a back-handed compliment from Tehran. A friend of a friend sent Mithal word that he wished to bring him a message from the Iranian government. Mithal received him, and when the meeting got down to brass tacks, as Mithal recalls, the man said: "Iran is very strong. It is supporting all the parties, and parties need money. There are only two whose leaders have not visited. The imam [spiritual leader Ali Khamenei] and the president [Mahmoud Ahmadinejad] would like to see you in Iran."

To avoid any covert dealings with Iran, Mithal replied that he would only consider a formal invitation. Before long the Iranian ambassador asked for a meeting. Early in that sit-down, Mithal complained about Tehran's hand in Iraq's violence, which the ambassador denied, protesting, "We are Muslims, we are neighbors, we are brothers." Then Mithal turned to another grievance: "Your atom program cannot endanger New York or London, but we are neighbors. I am afraid of it." To this, the ambassador replied that the program was peaceful, designed to produce electricity which Iran would be willing to sell to Iraq cheap. Then Mithal says he answered: "Your Excellency, because we are Muslims, because we are neighbors, because we are brothers, if you make an atom bomb, please make two—one for you and one for me."

On top of this, Mithal reminded the Iranian that he advocated a strategic alliance with the United States and had visited Israel twice, but the man brushed that aside, asking nothing in return for Iran's beneficence. "So they came in a very fine way," says Mithal. "But once they invest in you, the game is over."

He declined to visit "the imam and the president." Such a pilgrimage would have conflicted with his party's nationalistic stance. In some ways, Mithal's party resembles political forces in Europe in the nineteenth century that combined nationalism and liberalism and sought to build democratic states. Mithal says:

> There is no Arab nation. I am an Arab man. My father is Arab, my mother she is Arab, but when I went to Jordan they told me I am Iraqi. When I went to Syria, I have the same problem. When I go to Egypt, when I go to Saudi Arabia, to Kuwait and those countries they are not dealing with Iraqi as Arab. They are dealing with Iraqi as Iraqi.

Underscoring his point with a dramatic flair, he told an Iraqi television audience, "I would not spend one cent to rebuild Mecca if it is damaged. That is not my job. My job is just Iraq."

Not only does he believe Iraqis should distinguish themselves from other Arabs, but with equal fervor he discourages them from dividing themselves from one another: "Iraqis must consider themselves Iraqis first—before they consider themselves Muslims, Sunni, Shia, or anything else." When, in September 2007, the U.S. Senate passed a resolution introduced by Joseph Biden that pushed "federalism" in Iraq in a way that many Iraqis thought was tantamount to partition of the country, Mithal took the lead in opposition. He introduced a bill in the national assembly declaring Biden *persona non grata* in Iraq.

In his campaign against Biden, Mithal showed himself once again to be a man of contradictions. He was a democrat who once conspired with Qaddafi. He was the living embodiment of the "radical middle." He put it:

> I do not believe in a passive liberal position. Normally, we got the feeling here in the Orient, "You liberals, you are so fine, so kind, you do nothing but have liberal values." I believe if you are liberal you have to fight for your liberal space and to make it real but in liberal terms, not revolutionary terms, not extremist terms.

By the same token, Mithal is in some sense the most pro-American of Iraqi politicians, thanking America for ousting Saddam and advocating democracy more convincingly than any other Iraqi politician. But at the same time, his relations with the Americans are often testy. This was exemplified by his denunciation of Biden, his battles with Paul Bremer, and his criticism of the State Department for its fear of mentioning Israel to Iraqi audiences.

By far his sharpest clash with the Americans came in June 2007 when Iraq investigators found two men who confessed to taking part in the ambush that killed Mithal's sons, for which the Baath Party and an affiliate of al Qaeda had claimed responsibility.[26] According to the two, they had been hired for the hit by none other than Asad Kamal al-Hashimi, Iraq's minister of culture. Al-Hashimi, the former imam of a Sunni mosque, was an Islamist and a leader of the Iraqi Accordance Front, the main bloc of Sunni legislators.

Prime Minister Nouri al-Maliki had to sign off on arrest orders for high officials, and he was always reluctant to do so. In this case, the investigating judge had signed an order for al-Hashimi's arrest, but Mithal became convinced that Maliki was blocking it. He aired this belief in a television interview as well as a private face-to-face meeting, with the result that the order was issued.

A large contingent of Iraqi law-enforcers backed by American forces raided Hashimi's home and arrested many of his bodyguards, 42 according to a spokesman for his party.[27] But Hashimi was not apprehended and went into hiding. Mithal claims that Hashimi first found sanctuary in the home of Tariq al-Hashimi, who, as one of two Vice Presidents, is the highest ranking Sunni in the Iraqi government. Then, after some days the fugitive was spotted having taken up residence in the al-Rashid Hotel. The al-Rashid, a famous hangout for foreign journalists, was once Baghdad's leading hotel. It is located inside the Green Zone, a block from major U.S. military offices. Hashimi had apparently used his ministerial identity to enter the zone.

When Iraqi police went to the al-Rashid to arrest Hashimi, they were blocked from entry by heavily armed Peruvian contractors who maintain security throughout the Green Zone through scores of checkpoints, one of which controls the gate to the grounds of the al-Rashid. These contractors are employed by the Americans and answer to them.

Mithal publicly accused the Americans of sheltering the killer. This was sharply rejected by the U.S. embassy which issued a formal statement insisting that it had "not been involved or intervened in the situation.... The United States has not taken a position on the matter. This issue is for the government of Iraq to resolve in accordance with the rule of law."[28] But the Iraqi police could not enter the al-Rashid unless the Americans instructed the contract guards to let them in.

Why would the Americans abet Hashimi's escape from justice? Because the top U.S. political goal in Iraq was "reconciliation," and the Sunni bloc in parliament was treating Hashimi's indictment as a sectarian issue, notwithstanding that Mithal, too, is Sunni. The Iraqi Accordance Front withdrew its members from the cabinet and announced they would not return until the indictment of Hashimi was quashed. According to the *New York Sun*:

An administration official yesterday also pointed out that there are Shiite politicians in the Maliki government that have outstanding warrants who have not been apprehended. "It's like handing out speeding tickets at the Indy 500. There is no way this will not look sectarian," the official said.[29]

Mithal dueled with the embassy, speaking to the press repeatedly to build pressure on the Americans to allow Hashimi's arrest. "If we move now, we will have him," he said. "But if we lose time, he could flee the country."[30] These fears were borne out, and after some days all signs of Hashimi disappeared from the al-Rashid. According to some reports, he had made his way to Jordan.[31]

Nonetheless, Mithal pronounces confidence that justice will in time be done. "I will have him—if not today, tomorrow—and through the law." Some of his followers, he says, have proposed to find Hashimi and settle the score, but Mithal insists that he wants his own case to be a model of democratic legality:

> Justice must work. This system must exist. We cannot work against the system. We cannot work outside the system. And he has the right to have lawyers, to go to court, and we have the right to wait on the judge. If the justice says, "One year," I will say, "Okay." If the justice says, "10 years," I have to say, "Okay," even if I do not like it. How can we build the system and say we have the values if we do it like criminals?

While Hashimi remained a fugitive, apparently outside of Iraq, the wheels of Iraqi justice did indeed turn, and in August 2008 he was convicted in absentia of the murder of Ayman and Jamal and sentenced to death. The legal system also worked in November 2008 when the Iraqi supreme court overruled a vote in the legislature to strip Mithal of his parliamentary immunity so that he might be prosecuted for the capital offense of visiting Israel which he had done yet again earlier that year.

While the hearing proceeded, a petition defending Mithal garnered the signatures of some 400 Iraqi intellectuals. The court threw out the charges, which had been based on a 1950s law, as "illegal and unconstitutional because the current constitution does not prevent citizens from traveling to any country in the world," according to the court's spokesman,[32] and Mithal's standing was fully restored.

Ideologically, Mithal stands well outside the Iraqi mainstream, but he is more charismatic than most Iraqi leaders. So his hopes of rallying Iraqis to his unusual views are not necessarily pipedreams. "For me, it is not a dream; it is a goal," he says. His party central headquarters in Baghdad's Red Zone, closely guarded by his own men, bustles with the activity of staff and volunteers who dote on him. His large office is modestly furnished. Little hangs on the walls except two oil portraits—one of Ayman and one of Jamal, both made when they were boys.

His responsibility, as he sees it, is to "push people to be free" because "if they are free .... they will not follow war or fascism." And, yet, even if it requires pushing people, he insists that in propagating a liberal system, he is not trying to create something of whole cloth but to revive something. He puts it:

> Iraqi society, especially Baghdad society, is liberal; the city society in Iraq is liberal. So you do not need to wonder that an Iraqi has it [liberal values]. He is liberal compared to Saudi Arabia, compared to Turkey, compared even to Iran in the Shah's time, compared even to Syria whose people are liberal. Here, there are liberal values. But the fight between the socialist Ba'ath Party and the Islamic party and the long dictator system and militarism crushed all of the values in the Iraqi society.

Mithal believes he can resurrect this tradition and build a larger political base for his ideas. "Then we will have a new state, new majority, new people. One day I will guide this Iraqi nation," he says with supreme confidence. But at other moments, he admits to one critical doubt about this vision: that the assassins who killed his sons will eventually find their true target.

No doubt the assassins will keep trying. They will have various reasons, but the one that will surely keep them trying is the same one that prompted the attack that killed Ayman and Jamal—Mithal's extraordinary position on Israel. Far from backing away from it, he regards it as central to his vision. For one thing, he believes that the strategic interests of the two countries mesh. Not only are they both plagued by terrorism, but they have another common foe. "Iran would like to divide Iraq and eliminate Iraq," he says. "But Iran is also the enemy of Israel."

In addition, he sees an ideological affinity, believing that Iraq can be the region's second democracy:

> I do not believe we can [achieve] democracy in the Middle East in five years. You need time, and a base of Middle Eastern powers, two poles pushing for democracy, pushing for free economy, pushing for a free way of understanding, pushing for peace.

"We need each other," he says. He ticks off the assets that Israel brings to the table: "know-how, money, good connection to the international community, a democratic system. And ... many Iraqi-Israelis." But Israel also needs Iraq. "They cannot do without us if they want to exist in safety, be a normal society instead of [having to] fight terrorism, and the social pressure, psychology pressure, of feeling everybody is against them," he says.

When he sat in the Istanbul coffee shop in 2004, inhaling the shisha and trying to make a decision, he knew he was about to enter a storm that would be neither brief nor easily escaped. But the journey he chose to make was integral to what he hoped to help his country achieve, which is his life's mission. He puts it:

> This nation has the role to be part of the modern international community. My neighbors are not my geographic neighbors. My neighbors are my ideology, the way of life, or [strategic] interests. They are more close to me than my geographic neighbors. There is nothing can make you happy or make me happy more than to see your people successful and enjoying their chances—normal chances. This is my goal.

The Revolutionist

Iran: Mohsen Sazegara

Mohsen was the last to board, stepping onto the gangway at Charles DeGaulle Airport just a moment before the gate closed. It was one o'clock in the morning of February 1, 1979. The craft was an Air France jumbo jet, chartered to carry Ayatollah Ruhollah Khomeini home in triumph to Iran after 14 years of exile. The revolution he had inspired had been rising fast and was approaching its climax. The long-ruling Shah had departed the country two weeks earlier for "vacation" after installing a provisional government. It was not hard to predict that Khomeini's return would give a final push to the system the monarch had left behind.

Hundreds of supporters and recent converts to Khomeini's cause had rushed to Paris, hoping to garner the prestige of accompanying the Ayatollah on his flight home. But Khomeini opted to take only the dozen aides who had surrounded him in his final exilic headquarters in Neauphle-le-Château, as well as two or three other old comrades. The rest of the 380-seat Boeing 747 was reserved for the press.

Not only would the Islamic revolution reap a bounty of publicity that would be useful in the final grasp for power. But the presence onboard of these journalists would assure that neither the Iranian military nor the Americans would try to down the plane.

Mohsen and his colleagues in the Ayatollah's headquarters had printed tickets for the flight which they distributed to news organizations, based in part on the importance of the company and in part on "how cooperative, how pro-revolution" their reportage had been, as Mohsen puts it.[1] There were many more requests than seats, and just forty-eight hours before flight time the problem was severely compounded. Air France decided that it would need to load extra fuel in case the plane was barred from landing and forced to return. Iran's provisional Prime Minister had closed the country's airports for four days to block Khomeini's return before yielding to pressure to reopen them. What if he reversed himself again? The weight of the extra fuel meant that the plane could only be filled to half capacity with passengers although it was already sold out.

The task of selecting the two hundred journalists to be bumped from the flight and informing and placating them made these last two days in France an ordeal for Mohsen.

He was haggling over it at the airport right down to flight time, which is why he was the last to board. In the air, the Ayatollah went to the comfortable berth that had been prepared for him on the 747's upper deck and went to sleep. Mohsen, however, had work to do. On the ground in Iran, the revolutionary movement was issuing its own press credentials, acting as if it was the government already. Thanks to all the last minute changes, there was no accurate list of the journalists arriving with the Ayatollah. So it was Mohsen's duty to make his way through the cabin to record the names and affiliations. Although he had slept little the last few days, his adrenaline was flowing, and he was young, having just turned 24.

On arrival, Mohsen escorted a caravan of Western reporters endeavoring to follow Khomeini, but when a helicopter plucked the Ayatollah from the throng of millions who clogged the streets to hail his return, Mohsen led his charges back to their hotels. Once the last of them had disembarked, he hailed a taxi to his parents' home.

No one was expecting him. For reasons of security Mohsen had made only one call to his parents during his months in Khomeini's headquarters near Paris—to let them know where he was, since he was no longer in the U.S., as they thought. He hadn't dared phone again to say he was coming home.

The doorbell was answered by his father. His mother and siblings were out amidst the crowds. But his father scorned mullahs, disliked politics, and had always frowned on Mohsen's activism. When the older man saw who was at the door, however, "For the one and only time he kissed me," recalls Mohsen.

Even more surprising than this unwonted gesture of affection, were the words he spoke. "My son, I congratulate you. You succeeded in ousting the Shah. I did not believe you could do it." Perhaps he was overwhelmed with joy at seeing his boy safe, or perhaps he was caught up in the excitement of the times, but this seemed to concede the validity of the younger man's activities. "That was very sweet for me," recalls Mohsen, as it would have been for any son who had ever quarreled with his father.

Mohsen could not have imagined at that blissful moment that the taste in his mouth would gradually turn bitter, that he would grow disillusioned with the revolution that he, in his short life, had done much to bring about, that his revulsion at its cruelty would lead him to reconsider all of his beliefs and even to embrace key ideas of the despised West. Nor could he possibly have foreseen that he would leave a high perch in the regime that he was still fighting to install to become one of its most tireless and effective opponents, a beacon to the next generation of rebellious youth, which would bring him to experience the torments of prison and the loneliness of exile.

Mohsen Sazegara had been born on Christmas day of 1954, according to his mother, although his birth certificate puts it ten days later. Theirs was an old Tehrani family living in the southern reaches of the city. His father, Muhammed Ali Mullah, was a storekeeper, selling bedding, a trade he had plied from the age of five, working in *his* father's store. Before that, the men in his family had been "mullahs," a term that did not then mean cleric, but rather designated those who, before there were schools, offered rudimentary instruction in reading and writing using the simpler verses of the Koran.

When, under Reza Shah who ruled from 1921 to 1941, Iranians first assumed family names, often reflecting their occupations, Mohsen's forebears became the Mullahs. But as that word evolved to connote clergyman, Muhammed Ali grew uncomfortable, so he changed it. The name of his shop was Sazegar, a Farsi word meaning agreeable or accommodating, and from this he fashioned the moniker, Sazegara.

Mohsen's mother, Aghdas, was from a family named Anisi Tehrani. The latter part signified their home city and the former part reflected their pride in being distantly related to Anisoddoleh, the favorite wife of the nineteenth century ruler, Nasser Al-din Shah. Aghdas was fourteen when she wed Muhammed Ali, who was thirty at the time.

Although Aghdas's mother, a widow, cared deeply for her, she had already caused the girl a bitter disappointment that was to stay with her the rest of her days. Aghdas had graduated from six years of grammar school at the head of her class and looked forward eagerly to the next six grades. But Reza Shah, trying to modernize Iran as Ataturk had modernized Turkey, had banned the wearing of the veil. Aghdas would have been happy to go to school without one, but her mother was appalled at the idea that her pubescent child would go about with her hair uncovered. Then, she attended a ceremony at which the recent graduates were processed for entry to the next level of schooling, and she saw the state-issued school uniform that Aghdas would have to wear: a skirt that she thought much too short. She pulled Aghdas out of line, took her home, and forbade her from high school, enrolling her instead in a typing class. Aghdas cried for three days.

But at least her marriage was to give her happiness. Mohsen recalls her telling him often that his father was "najib," noble. He never drank, she said, nor so much as looked at another woman. And he left for his shop at seven each morning except Friday and returned only at nine at night to provide for her and their five sons and two daughters. Mohsen was the sixth of the seven, and all received the education that poverty and tradition had denied to their parents.

Mohsen's childhood was a happy one. His green eyes and light complexion were unusual for an Iranian, bringing him lots of fawning attention from adults and older children. And he was a prize student, earning one of the top scores in the country on the uniform exams given to grammar school graduates. If his stellar success evoked any jealousy among his peers, he subdued this by volunteering to tutor them and even giving them the answers during tests. He was often accepted as leader in the games played with other boys, including the games he invented reenacting the many movies his older siblings took him to see.

When Mohsen was fifteen, he discovered he carried "a political gene." The Tehran government had announced a doubling of the highly subsidized municipal bus fares. Opposition voices called for citizens to protest by boycotting the buses. The next morning when Mohsen headed to school, he found the streets teeming with pedestrians observing the boycott. He had not yet formulated political ideas, but he was swept up in the protest. He stopped a few buses, hopped on, and urged the riders to join the boycott. "I was really excited," he recalls. "I do not know why."

When he reached his high school, two hours late, he found that the adjacent Polytechnic was roiling with protests. He decided to skip classes for the day to soak in the events. When police charged, some of the protestors escaped onto the high school grounds where Mohsen helped guide them to hiding places. By the end of the day, the government announced rescission of the fare increase. That evening, Mohsen rode the bus home at the old fare. "That experience was wonderful for me," he recalls, and the victory was "very sweet.... Politics suddenly came into my soul. After that I started to follow all the news and to read about it in books."

He read a lot, not only about politics. At sixteen he read a life of the Prophet, and was captivated by it. He worked his way through the Koran in Farsi translation, then again in the original Arabic, which was taught in Iranian schools. "I started to think about the part of life that does not have to do with reason," he recalls, "about the part that goes to your heart, the experience of touching the supernatural." Over the next year he read other religious books and books about religion. Then, he says, "When I was in the eleventh grade—17 years old—I decided to pray and be a Muslim."

Of course he was Muslim by birth, but Muhammed Ali was not devout. He did not go often to mosque or take his sons there, and he was disdainful of the clerisy. It is traditional for Iranians to hire clergymen to come to their residences to chant mournings for the missing Imam Hussein around whom much Shiite theology revolves. Muhammed Ali, however, said that mullahs were "liars," and he would never allow one in his home. In this laissez-faire environment, the Sazegara girls did not cover their hair, and neither they nor their brothers much practiced their nominal faith.

Mohsen was the exception. He decided to "pray and fast and participate in Islamic rituals." His older siblings did not let this pass easily. They argued with him about the validity of religious belief, but apparently the atmosphere in the home was sufficiently friendly that these arguments were not angry. Even though the high school-aged Mohsen could not have had the intellectual tools with which to contend with his university-educated brothers and sisters, he loved the intellectual challenge. It drove him to absorb books criticizing or defending religion, an intellectual interest that was to continue all his life.

He found a single friend, Saeed, who shared his feelings. The two of them began to take an interest not only in religious observance but also in some of the political ideas built around Islam that were beginning to be circulated. They were especially moved by the thoughts of Jalal Al-e Ahmad. He was a writer, still in his thirties, of novels and other genres but most importantly a voice of protest against the global dominance of the Christian West. The title of his most noted work was translated as "Weststruckness." Its thesis was that:

> Our world is a world of confrontation between the poor and the rich. . . . We've not been able to retain our own cultural/historical personality during our encounter with machines and in the face of their inevitable assault. In fact we've been destroyed. . . . [W]e've been unable to take a calculated and well-assessed position in the face of this monster of the new century . . . . The point is that as long as we don't perceive the nature and philosophical basis of Western culture, and continue to behave as Westerners superficially, we'll be like the donkey who posed as a lion and ended up being eaten by one.[2]

This book had been banned by the regime, but Saeed, who, unlike Mohsen, came from a deeply religious family, had gotten a hold of a copy. He and Mohsen liked it so well that they reproduced seven or eight contraband copies. Copying machines were in use in Iran by that time, but as in the Soviet Union, they were carefully controlled to prevent subversion, so the two copied the book by hand, using carbon paper. It was Mohsen's first act as an Islamic revolutionary.

Upon graduation, Mohsen ranked 96th out of a quarter million students on the college entrance exam. He wanted to study physics, but his older siblings told him that he must qualify himself for a remunerative job, and thus he opted for engineering, entering Aryamehr University. In the U.S., technical colleges are usually quiescent, but in Iran they were hotbeds of political activism, probably because the best students chose them, motivated like Mohsen by financial considerations.

To his delight, Mohsen found Aryamehr throbbing with political activity. "I was like a fish in the sea," he recalls. "Every day we had some protests against the Shah. We were just looking for some reason to start a demonstration." Usually, these were launched by older, more seasoned activists, and as a freshman Mohsen was happy to become one the foot soldiers whose job often was to run from class to class spreading word of the time and place.

The student activists formed two camps, Marxist, and Islamist. Each was spearheaded by a guerrilla organization, raising the stakes of the sparring between the students and the regime. A police regiment was stationed permanently on Aryamehr campus, and the Marxist guerrillas managed to assassinate the commander. In this atmosphere, students could be arrested for possessing a subversive leaflet and certainly for distributing them. Mohsen and his comrades resorted to tossing them from windows or leaving them in dining halls. Readers did not have to pick them up but could peruse them on the ground or on a table. When you entered a dining hall, says Mohsen, if you saw students clustered, "you could be sure there was something on the table."

Mohsen drank in the works of Ali Shariati, the intellectual fount of the Iranian revolution, who had studied with Jean-Paul Sartre in Paris and who reinterpreted Islam as a higher form of Marxism. Shariati's approach substituted the Muslims for the proletariat as the engine of revolution. Mohsen puts it:

> Any element that counts in Marxism, [Shariati] tries to persuade you that we have the same in Islam. It was very attractive to believe that Islam is the best religion in the world, the last religion. So not only revolution but politics, economics,

culture, everything must come out of Islam. We have the solution for everything.

Inspired by this "maximalist theory of Islam," Mohsen joined the underground Muslim student association. He considered becoming a guerrilla, but neither of the existing groups suited him. He rejected Marxism, not realizing how much the philosophy he embraced was modeled on it. Even the Islamist fighting group, the Mujahideen e Khalq (which still functions in Paris and Iraq), was infused with Marxism to a degree that put Mohsen off. "It was clear that they had chosen Marxism and just painted a thin coat of Islam on it," he says.

To deepen his Islamic understanding, Mohsen made himself an acolyte of two different clergymen. One was an ayatollah who downplayed politics in favor of theological questions. The other was deeply political. He was a disciple of Grand Ayatollah Mohammad Bagher Sadr.[3] That Iraqi sage had written two master works, *Our Economy* and *Our Philosophy*, extolling Islam in contrast equally to Marxism and capitalism. In this, as well as the thought of Shariati, Mohsen found an ideology with which he felt at home.

Because the university was located in Tehran, Mohsen, like most of the students, lived in his parental home, and his mother, Aghdas, became a key accomplice. He recalls:

> Most of the time I came home late at night. My father was asleep because he was tired from a long day's work, but my mother was awake, waiting for me. She encouraged me to be active politically. I always knew that somebody at home supported me.

If Muhammed Ali had been awake, he would not have given Mohsen his approval, because he was more conservative politically and fearful of the consequence of Mohsen's activities. But Aghdas was not afraid, and she gave Mohsen more than words of approval. "Whenever I wanted to hide something from the hands of SAVAK [the security service], such as prohibited books, I gave it to my mother," recalls Mohsen. She knew how to hide things where they would not be found if our house was searched."

Despite his mother's help, Mohsen realized that he was destined for trouble with the authorities. Although he had not become a guerrilla, he was an activist and agitator. His oldest brother, an air force helicopter pilot, was summoned for questioning about him, leading Mohsen to realize that SAVAK was aware of his doings. Rather than wait to be arrested, Mohsen, who had by now spent two years at university albeit not always studying, decided to continue his education in the U.S. In addition to keeping him out of SAVAK's clutches, this would shelter him from the draft to which he would have been subject immediately upon graduation.

If it was odd for a young revolutionary suffused in anti-American ideology to want to go to America, it was far from unusual. The Shah himself once commented that there were fifty thousand Iranian students in the U.S., but not more than five thousand were pro-American. Mohsen, laughing in hindsight, speculates that the number was probably smaller.

In 1975 Mohsen entered the Illinois Institute of Technology in Chicago. Although he supported himself by working on a university research project in physics and delivering groceries, he did not much integrate into the U.S. He lived, as he puts it, "in an Iranian Islamic subculture." He joined the Muslim Students Association and became the organizational secretary for the northern region of the U.S. Its activities were mostly cultural and religious. For politics he helped found the Young Muslims Organization.

One day, Reza, his roommate and fellow activist, asked Mohsen what he thought of the idea of the two of them joining the Liberation Movement of Iran. Led by Mehdi Bazargan, the Liberation Movement of Iran had been formed in 1961 by three prominent intellectuals of Islamic orientation, the only political formation of this ideological and sociological composition. It soon became a vanguard of opposition to the Shah, coming to the fore in the bloody 1963 uprising sparked by the arrest of Ayatollah Khomeini. The leaders of the organization were given jail terms; Bazargan's ten years was the longest. The Movement commanded evident grass-roots support, but because it was illegal it admitted few members and functioned clandestinely. It also had branches in the United States and Europe and in Lebanon where it created the Shiite militia, Amal. The Mujahideen e Khalq grew out of this group but soon went its own way.

Because it was underground, one could not apply for admission. But Reza had been approached by a recruiter who had observed his and Mohsen's activities in the open groups. Mohsen said he would have to think it over, which shocked Reza who was thrilled to be invited into this exclusive vanguard. Mohsen, though, knew it meant risking a long sentence. Also, being of ideological temperament, Mohsen wanted to read or reread the group's policy tracts. After a week he told Reza he was ready. During the next two years, his activity in the other organizations tapered off as the Liberation Movement of Iran absorbed his time. In the process, he grew close to the LMI's public representative in the U.S., Ebrahim Yazdi, a pharmacologist at Baylor University some twenty years Mohsen's senior, who served as Khomeini's representative in America.

During this period, Mohsen made four trips home, each time carrying out missions for the LMI. In America, the movement published literature that was banned in Iran. This included not only theological and ideological tracts, but also manuals on underground operations and guerrilla tactics. These materials were printed on thin paper and in fine type to make them as small as possible, then packed into the false bottom Mohsen had rigged up in the suitcase he carried to Iran.

In 1977, the inauguration of Jimmy Carter, whose emphasis on human rights clouded Washington's support for the Shah, dispelling his aura of invincibility, stirred new hope in the members of the LMI. By 1978, the time of Mohsen's last trip home before the revolution, opposition to the Shah's rule had advanced considerably as had support for an Islamic revolution. Mohsen observed a change in his own family. Once he had been the only devout Muslim and the only political activist among the Sazegaras (except for his mother's quiet help). But now his two sisters took to covering their hair and his brothers became supportive of his activities. One of his brothers, Mehdi, had just opened a small business. He had a mimeograph machine, with government authorization that was still required for any copying equipment. Mohsen asked Mehdi if he would report the machine stolen and let him take it to an LMI office inside the country. He told Mehdi that if investigators pressured him he could name Mohsen as the culprit—so that he rather than Mehdi would take the heat. To Mohsen's surprise, Mehdi was far from reluctant. He physically assisted Mohsen in "stealing" the machine during the night and transporting it to a secret location.

In October 1978, as the Iranian revolution gained momentum, the Shah struck a deal with Saddam Hussein, each of whom had supported opponents of the other's regime. Saddam agreed to expel Ayatollah Khomeini, the inspirational figure of the revolution, from the Shiite holy city of Najaf where he had taken exile in 1965. By chance, Yazdi, the Baylor University pharmacologist and Mohsen's mentor, was visiting Khomeini when Saddam ordered him to leave Iraq. After being turned away at the Kuwaiti border, the ayatollah decided to move to a Western country.

An exiled Iranian sympathizer owned an orchard and country home in Neauphle-le-Château, a half hour from Paris, where Khomeini took up residence, although at first his whereabouts were not revealed. A couple of days later, back in his student apartment in Chicago, Mohsen received a call from Yazdi. The essence, he recalls, was: "We are in Paris. We have brought Ayatollah here. We need you."

That was afternoon, Central Standard Time, seven hours behind Paris. Mohsen had only 8 dollars in cash. He called a local LMI supporter and arranged to borrow $230 for airfare. Then he told his two roommates to take care of his belongings, and he left for the airport. (Fortunately, they were members of the Muslim Students Association and agreed with his activities, so they were willing to indulge this abrupt departure and worry about the rent later.) He flew that evening, and at 9AM, local time, he landed at Charles DeGaulle. He had only summer clothes with him, although this was late October and days were growing cool.

Khomeini's command center in Neauphle-le-Château was made up of fewer than a dozen people. At first they all bunked in the small country house, but when Khomeini's wife and some other family members arrived, a cottage across the street was rented for him and them. The village had a single inn, and Yazdi took a room there for himself. Since there was also a heavy traffic of visitors to "the Imam," they leased a large tent and set it up in the orchard to serve as a mosque. On Christmas, Khomeini sent greetings to the villagers, apologizing for the disruption his presence had caused.

While Khomeini mostly remained aloof, for Mohsen, long days of work were followed by long nights of debate over tactics with Yazdi and a few other members of the Liberation Movement of Iran. The group made a point of keeping a penurious menu that they deemed appropriate for their revolutionary mission and circumstance. Mohsen began to suffer from a vitamin deficiency. Penniless, he borrowed enough to purchase some fruit to supplement the collective meals. He also prevailed upon an Iranian exile who arrived from Germany to get him something to ward off the cold, and the fellow supplied him with a German army jacket.

Mohsen's duties included handling press relations for Khomeini, and preparing a daily news summary of the international media, including translations of key items from English. This synopsis was ordinarily the last thing the Imam read before turning in for the night. Mohsen also began to teach a one-week course in such things as surreptitious communications to a few cadres who came for the training. He, himself, had limited experience in such actions, but, always the avid reader, he had consumed books on clandestine operations.

In November 1978, struggling against a rising tide of opposition, the Shah resorted to a military government. A group of Khomeini's close clerical allies sent him a message proposing that he issue a *fatwa* calling for *jihad* against the regime. That evening, Mohsen and two other young activists discussed this idea with Yazdi, and they reached a consensus that such a move should be held in reserve as the revolution's "nuclear option." Instead, they devised a series of peaceful measures to undermine the authorities—strikes, boycotts and desertions by soldiers. Mohsen described his own brother, the pilot, whom he was sure was more a nationalist than a monarchist and could be won to the revolution.

Yazdi presented this alternative to Khomeini who embraced it. He issued a *fatwa,* calling for soldiers and junior officers to abandon their posts and another to the wives of officers, telling them to treat their husbands as *haram,* or forbidden, if they remained loyal to the Shah's army, meaning not to cook or provide other services for them.

These subversive tactics worked, and the army slowly began to disintegrate. A spirit of disobedience spread among a once cowed population prompting the Shah to dismiss the military government and reverse course. Hoping to placate the opposition, the Shah appointed Shahpour Bakhtiar, a lifelong opponent of the monarchy, as Prime Minister and agreed to leave the country for "vacation." With momentum quickening in his favor, Khomeini decided to return to Iran to help tilt the balance against the remnants of the Shah's rule.

Yazdi tried in vain to dissuade him, but this was one occasion when Mohsen was at odds with Yazdi. Later, when the two were alone, Yazdi explained his reasoning to Mohsen in words that proved prophetic. Mohsen reconstructs what he heard:

> Do you know why I bid him to stay here? Because here in Paris we have very few clergy, mostly young, and things have been in our hands. But as soon as Ayatollah Khomeini goes back I'm afraid high-ranking clergy will surround him, and they will take over from us. Here, we are his advisers and he listens to us. I am afraid that as soon as he goes to Iran, we will not see him anymore. He will be in the hands of those clergy and I'm afraid that they will ruin everything.

Recalling this warning, Mohsen adds, "I remember standing in the dark street where we were discussing this and saying to myself that Yazdi is too hostile to the clergy." He and Yazdi, after all, were intellectuals who took Islam as their guide. How different could the clergy be from them? "I was not experienced enough," rues Mohsen. "What he predicted is exactly what happened."

On the night of January 31st, Khomeini, Yazdi, Mohsen, and a handful of others who had constituted the revolution's command center boarded their "victory flight" to Tehran, carrying along the throng of reporters that Mohsen and a few colleagues had selected.

After an emotional reunion with his family the evening after arriving, Mohsen went back to work early the next morning, showing up at Refah High School which the Council of Revolution had turned into a headquarters for Khomeini. Portentously, however, Khomeini had already abandoned this headquarters, taking up residence at a different Tehran high school that had been set up for him by his clerical followers.

For the moment, with Bakhtiar still sitting in the seat of government and commanding the army, there was no time to focus on divisions with fellow revolutionists, but this episode resonated with the foreboding Yazdi had confided to Mohsen a few nights before. Already the mullahs were gaining control of Khomeini.

Mohsen, the revolution's liaison with the international press flooding into Tehran, was too busy to dwell on it. On February 5th, four days after his arrival, Khomeini announced that he was appointing Mehdi Bazargan as Prime Minister. Hours before the announcement, Bazargan hosted a lunch at his home for the members of the Liberation Movement of Iran. About thirty other men were there, constituting the majority of the group's membership. They had ample cause to celebrate. This compact elite had formed the cutting edge of the revolution that had turned their country upside down, and it was now about to lead the government. Mohsen was the youngest member.

For the moment there were two governments in Iran, Bazargan's and Bakhtiar's. But six days later, when the army's commanders declared neutrality in the struggle for power, Bakhtiar resigned and went into hiding. The triumph of the revolution was complete.

Although the old regime was gone, the new government did not yet control the country which was awash in arms thanks to the collapse of the army and police. Various splinters laid plans to seize power, national movements of Iran's minorities glimpsed a chance for independence, and bitter-enders loyal to the Shah set out to exact revenge. As a first step in solidifying the new regime's grip, Khomeini tasked Ayatollah Hassan Lahoti with collecting weapons from the public, and Lahoti, who had gotten to know Mohsen in Neauphle-le-Château, asked to him to serve as his deputy.

They set up operations in a large military base in the middle of Tehran called Baghe Shah, and when night came,

Lahoti went home after instructing Mohsen to remain there alone in charge of the facility. There was lots of shooting in the streets those unsettled nights, and suddenly Mohsen heard automatic weapons fire that seemed to be coming at him from the direction of a Special Forces barracks located in one corner of the base. He pulled his only weapon, a Colt 45, and fired a few rounds toward the source of the sound, although he had no formal weapons training and suffered from an eye condition that impaired his vision. "I figured out that this was useless," recalls Mohsen, "and that I better go hide." The next morning some of the Special Forces members, who for the moment had to obey Mohsen however they may have felt about it, admitted that they had been shooting in his vicinity, "just to tease you."

This joke underscored the need to damp down chaos and the fact that the victorious revolutionists could not rely on the existing forces of order, many of whom had left their posts. In the next days Mohsen and more senior figures— Lahoti, Yazdi, and a few others—discussed this issue and came up with the idea of forming a Revolutionary Guard to enforce civic peace, suppress armed opposition, and defend against foreign enemies. In late February the Guard was launched with a team of five provisional commanders. Mohsen was one, in charge of intelligence and with some responsibility for recruitment. The latter assignment came easily since Mohsen had scores of friends and contacts from his years in the student movement, and he brought about 65 of them into the nascent Guard Corps. But he knew little if anything about intelligence. So he went to the headquarters of SAVAK, the Shah's secret police, and found training manuals to read.

One in particular riveted him, a manual on interrogation. A sentence leaped out at him. It said that an interrogation was a contest between the interrogator and the prisoner. As he absorbed that and read on, he had an epiphany. SAVAK's

infamous tortures had been the symbol of everything the revolution was against. Mohsen had always assumed that torture was just in the nature of SAVAK, but now he realized that
torture flowed from the logic of the situation. The implication
disturbed Mohsen. The new regime also had serious enemies.
Would they, too, become torturers?

Mohsen shared this concern with a clerical authority he
knew, Ayatollah Mojtaba Tehrani, the imam of one of
Tehran's largest and most important mosques. Tehrani
assured him that from the point of view of *sharia*, "if you are
interrogating an accused person and think he is lying, you
can sentence him to 80 lashes." The holy man went on to say
that you need not deliver all 80 blows at once but could
spread them into groups of five or ten until you got the truth.

Mohsen says this made him "really upset." Tehrani's
answer was a sophistry to justify torture. So Mohsen sought
out his friend Abdolkarim Soroush, a leading religious intellectual. Soroush understood Mohsen's worry and said that
the best preventive would be to disallow confessions in court,
as French law does, therefore lessening the incentive to
extract them. Unfortunately, added Soroush, in Islamic
jurisprudence confessions are regarded as the most important
evidence. Therefore, a big change in thinking would be
required.

This, and the fact that Mohsen, who was a natural publicist, found he disliked secret activity, convinced him that his
future did not lie in the Revolutionary Guard. In May, the
Guard was reorganized, absorbing two other armed groups,
and new commanders were elected. Although Mohsen is confident he could have been chosen, he was ready to move on.

He joined the national radio and television authority and
forged a position for himself as deputy director for politics,
charged with overseeing the ideological content. He also produced a daily assessment of national and global politics that
he read out each day on the 2PM radio news. Shortly after,

Mohsen was appointed as overall chief of the national radio. Already, a vicious power struggle was underway between the Islamists and the Mujahideen e Khalq, and one goal that Mohsen was supposed to achieve was to purge the radio of a slant that was alleged to be pro-MEK.

During his stint at the helm of the national radio, two major developments unfolded in Mohsen's life. One was personal; the other, political. The former concerned a cousin of his named Soheila whom he had known since her birth. Her older brother, Saeed, was Mohsen's age, and the two boys had been playmates at myriad family gatherings. Mohsen had taken scant note of Soheila, six years their junior, until she began to grow up. When he left for the U.S. at age 20, she was 14 and in the process of pleasing changes. Mohsen liked the way she looked, but he says that he was struck even more by how bright she was, first in her class just like him. And, too, he liked her mother very much and bore in mind a Farsi proverb that if you want to pick a wife, study her mother because that is who she will become.

When Mohsen returned to Iran, Soheila was a first-year college student, majoring in medicine, and he found her just as appealing as he had remembered. Mohsen was ready to make the big move, but he was afraid of rejection. So first he sounded out Saeed: "If I propose to Soheila, do you think she will accept?" Saeed said he would find out. Meanwhile, Mohsen shared his hopes with his mother, who strongly approved. Some discussions ensued between the sets of parents, and finally Mohsen got his answer. Soheila was prepared to accept his proposal if he came to Shiraz, where she was studying, to deliver it himself.

Mohsen flew to Shiraz, more than six hundred miles from Tehran and picked up Soheila at her dormitory. So innocent was he of women that he was surprised when she told him later that her girlfriends had been watching through the windows to check him out. They went to lunch, and Mohsen dominated the conversation. He spoke of the revolution and their revolutionary duties and all the important political things they would do together. He apparently had no idea that this was not the kind of proposal that girls dream of. Fortunately for him, Soheila had already decided that she would have him. Finally in frustration and boredom, she said: "Okay, okay. Go back to Tehran. We'll talk some other time. I accept."

The political development that affected Mohsen arose within the Liberation Movement of Iran. During its years of struggle, the organization had no semblance of internal democracy. Given its illegality and the necessity for secrecy, it was compact, top-down, and functioned in cells. Because the LMI professed democracy, the triumph of the revolution at once posed the question of internal democratization. For the first time, the group elected a central committee. It consisted of thirty members, which was about half of the total membership, and it in turn named a five-member executive committee. Mohsen was chosen to both.

Frictions soon emerged between Khomeini and Bazargan, reflecting a broader division between clerics and intellectuals, of which Yazdi had forewarned Mohsen. As Prime Minister, Bazargan was making all sorts of compromises, even suggesting a modus vivendi with the United States. Within the Liberation Movement of Iran, Mohsen and other radicals deplored this loss of revolutionary zeal. Although a minority, they mustered enough votes to block Bazargan from being the LMI's candidate for president in elections scheduled for January 1980.

Some months later, the radicals, 12 of the 30 central committee members, left the LMI, but their efforts to launch a new organization came to naught as they fell out among themselves. While these factional quarrels were barren, they did bring Mohsen an important benefit. He grew close with two older and influential men who advanced his career: Mohammed Ali Rajai and Behzad Nabavi.

That summer, Rajai was named Prime Minister, and he immediately asked Mohsen to come work for him. When Rajai formed his cabinet, he named Nabavi Advisory Minister for Executive Affairs, and Mohsen became his political deputy. The new cabinet was approved on September 21, 1980, and that same afternoon Iraq invaded Iran. Now, on top of the challenge of creating a new system of government and restoring domestic tranquility, the country was at war. But the internecine power struggle continued unabated.

In his new post, Mohsen devised a plan to reduce internal turmoil. It consisted of a simple carrot and stick. All political groups would be allowed to participate in political affairs, even Marxists or other non-Islamic groups, but not if they engaged in armed struggle. After months of meetings Nabavi and Mohsen succeeded in getting the top officials of the regime to agree to this plan, which was called the 10 Articles Declaration. Mohsen and two other second-tier officials were named to implement it. They were thwarted by resistance from two directions.

On one side was the Mujahideen e Khalq, whose daring attacks against the Shah had drawn thousands of young radicals to its ranks, and which now emerged as the country's most formidable anti-clerical faction. Its leader, Massoud Rajavi, had been arbitrarily disqualified from running for president, and its candidates for the *Majlis* were all defeated amidst sundry electoral irregularities. It denounced the 10 Articles plan as a trick designed to get its members to lay down arms and leave themselves at the regime's mercy. On the other side was Asadollah Lajevardi, who functioned as the regime's Quasimodo. The warden of Evin Prison, he exercised wide-ranging prosecutorial and investigative power, buttressed by links to Khomeini that made it hard even for officials of higher rank to overrule him. Lajevardi insisted that the MEK should not be given political rights under any circumstances. Nor was the MEK his only target. No sooner had the declaration been issued than Lajevardi closed down sixty newspapers and journals, sending a signal that a new era of political tolerance was nowhere near.

Punctuated by numerous executions and assassinations, MEK's battle with the new authorities came to a head when its members and sympathizers took to the streets on June 20, 1981 for a massive show of strength. The timing could not have been more difficult for Mohsen. Soheila was pregnant beyond term with their first child, and on that day the doctor administered a drug to induce labor. Mohsen was too busy in the Prime Minister's office to accompany her to the hospital. The doctor told her to return the next day, and this time her parents went with her because Mohsen felt he could not miss an important meeting with the Prime Minister. While it was underway, Rajai's secretary interrupted to say there was an urgent call for Mohsen. It was Soheila's mother in tears, saying that something was wrong that might require emergency surgery. Rajai told him to go to the hospital at once promising to "pray for your child and also that you will be a good father."

Streets all around were blocked with burning tires from the skirmishes, so Mohsen ran the two kilometers to the hospital. When he arrived he found his mother-in-law sitting in a stairway leading to the obstetric department, crying. She said she did not know what was wrong, but that the delivery was terribly delayed. At that moment the obstetrician came out to tell them that mother and son were both safe. Whatever anger his mother-in-law may have felt at his absence was dispelled by joy. Drying her tears, she joked, "He was just waiting for his father." Mohsen went to the public phone to get the latest news from the office.

In mid-1981 the struggles quickened. President Abolhassan Banisadr, who had been constantly at odds with Prime Minister Rajai, lost the backing of Khomeini and was impeached in June and forced from office. Such was the nature of Iranian politics that he felt compelled to go into hiding, assisted by the MEK with which he now formed an alliance. New presidential elections were held in July, and Rajai was elected president. A cleric, Mohammad Bahonar, was named Prime Minister. Meanwhile, the authorities continued to exact fearful reprisals against the MEK which carried out a campaign of bombings that took the lives of many top officials.

In August, while Mohsen was working in his fourth floor office in the executive building, having assumed responsibilities in the new administration similar to those he had held in the previous one, a massive blast shook the structure. It emanated from the first floor where the High Council of National Security, which included the President, the Prime Minister and several cabinet ministers, was meeting. Mohsen rushed downstairs, but there was nothing he could do. The bomb had ignited a blaze, and smoke was everywhere.

No one knew exactly who had been in the room at the time of the detonation, so Mohsen and some colleagues made the rounds of hospitals and reconstructed a record of who had been in attendance and who among them was dead, who injured, who relatively unscathed. In the end, there were three participants unaccounted for: Rajai, Bahonar, and the taker of minutes, a secretary to the High Council named Massoud Keshmiri. There were two bodies burned beyond recognition, having been at the head table, the epicenter of the explosion. Eventually, dental records identified them as Rajai and Bahonar.

The next day a funeral was held with some half a million mourners. Mohsen was concerned about doing right by poor Keshmiri whose body had been entirely consumed by fire. Mohsen had sent a member of his staff to consult with religious authorities about the applicable *sharia*. They ruled that ashes gathered from the spot where Keshmiri had been sitting could be assumed to include some of his remains.

Ali Tehrani, a member of Mohsen's staff who was Keshmiri's best friend, performed this task so that Keshmiri could be buried along with the others. In the funeral procession, Rajai's and Bahonar's bodies were carried wrapped in white shrouds, followed by another stretcher, bearing a plastic bag containing what was deemed to be left of Keshmiri.

That evening, with a heavy heart, Mohsen went to a weekly dinner with a circle of friends from the old days of struggle. It was in the home of Kamal Kharrazi who was to become Iran's Foreign Minister in the 1990s. All of the guests were also in the thick of political life, and they took turns sharing news. When Mohsen told the pathetic story of Keshmiri's remains, his friend Abdolkarim Soroush interrupted: "Mohsen, do you mean to say that they did not find anything from him? Didn't he wear a ring or watch or belt?" Mohsen replied that of course Keshmiri wore those things, but "we did not find anything." Then, Mohsen recalls, Soroush said:

> It does not make any sense because if you burn a body in high heat the skeleton will be left; at least 15 kilograms will be left. Bones burn only in exceedingly high temperatures. So it makes no sense that you did not find anything of him. Maybe he planted the bomb and left the room and disappeared.

"It was like a light switched on in my mind," says Mohsen. "All night I had nightmares. I saw Keshmiri killing Rajai and Bahonar, and I was chasing him." He rose even before pre-dawn prayers and went to the office. There he found an investigative committee of the intelligence branch already at work. He asked one of the members to come out, and he shared with him Soroush's insight. The interlocutor replied: "Mohsen, do not tell anybody else. We have reached the same conclusion because we have not found his car, and usually he parked it somewhere around here. Also, his wife and two children are not at home."

Investigators tapped the phone of Keshmiri's parents and captured a call from his wife, reporting blithely that she and the children had gone on a trip and would be back soon. She sounded nothing like a woman in mourning which seemed to confirm that Keshmiri had carried out the bombing. Neither he nor she and the children were ever heard from again.

The case was referred to the judicial branch, and it fell to Lajevardi, the vindictive investigator who had foiled Mohsen's "10 Articles" plan of reconciliation. Lajevardi at once convinced himself that Keshmiri must have been aided by accomplices within the government.

Keshmiri's supervisor was Khosrou Tehrani, a deputy to the Prime Minister in charge of intelligence who had recruited Keshmiri from Mohsen's staff. Lajevardi demanded to interrogate Tehrani as well as Mohsen and more than twenty other members of the Prime Minister's staff. But Nabavi, Mohsen's immediate superior and a cabinet member, was able to block Lajevardi from hauling in Mohsen without any evidence against him. Khosrou Tehrani was similarly protected by the Prime Minister, so Lajevardi had to content himself with the others. All were eventually released except Ali Tehrani, the best friend who had collected Keshmiri's ashes who was also the one who had first introduced him to Mohsen. (The name Tehrani, meaning someone from Tehran, is extremely common. Khosrou and Ali were not related.)

Trusting Ali Tehrani's innocence but fearing that he would nonetheless be held at great length, Mohsen and his friends proposed that the case be transferred to a "revolutionary court" because these operated more swiftly. It was, they later realized, a foolish mistake. Ali Tehrani was taken to Evin Prison and delivered to the notorious "seventh branch," a "revolutionary court" specializing in security matters and notorious for its cruelty.

The bombing led to a shift in the ideological tenor of the regime. A new presidential election, held to replace Rajai, was won by Ali Khamenei who later succeeded Khomeini as Supreme Leader, and another hardliner, Mir-Hossein Mousavi, was named Prime Minister. "I felt I was defeated," says Mohsen. His plans for civic peace, by means of the Article 10 Declaration, had come to naught, as had his lobbying to bring the war with Iraq to an early halt. He had pictured a "revolution whose face was a religion full of kindness for the people" and instead "it became a brutal regime of torture, suppression, and killing."

In November 1981, Nabavi, Mohsen's boss in Rajai's cabinet, was named Minister of Heavy Industry in the new government, and he asked Mohsen to join him in that office. This was a post at which he felt he could help to build the country while remaining aloof from the political fray that had played out so disappointingly.

After ten months, Nabavi made him the head of the Industrial Development and Renovation Organization. Founded by the Shah's government in the 1960s in order to interface with similar organizations in the Communist countries, IDRO had grown into an enormous holding conglomerate comprising 142 separate companies accounting for one-sixth of the country's industry. Its various entities produced automobiles, trucks, tractors, construction equipment, boilers, pipes, metals, motors, railway cars, ships, oil drilling equipment, and other heavy products.

On his first day as chief, Mohsen assembled the two hundred staff of IDRO's headquarters and beseeched their help, admitting disarmingly that his only factory experience was as an agitator trying to foment strikes. He threw himself into this new work with verve and surrounded himself with young managers. He ordered production accelerated by going to two and three shifts a day. In addition, in the first two years, IDRO accomplished 86 new projects, either building a factory or expanding an existing one. When the war front moved to marshland, the army for the first time requested floating bridges, and somehow, by adapting existing assembly lines, IDRO produced 2.5 kilometers of bridge within a matter of days.

While Mohsen basked in his success at boosting production, he ran into difficulties elsewhere. Iran Khodro, a part of IDRO, was the biggest auto manufacturer in Iran. Its principal product was called the *Peykan,* Farsi for Arrowhead, which was modeled after the 1960 Hillman, a British make. Mohsen remembers:

> The quality control department of the company had a list of more than 300 problems that they wanted to solve. The company is about 14 kilometers outside of Tehran. Sometimes, when a customer bought a car there, he did not even reach Tehran before he had a problem with the car. People knew they had to go to private shops to repair the cars they had just bought.

After experimenting unsuccessfully with all manner of exhortation, trying to inculcate managers with the mantra of being "customer-oriented," he had an epiphany:

> If you want to have a good product you need competition, because if you are exclusive, people will buy your cars even if you do not assemble them. You could put them in a plastic bag and give it to them and say, "Go home and assemble it yourself." They have no other choice.

This experience led him to reexamine his ideas about economics. Although he had rejected Marxism, Mohsen thought of himself as a Leftist "like the other Islamic revolutionists." The ideas he held, learned from Shariati and especially Mohammad Bagher Sadr in his book *Our Economy,* were socialist ideas that frowned upon private property. "But when I went to the industries I found that this does not work," he says.

The year he took over, the state budget allocated $100 million to IDRO to cover its losses. Mohsen concluded that the whole idea was wrong. "The first lesson of business is that you have to make profit," he says. "Everybody in the world makes a company to get profit out of it. You do not make factories just to have factories." So he laid down a new policy: "If your company does not produce any profit, we will close it."

Mohsen's insistence on profitability met resistance. First, there was the issue of putting people out of jobs. Even more important, the unprofitable industries were undergirded by a philosophy of autarky rooted in the anti-Western philosophy of Islamic revolution. By these lights, it was important for Iran to produce everything to demonstrate its independence.

Experience taught the folly of ignoring economies of scale and comparative advantage. "The investments that we needed to make many goods inside Iran were not compatible with low quantities of production," he explains. Iranian industry might need one hundred thousand of a certain part, but it might only be economic to produce at least a million. If you could market the other nine hundred thousand abroad, everything would work out fine. But if you could not, you were better off buying the one hundred thousand that you needed from another country.

Mohsen recalls a visit to Iran by Turkish Prime Minister Turgut Ozal, who championed free market reforms:

> Nabavi, the Minister of Heavy Industries, was explaining to Turgut Ozal one of our 86 new projects. A company that we established in Tabriz under license from Switzerland started to produce textile machines to sell to the textile industries of Iran, and we were proud of that. I remember that Turgut Ozal looked at that machine and said, "Yes this is very good. I congratulate you. But I prefer that textile industries of Turkey buy these machines from Sulzer in Switzerland directly in order to have better quality and to be able to sell the textiles in European countries."

He was right. We were happy that we had self-sufficiency in the machinery of textile industries, but our textile industries went bankrupt and Turkish textile industry has a record of $10 billion per year in exports of textiles, cloths and products like that. They have gotten the Iranian market as well.

A far bigger project than textile machines was automobiles. They already produced the *Peykan,* but that was not enough. "We were very eager to make a car by ourselves," recalls Mohsen. "Not only to produce it, like the *Peykan,* but to design it, to prove that we can make a car from A to Z and be able to say, 'this is an Iranian car.' And we did that." But the results were not all that was wished for:

> It took ten years and lots of money. Iran Khodro even hired a British engineering company with more than 40 engineers, and we tried hard. At last we made a fully Iranian car; its name is Sahand. But it is not viable because we do not have much market for it. Our domestic market is not big. We have spent so much money to design that car, to make the parts in Iran, because you need lots of tools to make any part, lots of investments. For a car of this price you need to sell a minimum of about 2 million cars to reach to the break-even point.
>
> But you do not have such a market in Iran, and it is impossible to sell these cars to other countries. The only country that imported this car is Syria just to say that we have exported an Iranian car to another country, although they make this car much cheaper in Syria.
>
> The company does not make any profit out of that but we are happy that we are imitating the big companies that sell semi-knockdown, SKD they call it, and we can say that, "we are making an Iranian car in Syria." (And even a few in the Central Asian republics.) But we are unable to sell them any place in the world.

Mohsen succeeded in weaning IDRO from subsidies and operating the company in the black. This success confirmed him in his new opinions. "What I found out changed me from Left economic ideas to Right economic ideas." He believed it was detrimental that so many of the country's new rulers had come through engineering school, as he had. "They look at everything from an engineering point of view, which, especially in the economy is a disaster [because they want] to control everything," he observed. In contrast, he came to cherish economic freedom, and he began to take his economic counsel from Mohammad Tabibian, a professor who was called "the Milton Friedman of Iran."

Mohsen felt that the lessons he learned about economics held political implications. He formulated this catechism: "If you want to have a good business, you need competition. For competition you need a market economy, not a state-run economy. And for a market economy you need democracy." Why? Because, he says, "If you have a source of exclusive power, they can manipulate the sources of money as well." In other words, tyranny is contrary to rule of law, and rule of law is essential to the smooth functioning of markets.

In addition, Mohsen saw consequences for Iran's foreign policy. "To participate in the circulation of business in the world, you cannot fight with the world," he says. "You cannot deny Western civilization, and then say, 'we want to cooperate with you.'"

Mohsen had been at IDRO two years when one morning his secretary told him that a visitor insisted on seeing him right away. Mohsen asked if the person had an appointment, and when the answer was no, Mohsen said, "Tell him I'm busy." But his secretary replied, "Boss, I think you have to see him. He's from the Judicial Authority, and he has an order. A tall man with a black beard entered and said, "You are under arrest," showing Mohsen a warrant signed by his old nemesis, Lajevardi.

Mohsen picked up the phone and called his superior and friend, Nabavi, who spoke with the arresting officer, but the bearded man insisted that he had his orders. Nabavi got Ayatollah Ardebili, the head of the Judicial Authority, on the other line, but Lajevardi had his own sources of authority, so the best Ardebili could do was order a delay. Mohsen had to agree to turn himself in the next morning for interrogation.

The accusation once again was that Mohsen was a secret agent of the MEK who had conspired with Keshmiri in the bombing that killed Rajai and Bahonar. Ali Tehrani, languishing in jail for three years, had finally broken under torture and told his interrogators that he would sign anything they put before him. He "confessed" that he had worked covertly for the MEK and that he had collaborators in the Prime Minister's office who had promoted Keshmiri. That presumably meant either Mohsen or Khosrou Tehrani, and it was sufficient to give Lajevardi at last the authority to arrest Mohsen.

Mohsen arrived early at Evin Prison, where he was blindfolded, although not handcuffed, and taken by car to the appropriate building. He was seated in an empty interrogation room and left there for some hours. At noon someone came with a tray of food but he had no appetite. Then after lunch, an officer entered and said he needed the room. Mohsen was led by the hand down a long and wide corridor. He could see from under the blindfold, and what he saw was "a very sad scene." As they passed various interrogation rooms he heard shouting, and the corridor was lined with young male and female prisoners awaiting their turns. The young women looked particularly pitiful.

He was led down a flight of stairs, then seated on a crushed cardboard carton at the bottom of the stairwell and told to stay there, although his blindfold was removed. He could see another long corridor, again lined with frightened prisoners like the ones above. They reminded him of the baby chicks he had raised in boyhood "when they get cold or become ill and they don't move." He recalls the feeling that came over him:

> That was a turning point of my life. I said to myself, what is going on? Is this what we wanted to create—these prisoners, this atmosphere, that interrogator? I knew that I would be released because of pressure outside Evin. But what about these young people?
>
> I had heard several things about tortures, killings, executions. I had told myself that the opposition groups exaggerate. Lajevardi is cruel but not that cruel.

Now he wondered if all the terrible things he had heard were indeed accurate. Then he witnessed something that chilled him to the bone:

> While I was looking at that sad scene, an interrogator came out from one of the rooms and shouted, "Guard, come take this [bitch] to be beaten more; more lashes." She was young and blindfolded, and she started to cry. I heard her say, "I cannot bear more lashes." And the interrogator said that "Hah, you cannot tolerate a few lashes in this room? How can you tolerate the God's eternal punishment? In the next life you will be in hell." And they took her away.

Mohsen recalls, "That really shocked me. I asked myself, 'Who persuaded this interrogator that he is an agent of God?' A person who believes he has a mission from God can easily torture, kill, or do anything."

He was left in the stairwell until evening. Then he was taken to have his mug shot snapped. One of the interrogators told him that he was going to be released "because your friends have lied to Imam Khomeini, but rest assured you will be back here. We'll be waiting for you." He was turned over to a guard who led him outside the building where he was allowed to remove the blindfold, and suddenly roles seemed to revert to normal. As they waited for a car to the prison gate, the guard said, "Mr. Sazegara, I know you are the head of the automotive industries. I'm trying to buy a van. Can you help me?" Mohsen declined.

The next morning, Mohsen went directly to the office of Minister Nabavi, his friend and patron, to review the previous day's events. Nabavi told him that he had enlisted the help of Ardebili, the head of the Judicial Authority, and that the two of them had won over Ahmad Khomeini, the usually hard-line son of the Imam, who in turn went to his father and secured an order for Mohsen's release.

Mohsen told Nabavi of the disturbing things he had seen and heard in Evin. "I have to tell Ayatollah Khomeini what is going on," he said. Nabavi phoned Ahmad Khomeini and asked if they could come to see his father, and somewhat to their surprise, they were given an appointment for later that morning at the Ayatollah's home in Jamaran, a northern sub-urb of Tehran (where he had moved from the holy city of Qom).

The meeting consisted of just the four: Mohsen, Nabavi, Khomeini, and his son, Ahmad, who was a close aide. They sat on the floor of a small drawing room. Mohsen was not on personal terms with him, but the Ayatollah remembered the devoted young man on his staff in Neauphle-le-Château. Mohsen recited his experience at Evin, stressing the words of the interrogator who acted as if he was God's deputy. Mohsen felt tense and he thought that Khomeini, who listened care-fully, seemed to grow tense, too. Then, as Mohsen recon-structs it, he concluded with a bold albeit respectful appeal: "Imam, I have followed you from Paris. If you agree with what Lajevardi is doing, please tell me. Then I will know that I made a mistake and I will resign my position and ask God to forgive me. And if you do not agree, why don't you remove Lajevardi?" Khomeini did not respond.

Ahmad showed them out, and standing out in the yard, he bid Mohsen write down his account in large print so that his father could read it. Mohsen did it later that day, then had it copied over by Soheila's cousin who had particularly good handwriting, and it was delivered the next morning.

As they left, Mohsen and Nabavi shared their astonishment that Ahmad had gotten them the meeting with his father so promptly since they believed Ahmad was Lajevardi's sponsor. Apparently something was in the wind. Ardebili, the head of the Judicial Authority, had grown unhappy with Lajevardi. Ardebili was close to Khomeini, and Mohsen heard later that he had brought some other former prisoners to tell their tales to the Imam. A week or so later, Lajevardi was removed from his post.[4]

This, however, was not enough to make Mohsen feel whole again. After what he had seen in Evin, Mohsen says:

> Something was broken inside me, and I was not the same person. Put it this way: You have raised a child and you like him very much. But one day, you see that he is doing something very bad, a crime. Something will break inside you. Still, you love him; this is your son. But you do not like what he is doing. I had such a feeling. I still loved the revolution. I was about 30 years old. I had spent so far 13 years of my life from early morning until late at night on it. And I really loved the movement that we made, that great victory. But now, I did not like that face of the revolution, the face of this new child. Now, I began to believe many things that I had heard. Before that, I told myself, "No, they are exaggerating." But now, I believed everything.

Mohsen went back to work, but a need grew within him to understand what had gone wrong. The seventy hour work weeks he put in at IDRO left no time for reading, so he realized he would have to leave. In 1985 he submitted his resignation, although it took most of another year to extricate himself, signing on as an adviser to a few companies.

Altogether this work required about 25 hours a week and paid enough to support his family, which now included a second son, Shahab, who had been born in 1984, just before Mohsen's day at Evin. Most of the rest of his hours, Mohsen spent reading, or rather rereading. He began with the works of Ayatollah Khomeini, at the center of which lay the theory of *Velayat e Faqih,* the rule of the religious jurisprudent. Mohsen recalls:

> When I read that book the first time, I was 20. I did not notice the main idea of Ayatollah Khomeini. What was wonderful for me was his language against the U.S., the Shah, and Israel. This time, I did not care about the slogans. I was looking for the main ideas. And I said to myself, "Wow, what kind of political philosophy is this? So much authority for one person without any control, and a divine mission. This is despotism."

It was, moreover, a despotism whose scowl Mohsen realized he had seen with his own eyes on the face of the heartless interrogator who thought he was acting for God when he ordered more lashes.

He worked his way back through Shariati, Bahger Sadr, Al-e Ahmad, and others. Mohsen already knew that he no longer believed in their economic theories of Islamic socialism, but now he found that the rest of their ideas no longer rang true either. Shariati was the most prolific and influential on Mohsen and the entire revolutionary generation. "The pillar of Shariati's ideas is to make a revolutionary ideology out of religion," says Mohsen. On rereading he found some of what Shariati proposed "worse than what Stalin did in Russia." Mohsen's own thinking was stimulated by discussions with his friend, Soroush, the liberal religious thinker, and he embraced Soroush's "minimalist" idea that, as Mohsen paraphrases, "religion aims to answer only two main questions: Where have we come from? And where will we go?"

Looking back, Mohsen assesses:

> We are an undeveloped country because of undeveloped human resources and undeveloped intellectuals. Unfortunately, in Iran, most of the intellectuals, Islamic or non-Islamic, were affected by Marxist intellectuals. And Marxist intellectuals—maybe with the exception of Marx himself—decide about everything without using reason. They think that if they say that some idea is "bourgeois," therefore it is refuted.

He adds, "I don't know if it is more funny or more sad, that we thought we had a prescription for the whole world. When I see President Ahmadinejad, I think of Hegel's quip about history repeating itself: We were the tragedy version, and he is the farce."

Although Mohsen had been released within a day in 1984, Ali Tehrani, whose confession had been extracted by torture, was still incarcerated. By 1986, he had been held for five years. This meant that the cloud of suspicion puffed up by Lajevardi still hung over Mohsen and others who had served in the Prime Minister's office at the time of the bombing. Although Lajevardi had lost his formal position, he remained a leader of the hard line faction and the *éminence grise* at Evin, and he continued to circulate Ali Tehrani's signed "confession" in ruling circles to inculpate them.

When Muhammad Mousavi-Khoeini was named chief prosecutor of Iran, Mohsen saw an opportunity to close the file at last. Although Mousavi-Khoeini was not part of his circle, Mohsen trusted the man's fairness. So he and some others approached Mousavi-Khoeini and asked him to appoint someone to investigate the case, offering to undergo whatever interrogation would be deemed necessary to resolve it.

It was agreed, and Mousavi-Khoeini imposed only two constraints on the investigative team. Nabavi, who was still a cabinet member, was to be interrogated at his office, not at Evin. And none of the group could be tortured. Mohsen and a dozen or so colleagues reported to Evin Prison in March, 1986.

They were placed in solitary confinement, allowed no contact with the outside. Loud music was piped into the cells all night to deprive them of sleep. But the most searing part for Mohsen was the evidence of torture he could hear from other cells:

> I remember one night I heard the voice of a girl who was moaning, "Oh my God, Oh my Prophet, I do not feel good." I was walking in the cell and I knocked my head against the wall. I said to myself that, "Oh, Mohsen, this is the system that you have participated in creating. If this girl—I did not know who she is—in the Day of Judgment says to God that she has been oppressed and you have been part of this system, what will you answer? What will you say to God?" And that was very bitter for me, really bitter. And I decided much more not to cooperate with the system.

Mohsen was interrogated for twelve days and nights. He was blindfolded, and there were three interrogators, but the accusation that he was a secret MEK agent was absurd. Mohsen had a long and public record as an activist and had always been at odds with the MEK. Moreover, he and his circle reached the pinnacle of their influence in the administration of Rajai and Bahonar. Why would they kill them? Seeing that the case was going nowhere, Mousavi-Khoeini ordered the investigators to wrap it up, but they resisted, protesting that he had spoiled their work by disallowing the usual tortures.

After forty-nine days, solitary confinement ended for Mohsen and his friends. Only later did it become clear why. One of them, a former aide to Khosrou Tehrani, died in his cell. Eager to avoid blame, the prison officials immediately summoned Saeed Hajjarian. Hajjarian also had been an aide to Khosrou Tehrani and a friend of the deceased. He still held a position in the intelligence service, but he was not among the group being interrogated. They asked him to come to Evin at once to see the body before it was moved, so he could attest that it was a suicide. Hajjarian was shown his friend's body, hanging from his own belt—exactly as it was found, according to the warders. But Hajjarian later told Mohsen and others that the dead man's legs had been bent, apparently in rigor mortis, and it appeared that had they been straight his feet would have reached the floor—an impossible position in which to hang yourself.[5]

Whatever the truth about this death, it put the jailers on the defensive. Another prisoner was moved into Mohsen's cell, a high school student who said his only political act had been to distribute MEK literature. He had been sentenced to ten years, and he told Mohsen that he had been whipped on the soles of his feet until they bled and became infected. The young man's story and his palpable terror formed another burr on Mohsen's conscience.

A second consequence of the "suicide" was that it energized friends and sympathizers of Mohsen's circle who realized that similar deaths could follow. Sixty-nine senior officials signed a letter asking Khomeini himself to intercede. Khomeini convened the top judicial and prosecutorial officials, and Mousavi-Khoeini presented their opinion that no evidence existed. According to Mohsen, who heard the story from Mousavi-Khoeini, Khomeini said that he had known all along that there was nothing to the allegations. He ordered that the case be closed and that the accused be released within 48 hours. Mohsen left prison after serving a total of 75 days. Even Ali Tehrani at last was set free.

While this experience added to Mohsen's disillusionment with the regime, its aftermath compounded that. The dozen or so who had been through this ordeal and a few of their friends in government sought meetings with the regime's top officials. Saying that he had ordered an end to such practices, Hashemi Rafsanjani (who later became President) voiced shock and indignation so emotively that Mohsen believed him. But after the meeting, Hajjarian, who was still an intelligence official, expressed perplexity at this claim of ignorance. He said that two days earlier he had circulated a report to the regime's upper echelon, including Rafsanjani, about a prisoner who had died under torture.

Next they met Ayatollah Ardebili, the head of the Judicial Authority. Mohsen describes his response: "Ayatollah Ardebili laughed and said, 'There are lots of examples like that all around the country. I have some reports that somewhere they have raped some prisoners, not only tortured them.'" Mohsen says that he reacted angrily but Ardebili insisted that he was not to blame since he had not been directly involved in any of these cases. The only official who seemed to take to heart the accounts of abuses was Ayatollah Hussein Ali Montazeri, first in line to succeed Khomeini as Supreme Leader. Montazeri was later pushed out of the pecking order and placed under house arrest for challenging Khomeini and advocating fidelity to the revolution's democratic rhetoric.

In 1988, Nabavi approached Mohsen and asked him to return to the Ministry of Heavy Industry. Mohsen said he could do it only if he was authorized to initiate the privatization of the industries of IDRO. Nabavi was not sold on Mohsen's new Rightist economic ideas, but replied nonetheless that he was being crushed by the burdens of his office and would agree to any program for IDRO, if Mohsen would just take control of it again. A few months later, Rafsanjani was elected President, and Mohsen asked for an audience. He explained to Rafsanjani the need to privatize the economy and also to restore relations with the United States. Rafsanjani agreed.

Mohsen, however, did not remain long in his post. A new Minister of Heavy Industries was named to replace Nabavi, and although he and Mohsen had been friends in the fight against the Shah, Mohsen found he could not work with the man. Mohsen resigned and did not seek another post. Instead, in his mid-thirties and after years in the upper reaches of power, he returned to school. His revolutionary activities had cut short his university years and had diverted him from his studies during the time he was enrolled. His recent period of rereading the seminal texts of Islamism had convinced him that this ideology was wrong, but now he yearned to ground himself more widely in history and philosophy. He wanted desperately to understand why the revolution that had been the center of his life had turned out so differently from what he had hoped and expected.

He finished his bachelor's and master's degrees at the University of the Shahid Beheshti, renamed after an Ayatollah close to Khomeini who had been killed early in the revolution by an MEK bomb. He went on to enroll for doctoral studies at the University of London, much of which he was permitted to do from Tehran. He studied the Middle Ages, finding an analogy between Christian thought in Europe before the Renaissance and the current state of the Islamic world. He came to the view that the influence of Saint Augustine, in insisting on the subordination of reason to revelation, gave rise to what are sometimes called the "Dark Ages," and that Saint Thomas had inaugurated the liberation of the Christian world by arguing for concurrent respect for reason and revelation. He lamented that "in the world of Islam we still do not have our Saint Thomas," and he hoped that a path in that direction could begin with the thinking of his friend, Soroush, who argues that while religion is divine, knowledge of religion is mediated by humans and therefore is not intrinsically superior to other kinds of human knowledge.

A second problem within Islam that he identified through his comparative studies of other faiths is that "Islam was born with government" because the Prophet was also a ruler. Whereas in the Christian world the most important figures were theologians and philosophers, in the world of Islam pride of place belonged to jurists. Herein he saw the roots of Khomeini's theory of the rule of the clerical jurisprudent.

Reading contemporary political philosophers, he was especially gripped by Karl Popper's anti-totalitarian classic, *The Open Society and Its Enemies,* and also by the works of the libertarian economist Friedrich von Hayek. He came away believing in "pluralism, religious pluralism, modern rationality, and 'dare to know,' as Kant says—in short, liberalism." He embraced what he calls "the minimal theory of religion." This did not mean that one should be minimally religious. On the contrary, Mohsen remained as devout as he had been since seventeen, reciting the five requisite daily prayers (although Shiites combine these into three worship sessions), observing the fast of Ramadan and other rituals, abstaining from things designated as *haram,* or forbidden. What he meant, rather, was recognition that religion is not the answer for everything even if it addresses the most important things and therefore that it ought not to be inserted arbitrarily into other fields of inquiry.

Even while he studied, Mohsen kept up his political activity. With borrowed money he launched a weekly devoted to economic affairs. He hoped it would become an Iranian analog to the *Wall Street Journal* or *Financial Times.* But he only secured 300 subscriptions, not enough to survive. He rethought his strategy, and came up with a new plan. Instead of a serious weekly, he published an escapist magazine aimed at young people, called *Ayneh* (*Mirror*). It quickly turned profitable, corralling fifty thousand subscribers, and with the profits he sustained two serious monthlies, called (in translation) *Economic Mirror* and *Thought Mirror.* The latter was devoted to political topics, and each issue contained, among other pieces, an essay by Mohsen and one by Soroush.

Mohsen's journals pushed the envelope of permissible discourse, but this early phase of Rafsanjani's presidency was a relatively relaxed time. Mohammad Khatami was Minister of Culture, and publications fell under his jurisdiction. A couple of his deputies were friends of Mohsen's. One of them encouraged Mohsen to join a newly-formed cooperative of a dozen magazines, which he did and soon became its managing director. Within a year it had grown to include 450 publications. With backing from the Ministry of Culture, it purchased a building with good work facilities and an auditorium for public meetings. Mohsen saw it as the beginnings of an infrastructure for the liberal camp. But such hopes were soon dashed.

Ali Khamenei, who had replaced Khomeini as Supreme Leader upon the latter's death in 1989, maneuvered to concentrate power in his own hands at the expense of President Rafsanjani. In order to wrest the Ministry of Culture into his own hands, he launched a propaganda campaign against the "cultural invasion" by which the "enemy" (i.e., the U.S.) was subverting the Muslim faith of Iranians. Khatami resigned as Minister of Culture, and was replaced by Ali Larijani, a hardliner who was later to become internationally known as Iran's nuclear negotiator.

Larijani immediately banned *Thought Mirror* and took steps that Mohsen saw would soon lead to the closure of *Economic Mirror*. He went to see Larijani to protest, and he told Larijani that if his magazines were closed down, he would apply for a license to open a newspaper. "Close the door," replied Larijani, and then continued, as Mohsen recalls:

> Mohsen, sit down. I want to talk to you not as Larijani, the Minister of Culture and Islamic Guidance, to Sazegara, the

head of the press cooperative and publisher of *Ayneh* magazines. I want to talk to you as Ali to Mohsen, like old friends.

Let me tell you something. In the office of the Leader they have discussed this, and they will not let you publish anything. Do not go for a newspaper. If you do, I know you will have to borrow money. You may start it. But after a few weeks or a month, rest assured they will close it, and you will be left with lots of debt and no newspaper.

Mohsen transferred ownership of his escapist weekly to a friend, since he had published it only to underwrite his intellectual monthlies. Now that he was out of the magazine business, he made a living as a consultant to Iran's leading IT company, and while continuing his studies, he became active in a circle of some fifteen to twenty intellectuals centered on the quarterly *Kian*. The members arranged for publication of some classic works of liberal thought, held unofficial classes in people's homes, and gave lectures at universities. They employed what Mohsen calls "guerrilla tactics in politics. We put pressure on the regime, but whenever they wanted to attack us, we pulled back, not to let them have their final confrontation and arrest us, because we wanted to have time to spread our ideas." Nonetheless, they annoyed the authorities enough that the magazine's offices were sacked by the *Basij*. Called the White Shirts, the *Basij* were like Hitler's Brown Shirts or Mussolini's Black Shirts—thugs employed by an authoritarian regime to brutalize its opposition under the pretense of being socially-conscious or angry citizens.

Soroush was the group's star attraction, and his speeches at mosques and on campuses drew large crowds. Mohsen was often the organizer, and he developed close ties with leaders of student organizations that were growing increasingly rebellious. A highpoint occurred when Soroush was scheduled to speak at Amirkabir University, one of Tehran's most important. He waited at Mohsen's apartment while Mohsen proceeded to the campus to meet up with the student leaders. As Soroush readied to leave to join them, he saw a gathering of security forces apparently intending to detain him, so he retreated back. The students managed to put their phone into a sound amplifier, and in this manner Soroush delivered a brief address to the student throng. In content it was only a fraction of Soroush's planned lecture, but it was a triumph over the forces of repression, heartening the student protest movement.

Although Mohsen was deft at dodging the regime, he was helpless against human frailty, and in 1995, at the age of 40, he suffered a heart attack. While recuperating at home, he entertained a flow of visitors, hatching another political plan. He was ambivalent toward President Rafsanjani. He distrusted Rafsanjani enough that he declined a feeler about becoming an economic adviser. But he also saw Rafsanjani as a counterweight to Khamenei, the apotheosis of reaction. Mohsen remained friendly with a brother of Rafsanjani's and broached to him the idea of putting together a party of modernizers and technocrats to run in the 1996 *Majlis* elections. He helped to convince his old patron from the Ministry of Heavy Industry, Behzad Nabavi, to join forces even though Nabavi was still a socialist while Rafsanjani had to some extent embraced the idea of privatization. Mohsen recalls appealing to Nabavi in these terms: "I understand that you are leftists and you call Rafsanjani a rightist. But forget about left and right. We have only one dividing line in the country. That is between despotism and democracy."

Rafsanjani's new party succeeded in winning most seats, but it brought few of the results that Mohsen was hoping for. So by the beginning of 1997, with a presidential election scheduled for that June, the *Kian* circle decided to run their own candidate. At first, they did not think in terms of winning, but of garnering a large protest vote that would advance their movement. They were all too aware that they were not operating in a free environment, so the challenge was to come up with a candidate who would not be summarily ruled off the ballot as most candidates had been in each presidential election since the revolution. Mohammad Khatami fit the bill. He was a ranking cleric who was part of the establishment, so it seemed likely his candidacy would be allowed. But he had earned liberal credentials by resigning from the post of Minister of Culture and Islamic Guidance in opposition to Khamenei's overly restrictive policies.

Reluctantly, Khatami accepted their proposal. Ali Akbar Nategh-Nouri was the front-runner, and Mohsen's colleagues hoped that Khatami could poll a respectable five million votes, which would have made their movement an important opposition force. But Mohsen believed that the people were so disillusioned with the authorities that Khatami would win if they could make him the symbol of opposition. "Our trick was to keep Khatami away from the regime," recalls Mohsen, "and to encourage Nategh-Nouri to collect endorsements from government officials. That was a trap because if you wanted to win you had to show the people that you are as far from this regime as possible."

Once Mohsen found that a former deputy of his who was now a Khatami campaign official had printed posters showing Khatami posed with Ayatollah Khomeini and Ayatollah Khamenei, all three sporting black turbans, marking them as *sayed*s, descendants of the Prophet. Mohsen prevailed upon the man to take down the posters. "We tried to convey to the people that a vote for Khatami is a 'No' vote, not only to the regime but to Ayatollah Khamenei," said Mohsen.

The outcome was a landslide: Khatami carried 71 percent of the vote. Mohsen and his colleagues thought they were at the dawn of important changes. On the morrow of the vote, they sat down to draft a letter for Khatami, giving thanks to the nation. It included a list of reforms that Khatami would undertake and it also extended a hand of friendship to those who had opposed him—with one exception. Mohsen's circle was furious that national television and radio had tilted blatantly in favor of Nategh-Nouri. The broadcasting system was under the direction of Ali Larijani, the former hard-line culture minister who had closed down Mohsen's *Mirror* journals. He had been appointed by Khamenei, and the draft letter demanded his replacement.

But Khatami removed that demand and anything that smacked of confrontation. He told his supporters that publicly opposing Khamenei was a "red line" that he would not cross. And he held to this throughout his tenure. He met weekly with the Supreme Leader in private, and where they diverged he relied on persuasion or compromised or backed down. A further disappointment was in store for Mohsen when Khatami chose a cabinet that included few new faces. With a youthful population and a voting age of 16, young people had constituted an important base for Khatami, but he chose a Minister of Education who was notorious for suppressing student activism.

In all, it took Mohsen about a year and a half to lose all hope in the president. It took the nation as a whole six years, he estimates, to reach the same conclusion. The core reason for Khatami's failure, Mohsen believes, was not his cowardice or his poor choice of advisors. The root problem, he says, is that being "Islamists," Khatami and his inner circle, "cannot get rid of a maximal theory of religion. They do not believe in pluralism."

For the second time in his young life Mohsen had seen the political change he had worked for snatched away just when it seemed to be in hand. But, amazingly, it took none of the fight out of him. Since the Khatami administration refused to serve as a vehicle for major reform, Mohsen looked to create others.

Denied permission to start a party, he launched a daily paper. Although Larijani had warned he would not be allowed to do this, one of Mohsen's two partners, political sociologist Hamid Reza Jalaiepour, had had three brothers martyred in the war with Iraq which gave him a special status, making the authorities reluctant to deny him a license. Mohsen served as publisher, and Mashaallah Shamsolvaezin, the editor of *Kian*, became its editor.

In February 1998 they launched *Jame'eh (Society)*, a sixteen-page daily. In contrast to other Iranian newspapers which were composed of religious pap, cheerleading for the regime, and general grayness, *Jame'eh* practiced lively and irreverent journalism. It never ran a photo of a cleric, the likes of which filled the other papers. Instead, for example, one *Jame'eh* front page ran the photo of a beautiful girl playing the cello. To be sure she was decked out in a head scarf and full Shiite modesty, but the self-explanatory point of the photo (gasp) was her beauty. When authorities hauled in the mayor of Tehran on charges of corruption, many believed that the real reason for his arrest was that he had angered conservatives by backing Khatami's presidential campaign. *Jame'eh* ran a cartoon of a mayor posed in a mug shot, except the case number across his chest was the date of the presidential election.

To make the paper interactive, Mohsen offered free film to any aspiring photographer who wanted to submit shots for consideration, and he also invited submissions for the paper's daily cartoon. *Jame'eh* was the launching pad for satirist Ebrahim Nabavi, who ran a column called "Fifth Column," lampooning government leaders. When Rafsanjani dubbed himself the "general of construction," Nabavi invented mocking military titles for other high echelon officials. After a particular egregious tirade by Abbas Abbasi, an ultra conservative member of the *Majlis*, Nabavi filled his column with a photo of the man without any caption or other text. Since it was a humor column, it took the reader only a split second to get the point: Abbasi was a joke.

After its first 33 issues, Supreme Leader Khamenei attacked *Jame'eh* as "the face of the enemy" and a "cultural invasion." But the paper had taken off. Starting with a print run of fifty thousand, circulation grew to 350,000 in a matter of months. Overnight, it was the leading paper in the country. There was in fact demand for more copies, but production was constrained by printing facilities that were not equal to the paper's popularity. Revenue nearly reached costs, and plans were laid to establish *Jame'eh*'s own presses. It was on track to reach a circulation of one million and to operate at a profit by its first anniversary. But that date never arrived.

In July 1998, after five months of publication, *Jame'eh* received notice that its license had been lifted. Mohsen and his partners had been expecting that, so they had secured another license. The next morning—without missing a day—a new paper, called *Tous*, appeared on Iran's newsstands. It appeared identical in every respect to *Jame'eh*, except for its name. Mohsen ordered a reduced print run, but in this he erred, for the readers caught on instantly, and that day *Tous* sold out early.

After two weeks, an order came closing *Tous* on the grounds that it was simply *Jame'eh* in disguise. Then a supporter offered to let Mohsen and his partners use the license he held for a children's newspaper. They used that for some days, then won a court ruling allowing them to reopen *Tous* if they changed its appearance to make it different from *Jame'eh*.

It was of little avail. In September, Mohsen received a call while abroad, informing him that during the night the revolutionary court had sent officers to lock the offices of *Tous*. They had arrested his two partners, as well as the man who held the license for *Tous* and the satirist Nabavi. A warrant had been issued for Mohsen.

Mohsen was on a stopover in Kuala Lumpur on his way to visit New Zealand where his brother Mehdi, the one who had helped steal his own mimeograph machine for the sake of the revolution, was now Iran's ambassador. Mohsen said he would return at once to face the law, but the next available flight was not for three days. Waiting impatiently for the confrontation that awaited him at home, Mohsen, who had always avoided the limelight, decided to publicize his case. He announced to reporters that if arrested upon his return, he would go on a hunger strike because the regime had no legal right to arrest him or his colleagues.

He went to a local hospital to get a check-up so as to have evidence that any failure of health in prison was due to mistreatment or to his hunger-strike and not to a pre-existing condition. But the examination showed that his heart condition had worsened. He was hospitalized, and the Kuala Lumpur cardiologist would only release him when he signed a statement attesting that he was leaving against medical advice. The doctor also equipped him with nitroglycerine patches and a letter saying that he ought to be hospitalized as soon as he landed in Tehran. Soheila promptly read that letter in an interview on the BBC's Farsi service, declaring, "If the revolutionary court arrests him, his health will be its responsibility."

He was taken from the plane in a wheel chair and not arrested at the airport where hundreds of his supporters were waiting. He went directly to a hospital where he was placed in the critical care unit. A day later, two officers came to his bedside and declared him under arrest. A round-the-clock guard was left in his room.

Mohsen had bypass surgery, but he continued to work from his hospital bed. Soheila was Mohsen's collaborator, and from time to time during her visits, she would ask the guards to step out and give the couple some privacy to talk about personal things. During these moments alone, Mohsen would give her instructions to relay to the paper's business office which continued to function. Mohsen also enjoyed the collaboration of most of the hospital staff, who sympathized with his struggle against the reactionaries. When Mohsen was moved into intensive care after his surgery, the nurses insisted that guards were not allowed there and had to stand watch outside the door. But, unbeknownst to the guards, there was a second door, through which he received surreptitious visits.

Several days later, the mother of Mohsen's partner, Jalaiepour, appealed openly to Khamenei. She had four sons, she said, and had given three as martyrs in the war with Iraq. How could he take her last son from her? This was compelling enough to secure the group's release pending trial.

Convalescing at home over the next months, Mohsen had repeated discussions with Shamsolvaezin and Jalaiepour, and they came to a friendly parting of ways. The other two wanted to start a new paper, but Mohsen felt the effort would be futile. "Whatever we publish, Khamenei will close," he said. "He has realized the danger of newspapers."

The argument went deeper. Mohsen's position was growing more radical. "It is useless to follow the reform movement," he said. "Khatami did nothing for us. He was afraid even to phone us to say, 'I support you' or 'I worry about what has happened to you.'" Jalaiepour, however, was not ready to fight the Supreme Leader. Mohsen replied: "It is not our choice. Khamenei has already started the war. Maybe, if you go sit at home he will not do anything to you. But if you want to do something, then you have to confront Khamenei."

This stark assessment was vindicated when Khatami continued to bow to Khamenei even after town council elections in 1999 and parliamentary elections in 2000 had given the reformers control over most of the country's elected offices; Khatami kept his silence when, in April 2000, security forces closed down fifty publications, including *Neshat*, the newly founded paper by Mohsen's former partners, Shamsolvaezin and Jalaieipour.

Mohsen's idea was to launch a satellite television network that could operate from abroad and therefore would be difficult to suppress. He also wanted to form a political party, even though he was sure the authorities would not legalize it. But without partners and recuperating from bypass surgery, his preternatural energy failed him, and he could not mount the effort to initiate these two projects.

After completing his recovery, Mohsen found employment through another of his old friends from IDRO who managed Saipa, the country's second largest auto manufacturer. Mohsen proposed to form a subsidiary company for financing auto purchases and leases. Nothing of the kind existed in Iran. Later he expanded into insurance and also issued Iran's first credit card.

He did not, however, forsake political activity. In this period, from 1999 to 2001, no longer avoiding publicity, he began to give frequent interviews especially to the international press, above all the Farsi language broadcasts of Western radio services. Drawing on his circle of contacts in the student world, he traveled the country giving lectures at as many as 80 universities. These broke taboos, such as criticizing the founding principles of the Islamic Republic and advocating peace with Israel and reconciliation with America, and embracing globalization. He launched a website, AllIran.com, one of the first in Iran. On it, among other things, he posted an open letter to Khamenei, warning that he was alienating the people. The tone was respectful, but still it was rare for the Supreme Leader to be criticized directly.

Khamenei was denounced by student protesters who had demonstrated for more press freedom in June 1999. When security goons raided the dormitories of Tehran University injuring many and even killing several students, the protests, some of which grew violent, spread around Tehran and to seventeen other cities.[6] This helped to convince Mohsen that the prospects for change in Iran rested with the rising generation.

Disillusioned with Khatami, Mohsen announced his own candidacy for president in the 2001 election. He did not hope to win but to establish a base of support for his views. Not to his surprise, the Council of Guardians disallowed his candidacy, as it did most. Mohsen wrote a letter of protest, arguing that he met all of the legal qualifications, but the council did not deign to respond.

Blocked on this path Mohsen decided to create a student newspaper, which he thought would be easier to license and less visible to authorities than a daily but still reach the group in which he placed his hopes. He hired a twenty-one-year-old editor and a team of students to do the writing, tapping some of the professional journalists he knew to give guidance. It was launched at the beginning of the school year in 2002. Mohsen imagined the regime would eventually close this down, too, but he hoped it might fly under the radar screen of the security services long enough to rekindle student activism. On this he miscalculated; the venture was banned after two weeks.

Following that, he published an article that he knew crossed a "red line." Citing the illegal disqualification of his candidacy, he said that Iran needed a change in system, and he called for a referendum on the constitution. Two months later, in February 2003, two officers from the Ministry of Intelligence arrived at his apartment and placed him under arrest. They ransacked the apartment, confiscated his computers, as well as many of his papers and books, and made him walk down from the nineteenth floor, then blindfolded him and drove him to Evin prison. Some of their colleagues meanwhile raided the headquarters of his website and shut that down.

Before leaving the apartment, Mohsen told Soheila that he was starting a hunger strike to protest his imprisonment, and he asked her to act as publicist, to hold frequent press conferences and interviews to keep attention on his case. At Evin he would only consume a few sugar cubes and water each morning and evening. He told his interrogators that he would not answer a single question since the arrest was illegal.

After five days, a clever stratagem by his friends and followers, led by one of his brothers, won his freedom. They mounted a slate of fifteen liberals for the Tehran city council elections and declared that if victorious they would choose Mohsen as mayor. They printed up posters with Mohsen's picture and plastered them on every major street in Tehran. Fearing that this might attract a large protest vote, the authorities released Mohsen.

In June, demonstrations resumed at the University of Tehran, and while they were in train, security agents once again arrived at the Sazegara apartment. This time they had a warrant for Mohsen and for his oldest son, Vahid, who was then a college student and active in the protests. Trying to assure Mohsen that his own arrest was not on Mohsen's account, Vahid told him that all his friends at the university had been arrested.

They took Vahid first because he had fewer belongings to search. Mohsen embraced him and said, "Trust only in God, my son. And do not believe anything they tell you." Vahid replied, "Daddy, be sure that I will resist and that I am strong enough to confront them." Mohsen recalls: "I was really proud of him when I hugged him. And when his mother hugged him I cried. I did not want them to see my tears but I really worried about her because I knew that in a few hours I will go, too, and she will be alone." (Their younger son, Shahab, was at college in Scotland.) When Mohsen was taken, Soheila turned on the shower for the noise and wept in the bathroom. She knew the apartment was bugged, and she did not want "them" to be able to hear her "weakness."

Once again, Mohsen announced before leaving home that he was commencing a hunger strike, and he asked Soheila to publicize his three demands: that he be released; that the roughly 800 students arrested at that time also be released; and that Ayatollah Khamenei apologize to the people of Iran for trampling their liberties.

In solitary confinement at Evin in a 5 by 7 foot cell, Mohsen resumed his water and sugar cube diet and for good measure, refused to take his medications. He explains:

> I knew that it was dangerous to stop the drugs immediately, but it is important in a hunger strike to persuade them that you want to die. I do not recommend that any young prisoner go on hunger strike because it works only for a political prisoner whose death or life is important to the regime. I knew that they did not want me to die.

In retaliation, the three blankets that serve as mattress, pillow and covering were taken from him, leaving the cell bare.

He prayed and had an extraordinary feeling:

> The poet, Hafez, wrote that you are the main barrier between yourself and God, so you must transcend yourself. Everyone in an isolated cell, if he believes in God, finds that this is the sweet part of prison. You understand that you cannot do anything for yourself. So this barrier goes away, making the experience of praying to God especially sweet in prison.

After a day, fearing for his health, the authorities returned his blankets. They also allowed him a Koran. When taken to interrogation, he asked for a pencil and paper which his jailers furnished eagerly, thinking he would write a confession. Instead he wrote: "I protest. These are my demands [which he listed]. I will not answer your questions." He signed it, handed it to the interrogators, and said: "Do what you want."

They tried cajolery, telling him that if he answered they could complete the files on Vahid and all the other student prisoners and release them. So, although skeptical, he relented, telling them he would answer questions for ten days. At the end of that time, they did not keep their word. So Mohsen retaliated with the only club he had: a further threat against his own life. He ceased consuming water. That, they all knew, would kill him in a matter of days.

After 31 hours he passed out in his cell. "I dreamt that I was swimming in a pool and drinking lots of water," he recalls. He was taken outside and placed in a chair blindfolded. They tried to force some fruit syrup and then some yogurt into his mouth, but he resisted, and it poured down his beard and onto his prison pajamas. They had, however, succeeded in introducing about a teaspoon of the syrup, and Mohsen recalls, "It was fantastic because I was really thirsty."

Angry, one of the interrogators shouted that they had arrested his wife and other family members, which turned out to be false. The next day, after a prison doctor said his heart arrhythmia was worsening, he was taken by ambulance to Baghiyetollah Hospital which is connected to the Revolutionary Guard. Fluids were introduced through an IV, and "that was very delicious" he remembers.

A few days later, he collapsed in his cell, and while it turned out not to be another heart attack, he agreed after that to accept a daily IV. After a few weeks Vahid was released. After eight weeks of imprisonment, Mohsen had another collapse. He was taken back to the hospital where another attempt was made to force feed him, and again he resisted. Then the chief prosecutor arrived and told him the investigation of his case was completed so he could end his fast. Mohsen repeated his three demands, and the prosecutor replied that he would be released the next day, that the students had already been released, and that Khamenei had issued a pardon of the students which was as close as they would get to Mohsen's demand for an "apology."

Mohsen agreed to resume eating. His bail was met by pledging the homes of his parents and brother. But before he was freed, another branch of the revolutionary court initiated fresh charges against him. He renewed his hunger strike and soon again required hospitalization. His condition was dangerous, but he knew that he had increased leverage because he had gotten word about Zahra Kazemi. She was an Iranian-Canadian photographer who had been arrested outside Evin in July, taking pictures of the families of arrested students waiting for word of them. After a brief incarceration, she died in the same hospital to which Mohsen was repeatedly taken. The prison authorities announced she had had a stroke, but no one believed this,[7] and Mohsen felt confident that they would not want another death in custody to explain.

He refused the tests that the cardiologists said were needed, increasing the pressure on his jailers. But he believes that what especially helped him was that summer was drawing to an end and universities were to reopen. The students at Amirkabir University, where he had many friends, announced a sit-in and candle-light vigil on his behalf. Other universities said they would join. After 23 days of his second hunger strike, he was released. Altogether he had been incarcerated for 114 days, of which 79 were on hunger strike. He had weighed 160 pounds when he was arrested. He came out weighing 90.

His wife, son, brother and other kin met him at the gate of Evin and took him to his parents' home where the rest of the family awaited. His father, Muhammed Ali, was by now suffering from dementia, but he had a moment of clarity when Mohsen arrived. "Oh, my son, how long have you been in jail?" he asked.

The hunger strike had harmed his digestive system, but this was nursed back to health. More serious was the strain on his heart and the deterioration of his vision due to keratoconus, a defect of the cornea. His cardiologist and ophthalmologist each told him that he could receive better treatment in the West. This dovetailed with a meditation he had had during his months in Evin:

I said to myself, "Mohsen, you battled against Khamenei and despotism. You spent about four years mobilizing in universities. You had a website and friends amongst the businessmen everywhere. Then, they attacked you. They have arrested your friends, and they have destroyed you. What next?"

I concluded that I have to go out of Iran for a while to give myself a little time to study. I have to see the situation in the world, especially the United States, to learn how much I can rely on the international community.

To go abroad he needed his passport which had been confiscated. Upon release he had been promised that the papers the arresting officers took from his home would be returned. These included two book manuscripts: a memoir and a history of the triumph of Newtonian mechanics over Aristotelian and of Copernican astronomy over Ptolemaic. As an earnest of their good intentions, one of his interrogators had given his cell phone number. Mohsen rang up the man and said to him:

If I were you, I would let me to go out of Iran. You have the bail, and if you do not let me go, I'll give interviews and say that I need to go for medical and you won't let me. If I go, there are two possibilities. Either I'll come back and I'll be in your hands again, or I won't come back and you will be rid of one of the opposition.

After 41 days, the passport was returned, and Mohsen and Soheila made preparations to leave. But before their departure, Mohsen's father, Muhammad Ali, breathed his last. Shiites hold a ritual for the deceased after forty days, and Mohsen stayed to observe that. The next day, January 31, 2004, they left for Glasgow where their younger son, Shahab, was studying, and moved into his student apartment.

The Sazegaras were nearly penniless, but Iranian exiles rallied to their support. One lent him the cost of his eye treatment, which required two surgeries several months apart. Another provided him with a small apartment in London where he had to go for these procedures. Meanwhile, two months after his departure, Iranian authorities announced that he had been sentenced in absentia to a year's imprisonment.

Between medical treatments, Mohsen kept up political activity. He and seven others, one an exile, the other five inside Iran, circulated a petition on the Internet, demanding a referendum on the constitution of Iran. But before allowing it to go up, Mohsen had to take care of one urgent bit of personal business. Vahid, his eldest, had graduated and was working in Iran. For his own activities, he was under a 45-day suspended sentence. Mohsen feared that the regime would retaliate for the petition by re-arresting Vahid. With the help of the British government in expediting a visa, he was able to bring Vahid out.

Mohsen was told that the best treatment for his heart would be available in America, so he looked for a way to take his family to the United States. He accepted a three-month visiting fellowship at the Washington Institute for Near East Policy, a think tank known to be friendly to Israel. He knew he would be pilloried for throwing in with the "Zionists," but he also believed that this would show that he meant his words when he had advocated peace with Israel in his speeches on Iranian campuses.

His American cardiologist told him that, with a change in medication, he could avoid another surgery, provided he also avoided stress. Mohsen was not a good candidate for such advice. By September 2005, with his family settled in the U.S. and feeling his health problems under control, he made plans to return to Iran the next month. "If they put me in jail, I'll go on another hunger strike," he said.

He told his mother and some friends to expect him. The calls were apparently overheard by Iranian government eavesdroppers, and soon another announcement came out of

Tehran. Mohsen had been sentenced in absentia to an additional five years on top of the one pending. Apparently the authorities wanted to discourage his return. He said he would go back nonetheless, but with the election of Mahmoud Ahmadinejad as president, marking a further consolidation of power by Khamenei, he allowed himself to be dissuaded.

Over the next years, he took positions successively at Yale and Harvard Universities, subsidized by the Scholars at Risk Fund, and then moved to Washington, DC, where he created his own small research organization. He devoted himself above all to the idea he had first shared with Shamsolvaezin and Jalaiepour after the closure of *Tous:* creating a satellite television station to broadcast to Iran. With his affinity for business, he envisioned a commercial channel, relying on advertising, rather than accepting the stigma that comes with support from a foreign government. Satellite dishes are still illegal in Iran, but they are ubiquitous nonetheless. Mohsen estimates that nearly half of Iranian households have access to one. It is easy to find underground companies that sell and install dishes. Mohsen's goal is a full-spectrum station that would offer Western films and serials as well as news and talk.

For the short run, he feels this is the best path to change in Iran, because after the failure of "two big movements, the Islamic revolution and the reform movement," Iranians are suffering from "political depression." But they will get past this, and he believes that the next big leap can be to democracy and liberalism. The change, he insists, must come "without bloodshed" or "revenge," because they would only lead to "a new tyranny; a democratic regime will never come about that way."

In America, Shahab asked him one day: "Daddy, suppose you succeed. What next?" Mohsen replied: "I don't know, but I think that overturning two regimes is enough for one lifetime."

The Publisher

Egypt: Hisham Kassem

The images made his stomach churn: men beaten mercilessly or strung up in painful positions. He longed to turn from the page and think about other things, but he was not free to do that. He was not just reading these sickening stories. His job was to translate them, and much depended on doing it well.

Hisham Fayez Adb El Fadil Kassem had come to Cairo from his native Alexandria in part to move out of the shadow of his imperious father, in part because he loved the rhythm of the bigger city and yearned to carve out his place in it. After a few other jobs, he and a British friend, Roland Trafford-Roberts, had opened a firm offering high-quality translations between Arabic and English. Most of their trade was to companies, embassies, aid organizations, and foreign news bureaus. But on this occasion in 1993 they had a commission from the Egyptian Organization for Human Rights, the country's principal human rights group. The EOHR was widely respected although it was "illegal" because the government refused to license it. The UN Commission on Torture had invited testimony in Geneva, and the EOHR had prepared a report on Egypt. The organization's staff, mostly unpaid volunteers, had, at some risk and pain, gathered the testimony of numerous victims and compiled these into a devastating report titled *Crime Without Punishment: Torture in Egypt*.

Now it fell to Hisham to render the original Arabic into English which Trafford-Roberts would polish. Translating the report was "a massive piece of work.... wholly engaging for both of us," recalls Trafford-Roberts. "I have never worked so hard before or since."[1]

The difficulty of the task arose not just from the size of the document. Another problem was that it was hard to concentrate on the prose when the events being described were so distressing. They had not occurred in war zones but mostly in ordinary Egyptian police stations. "How could anyone do such things to another human being?" Hisham kept asking himself as he read on in agitation.[2] He found he had to leave his desk from time to time and go for a walk in order to soothe his nerves.

In the past, the two partners had sometimes quarreled over Hisham's more relaxed attitude toward schedules. But there was none of that this time. "We hit our deadline! I think Hish would rather have perished than let EOHR down.... anyone could see how fired up he was by the work (including his state security officer!),"[3] recalls Trafford-Roberts. The report was duly received in Geneva. For a moment, the spotlight of the UN body was turned on Egypt, and the Egyptian government was discomfited. But the commission has no enforcement power, and soon its attention turned to other countries with sadly similar stories. In the end, the greatest impact of the report was not on the readers for whom it was prepared but on the Egyptian who translated it.

Hisham Kassem's distress over the stories in which he had been forced to become immersed launched him on a journey that was to place him at the heart of the struggle for democracy in Egypt. Although neither he nor his loved ones had personal experience of torture, these awful accounts did more than kindle his outrage and pity. They stirred memories of the persecutions his family had suffered at the hands of Egyptian rulers. These reached back to Hisham's boyhood and well beyond in the family lore learned at his father's knee.

Hisham was the scion of Bedouin chiefs. The Bedouins are tribal nomads whose relations with any state authority have often been problematic. Relying on the oral tradition of his clan, Hisham can trace his lineage back to the Muslim invasion of Egypt by warriors who came out of Arabia. Among them, it is said, was a soldier who fought his way to Spain and left his bones there. But, as Hisham readily acknowledges, "the renditions vary," and the problem with this version is that there was a gap of 72 years between the Muslim conquest of Egypt in 639 and of Spain in 711. So perhaps it was the first warrior's son or grandson who joined the battalions that ventured on through Morocco to Spain.

However it went, some of their posterity returned eastward across northern Africa and their wanderings found an epicenter in the region south of Alexandria called Bahera. There they settled permanently when the nineteenth century Egyptian government under Mehmet Ali and his progeny offered inducements to lure the Bedouins into settling, making them more accessible for military service or corvee labor.

Even sedentary, the tribes retained their sense of unity, and members would rally to fight off conscription agents, tax collectors, or other predators. "I know lots of stories," says Hisham, "of my great grandfather's camels being stolen by bands coming from as far as Libya and then the tribe organizing a posse, chasing them back to the border, shooting them, and returning with the camels."

The tribe consists of 13 "houses," of which Hisham's, the house of Damain, has seven subhouses with Kassem being one of them. Each of these subhouses comprises hundreds of individuals. Since Kassem was far from the largest of the subhouses, it was especially proud that one of its own became chief of the tribe. He was Hisham's great grandfather, and he lived to a ripe age–100 it is said. Altogether, he had nine wives, although never more than the Muslim limit of four at one time. When finally he passed, one of his sons, still a teen, was elevated to chief.

Hisham realized that this man, his grandfather, was somebody special even when he was too young to understand why. "My memories of my grandfather were always of people bowing and kissing his hand and of wondering, 'why are they doing that?'"

As a family of chieftains, the Kassems owned considerable land and prospered from it. With modernity seeping into their lives, Hisham's father, Fayez, became the first of the clan to get an education, going on to become a lawyer. He married a city girl who worked as a French teacher, Samia Mohamed Hanafi, the daughter of an affluent and educated family that had moved to Alexandria from Cairo during World War Two. The couple had met at a concert by Umm Kalsoum, the poor daughter of a village imam who became the most beloved Arab vocalist of the twentieth century. In addition to Hisham, Fayez and Samia had two daughters, Hala and Hoda, and the family lived in a spacious, graceful flat in Alexandria.

Their comfortable life began to disintegrate with the rise of Gamal Abdel Nasser, mastermind of a military coup that overthrew King Farouk in 1952. In keeping with the wisdom of the times, the new rulers believed they could restore Egypt's dignity, power and wealth by strengthening the central government and instituting "Arab socialism."

Although Fayez and his family now lived in Alexandria, his father, Abdel-Fadil, remained on the estate in Bahera which qualified the Kassems as "big land owners" under Nasser's sequestration program. "Sequestration," which meant expropriation, was justified as a means of reducing undue privilege, but the criteria were ill-defined and were often political rather than economic.[4] Nasser was wary of the independent power of the Bedouin chiefs, so much of Abdel-Fadil's land was confiscated along with his cattle and horses, and he was placed under house arrest. Back in Alexandria, Hisham's father, Fayez, was barred from all legal work and put on a government stipend of 27 pounds a month, enough to feed the family but not much more.

There was also a loss of elementary personal freedoms. When his uncle died, Fayez asked permission to travel to the family home in Bahera to accept condolences as was customary.

The distance was not great, but even this internal travel now required a permit. The callous officer in charge asked in manifest indifference: "why don't you just send a telegram?" "I'm supposed to *receive* condolences, not give them," seethed Fayez, to no effect.

In addition to the loss of income and liberty, there was constant fear, as Nasser imposed a system of repression unlike anything Egypt had known under the monarchy or even the British. Borrowing from the Soviet lexicon, privileged people like the Kassems were branded "enemies of the people." Like many, Hisham's father nursed the timeworn illusion that the man at the top could not possibly know the awful things his underlings were doing. He wrote a letter to Nasser explaining that he was unable to sustain his family on his stipend. Next, recalls Hisham:

> One evening the doorbell rang, and two intelligence officers walked in. My father was very lucky. These were a couple of decent folk. They asked: "what's wrong with you? If this letter got into the wrong hands we would be here to arrest you." They handed him his letter back, warning: "If you do this again it will not necessarily come to us."

The final straw for Fayez came the day Hisham, too young to grasp what was happening to his family, arrived home from school with the sleeve of his jacket ripped and asked his father to buy him a new one. Fayez felt humiliated that he could not fulfill his child's request. He made up his mind at that moment to leave the country.

Fayez's father was friendly with King Idriss of neighboring Libya, a fellow Bedouin chief. Now Fayez wrote to Idriss asking for help. Idriss replied that he would give Fayez a job if he managed to get to Libya. But an "exit visa" was not easy to come by for an "enemy of the people." A friend of Fayez's knew the defense minister, Abdel Hakim Amer, Nasser's best friend and most potent rival. Amer had the power to sign exit visas, and the friend secured one for the Kassems. By family lore, Amer loved to smoke hashish, and he signed the document when he was stoned. Fayez swore he would not return to Egypt as long as Nasser was alive.

Although the Kassems arrived penniless, as Egypt's revolutionary law forbade taking more than five pounds out of the country, Fayez's legal training readily won him a good government job. Samia found work with Total Oil as a secretary, and they enrolled the children in the Franciscan Sisters School. Then, one day in the late summer of 1969, Hisham and his sisters heard the sound of gunshots. They thought it was a wedding. Revelers in that part of the world often discharge firearms in celebration. But in fact it was a coup by Muammar Qaddafi's Free Unitary Officers movement overthrowing King Idriss.

Fayez and Samia gathered their children into the house and stayed there for three days. Hisham says: "I remember my father saying 'there is a revolution going on outside' and not really understanding what a revolution was." Initially, Fayez's job as Legal Counsel to the Ministry of Tourism kept him out of the line of political fire. But as "popular committees" took over each workplace, Fayez felt he was on thin ice. In addition, the children's school situation declined precipitously as all British and American teachers were expelled from the country. Meanwhile, in Egypt, President Nasser succumbed to a heart attack in 1970 and was succeeded by Anwar Sadat, clearing the way for the family to return.

In 1974, the Kassems decided that Samia would take the children back to Egypt where they could receive better schooling than was any longer available in Libya. At 14, Hisham was too young to understand economic theories, but he could see what Nasser's Arab socialism had done to the Egyptian economy. "People would ask me whether they could buy my jeans because you couldn't find goods like that anymore," he recalls.

Like many boys in high school, Hisham became interested in his physical conditioning. He took up boxing in an

Alexandria club where he was the tallest boy in his weight class, giving him the advantage of long reach. Three days a week he would jump rope and pound the punching bags, and then on Fridays he would box against the other trainees in the club, taking pleasure in his growing mastery of the sport.

But then Hisham's trainer explained a final step to ready himself for official matches. He said that the first time a fighter takes a blow that breaks his nose he will lose the bout because it will compromise his balance or make his eyes tear. A repetition in subsequent fights will be less disabling because the first break will have an inuring effect. Thus, to avoid an unnecessary defeat, the trainer had his protégés' noses broken deliberately in a sparring match. For Hisham's peers who hoped to escape poverty through boxing, the price was worth paying. But for Hisham, the ring was a hobby and a way to get a vigorous workout. When it came time to get his nose broken, he recalls, "I said, 'I think I've gone as far as I'd like to go in this sport.'"

Despite his fling with boxing and a lifelong love of riding, Hisham had always been bookish. When it came time for college, he sought to study literature. He was drawn to drama and felt he had found his niche when a production of *Waiting for Godot* that he staged proved a big success.

He began to work professionally as a stage manager and assistant director, but he soon became disillusioned with what he found to be the low quality of theater in Egypt.

At the same time, his father was diagnosed with heart disease. A piece of the family's property had been returned to his grandfather by the Sadat regime, which reversed many of Nasser's more draconian measures. Soon thereafter, his grandfather had died, and Hisham's father, Fayez, had taken over management of the farm. Now, Fayez had to cease work, and it fell to Hisham to manage the farm. "In many ways this was convenient because I didn't know what I wanted to do," recalls Hisham. "I took my books with me, and I had little work to do other than making sure that the farm manager was doing his job."

After a year, restored by bypass surgery abroad, Fayez returned to work, and he and Hisham, who boasts that the farm earned more under his supervision, developed a rivalry. "In spite of the emotional bond between us, we could not survive together in one place," says Hisham. So he decided to follow one of his friends to the big city. The year was 1988. "It was a very sad day when my dad took me to the train station because it was like a declaration of the failure of our relationship," he reflects.

His friend told Hisham of an opening with a cruise boat company on the Nile, and after a few weeks of training, Hisham was assigned to manage one of the boats. Not long into the job, he was confronted with his first major challenge as an executive. He was notified that the boat had been hired for a three day holiday by a tour group of Israelis. Egypt had signed a peace treaty with Israel a decade earlier, but precious few Egyptians had actually met an Israeli, and much animosity remained.

He called a meeting to tell the staff what was coming. Anyone who was uncomfortable serving Israelis could take paid leave, he said. Whoever worked would be expected to treat these guests with the same hospitality for which Egyptians are justly famous. To his surprise, no one accepted the offer of leave, and the staff warmed to their task. The chef made breakfast pastries in the shape of a Star of David. (Hisham doubts that the story would have the same happy ending since the second Palestinian *intifada*.)

Some of the owners were launching a new company to provide provisions to the many Nile cruise boats, and they hired Hisham to manage it. But in the summer of 1990, the armed forces of Iraq occupied Kuwait, killing tourism on the Nile and with it the fledgling enterprise. Once again, Hisham had fallen victim to the caprices of Middle East politics.

One of his cruise customers was Roland Trafford-Roberts, an Englishman with whom he became friends. Trafford-Roberts had already translated and published an Egyptian play and was eager to get further into translation work. He and Hisham discussed the idea of launching a translation firm. Trafford-Roberts explains: "Hish and I got to talking, and the more we talked the more we liked the idea of working together. Within the month we had an office, about four thousand dollars worth of computer equipment and some business cards."[5]

It was his translation work that unexpectedly led Hisham to political activism. As a college student, he had spent long hours over coffee with his friends exploring all kinds of questions, with political issues high on the list. "There were Leftists, nationalists, all the various ideologies except Islamist," Hisham recalls. However, he had never found a satisfying political outlet. Political parties had grown up in Egypt early in the twentieth century, under British rule, and dominated politics through three decades of independence, starting in 1923. When Nasser imposed a military dictatorship he outlawed them. Later he created a single ruling party, called the Arab Socialist Union (ASU), which eventually was replaced under Nasser's successor, Anwar Sadat, by the National Democratic Party (NDP).

The purpose of the ASU and NDP was not to compete for power but to organize it. They put at the disposal of the regime a phalanx of aspiring cadres to perform whatever tasks of political mobilization or intimidation needed doing and served as conveyor belts by which ambitious young men could work their way into the establishment. At first, the ASU claimed to speak for the pastiche of Arab socialism and Arab nationalism that constituted Nasser's ideology. But over the decades, the ideology washed away, and no one could say what exactly the NDP stood for except its own perpetuation in power.

When Sadat eased state control, moving the country from Nasser's semi-totalitarianism toward a more ordinary authoritarianism, he allowed the old parties to resume functioning but kept them ineffectual through bribes, threats, and infiltration. If Egypt's parties came in a bouquet of colors, to borrow Mao Zedong's floral metaphor, the petals had long since been dried and pressed.

Hisham learned this lesson firsthand. Given the anti-revolutionary instincts that experience had bred into him, he decided to join the Al Ahrar (Liberal) Party. When the party leader was scheduled to speak in Alexandria, Hisham put on a suit and drove down to hear him. Twenty minutes after he was scheduled to begin, the leader had not shown up. So the nervous organizers asked Hisham if he would go to where the leader was staying to see what was detaining him. Hisham, however, suspected that the man was keeping the faithful waiting as a demonstration of his rank. "I was so annoyed at the lack of respect for his followers. I just denied that I had a car, and I walked off and never came back."

Following this disillusionment, his interest turned to Al Wafd, the party of liberal nationalism that had formed most governments during Egypt's thirty years of constitutional monarchy. But he discovered at once that this party was dominated by three families—the Badrawis, the Serageldins, and the Abazzas—and he was told that the only way to get ahead in the party was to attach yourself to one of these. Again, Hisham was repelled. He concluded that the NDP was the only party that mattered and toyed with joining. But friends warned him that he would taint himself by joining, and the appeal of the idea began to wane.

Instead, he stumbled onto his own political path, existentially as it were, by translating the report on torture. In the period preceding the epiphany of reading these appalling accounts, his political interests had taken second place to the demands of building his business. But the stories made him feel that the time had come for him to do something about public affairs. He turned to the Egyptian Organization for Human Rights (EOHR), his customer, and asked if he could volunteer.

His discoveries about torture had been upsetting. His first project with EOHR was no less so, although the subject was a different one entirely: genital mutilation. Often referred to as "female circumcision," which gives the misleading impression of an arbitrary but benign procedure like male circumcision, it in fact involves excision of such substantial parts of the genitalia that some girls die from their wounds.

Although Egypt is in many ways a culturally rich and cosmopolitan country, this brutal practice is ubiquitous, common among Copts (who are Christians) as well as Muslims, and may originate before the arrival of Islam. Survey data show that upwards of 97 percent of Egyptian women in the age range of 15 to 49 who had ever been married reported having undergone the procedure.[6] Only a narrow highly-educated elite stratum and, interestingly, some Bedouin tribes, abstain from it.[7]

As Hisham began to look into the issue, he recalls,

> My feeling was sheer horror. Even though I knew that the practice did exist in Egypt I had no idea of its magnitude or the inhuman conditions that the mutilation was carried out under. In the course of educating myself about the subject, I came across real sad stories. The idea that a girl's virtue could be protected by mutilating her sexual organs was the equivalent to me of a poor child having his hands hacked off so that he would not steal when he gets older.[8]

In 1994, a UN conference on population and development drew the world press to Cairo, resulting in a CNN broadcast of a live operation. Ten-year-old Negla, screaming protests, was operated upon without anesthetic by Hag Omar, a traditional "hygienic barber" who did not "bother to wash his hands or the child," said the correspondent.[9] The film stirred a response not only among American viewers but in Egypt where Hisham and the EOHR and other NGOs demanded action against the mutilations. In addition to public agitation, Hisham and several other individuals brought a suit against the Minister of Health to force him to take measures against the practice.

In response, the minister reversed a 1959 decree that had barred medical personal from performing such mutilation. Now doctors would be allowed to do it, but not non-medical personnel like Hag Omar, who, according to CNN, "circumcises thousands of girls each year as did his father before him."[10]

To Hisham and his colleagues, while this new measure would (if enforced) spare some girls from infection or hemorrhage from backyard operations, it also would legitimate a practice they wanted to abolish. They amended their suit to demand a total ban. In 1995, with their suit pending, the minister met their demand. Even with this victory, surveys show that Hisham and his fellow campaigners have made at most halting progress although another decree against the procedure was announced in June 2007, following news reports of the death of a twelve-year-old girl, apparently from the anesthesia, while being circumcised by a physician.

In addition to his volunteer work for human rights causes and his translation business that was humming along, Hisham began to dabble in journalism, writing a little, contracting for the occasional research assignment, and working as a "fixer" for correspondents from the *Wall Street Journal* and other foreign papers—setting up meetings for them, translating, and generally showing them the ropes. His interest in newspapers quickened, although he saw himself more as a manager than a reporter.

A friend of his worked for the *Middle East Times,* an English language weekly published in Cairo by the followers of

Reverend Sun Myung Moon. Hisham began to discuss with him the prospects for a different English periodical. The main Egyptian newspaper, *Al-Ahram*, publishes a weekly in English, but this is a government publication. And the *Middle East Times* bore the stigma of a "Moonie" paper. Hisham saw a niche for a fully independent English newssheet.

These deliberations were brought to a head unexpectedly in 1997 when the editor of the *Middle East Times* was fired and the rest of the staff walked out in protest. Suddenly Hisham saw that if he seized the moment he could have the pick of this experienced English-speaking staff (none of whom were themselves "Moonies").

He had an advance on his inheritance from Fayez who had sold the farm and shared the proceeds with his children. He found a partner and, at age 38, launched the fortnightly *Cairo Times*. The new venture almost died after just three issues when the partner got cold feet. Hisham agreed to try to buy him out, but he had exhausted his own capital. Then a young Japanese woman named Mika came to the rescue and bought the other half of the ownership. She happened to be Hisham's fiancée.

Because of his work, Hisham had many friends in the English speaking "expat" community in Cairo. One of them had introduced him to Mika, who had come to Egypt as a teacher for the Japan Foundation and the two took an interest in each other. Parents were appalled on both sides. Hisham's adoring mother would have gone along with whatever he wanted, but not his stern father. "He wouldn't mind if I married a Christian or Jew because these are the religions the Koran recognizes. But Buddhism was out of the question," recalls Hisham.[11] For their part, Mika's parents, who had never been near Egypt, "thought Cairo was a place filled with camels and tents."

While the young couple wrestled with their parents' misgivings, Mika's tour with the Japan Foundation expired. But she wanted to stay on, so Hisham offered her a post managing accounts for the newspaper. When suddenly Hisham found himself in urgent need of a new investor, Mika, already involved in the paper, stepped forward. Sadly, when parental objections to the match finally evaporated the relationship grew rocky. The romance failed even as the newspaper took off.

To publish, however, required more than capital. It also required a license from the Higher Press Council which sometimes took years to issue one. An alternative was to publish outside of Egypt and import the copies. This, however, subjected a publication to formal censorship. Much of the domestic press was government owned. And the rest practiced self-censorship. But foreign publications must pass advance scrutiny to assure that none of their words damage Egypt's security or undermine its moral standards.

Making it easier logistically there was a "free zone" in Cairo, near the airport that was treated as extraterritorial. It was home to two printing houses issuing dozens of "foreign" periodicals. The *Cairo Times* began to publish there, and Hisham launched into a long career of wrestling with the censors.

His troubles began when Roger Garaudy, the leftist-turned-Muslim French Holocaust-denier who enjoys considerable popularity in the Arab world, came to lecture in Cairo. A reporter and photographer from the *Cairo Times*, one British, the other Italian, covered his lecture and were arrested for reasons that never became clear. The plain-clothesman who interrogated them kept asking if they were Christian or Jewish. Hisham speculates that the arresting officer "thought it was his big day, that he had caught two Zionist agents who had been sent here to assassinate Garaudy."

The two were held for more than six hours, a large part of it on their knees, and threatened with other physical abuse. They shared a paddy wagon with four locals whom they saw and heard being subjected to far rougher treatment. When

Hisham lodged an angry protest with the Minister of Interior the next day, he was stonewalled. So he told the reporter, Andrew Hammond, to write an account of the experience. It was titled "An evening in the life of a *Cairo Times* reporter and photographer."

When the censor read the galleys of that issue, he demanded that Hammond's story be pulled. Hisham tried to bargain. "I'll pull any other story you want from this issue but not that one," he offered. But the censor was adamant, so Hisham defied him. The paper appeared intact on Thursday.

Hisham thought he had gotten away with his defiance. But on Monday, the distribution company called him to report that they had received instructions that the issue had been banned. "How can it be banned?" he asked. "It's already been on the market for five days." "Just keep quiet," came the response. And Hisham realized that the distributor was willing to work with him as long as the disobedience was not flaunted. Issues could be banned, but they would somehow find their way to the newsstand nonetheless.

Hisham's enjoyment of this sly victory was short-lived. When it was time to meet the censor with the galleys for the next issue, he recalls, "It was a massacre. They said: 'this out, that out, this out, that out.' And I sat there thinking, this isn't going to work." He turned to the censor and said:

> I am understaffed, and we barely put an issue together. I can't store a substitute issue with extra articles each time to replace what you veto. If I start missing my market day, I'll lose advertising. I'd rather close it with a big bang than have you push me into bankruptcy. No more galleys for you. I'm going to publish, and if you are not happy, then ban it, and I in turn will go public.

After this, Hisham's tussle with the censors turned into cold war. That issue was banned, and Hisham retaliated by "going public," reporting the banning to western news organizations which carried disapproving stories. Counseled by a sympathizer to avoid confrontation, Hisham replied, "I am a third generation victim of military harassment. I've seen it happen to my grandfather and my father, and both died proud men." At their next meeting, while complaining that Hisham had made his office look bad, the censor treated Hisham more gingerly.

In a subsequent issue, a light-hearted feature on "Ideas for Your Birthday in Cairo" closed with the jest: "invite the President [but] make sure there is a lot of parking space because his motorcade is so big you'll need an entire lot." As ridicule goes, this was pathetically weak tea, but nonetheless it crossed a line. No explicit criticism of Mubarak was tolerated. Hisham knew that if the *Cairo Times* went after Mubarak directly it would be shut down. Even this gentle spoof was bound to be killed by the censor. Hisham had put it in just to tweak him. But he was not prepared for what came next.

His printer called. "They've banned printing magazines in the Free Zone," he said. Liberals within the regime privately demurred from this action, and counseled their publisher friends to take a conciliatory posture. But Hisham asked the printer to fax over the formal order he had received and then in turn faxed it to every foreign news organization and human rights and civil liberties organization that he knew.

Nor did he rest there. With the Free Zone unavailable, Hisham found a printer in Cyprus. He flew to the island with layout of his next issue on film, had it run off, and flew back with the entire print run of 5,000 copies as baggage. The issue featured an account of the closing of the Free Zone to publishing. Of the 58 publications that had relied on the zone, only the *Cairo Times* dared to write about what the regime had done to them. But the authorities were waiting for him at the airport. They seized the copies and banned the issue. On subsequent occasions, however, he succeeded in making the round-trip unmolested.

He also thought up a new method for striking back at the censors. The *Cairo Times* created a website, and its hottest feature was called "The Forbidden File." At the top it read:

> As a foreign-licensed publication, the *Cairo Times* must go through a censor before it enters Egypt. There's a rough guideline of things we're not allowed to write about, but sometimes it seems the goalposts change every week. You never know what they'll accept and what they won't. Usually we have to take out a paragraph or two (we've marked these parts in red), but sometimes they'll want a whole story removed, and if we don't comply they can ban the whole issue.

Then, the banned or cut articles would be posted. They were the likes of:

- "A Sweetheart Economy?: Just how bad is corruption in Egypt?"
- "Reading Between the Tank Tracks: Interpreting Egypt's military maneuvers."
- "Reining in the Police: The wall of official silence over routine police brutality is finally being breached ... or is it?"
- "58 Publications Kicked Out: The government shoots itself in the foot with a printing ban in Cairo's Free Zone."

Just as the imprimatur "Banned in Boston" was once the teaser sure to draw American readers to novels considered racy in their time, so the *Cairo Times*'s "Forbidden File" probably drew more readers to the censored articles than would have read them on paper.

The proscription on printing in the Free Zone was lifted after a few months, but Hisham's publisher told him that the administrator of the zone had let him know that it would be unwise to resume printing the *Cairo Times*. Fortunately for Hisham, the manager of the zone's other printing house was braver and said he would print the paper unless he received a written order not to.

When the *Cairo Times* was one year old, a dramatic incident in the predominantly Coptic village of Al Kosheh ended up having a powerful impact on the paper and on Hisham's career as a human rights activist. The Coptic denomination traces its roots back to Saint Mark who is said to have built the first church in Alexandria in the year 42, converting many Egyptians to Christianity. It was Egypt's predominant monotheistic faith until the Arab invasion late in the seventh century when Egypt became Arabized and Islamized. A minority resisted conversion, and ever since relations between Muslims and Copts—who are variously estimated to constitute from 6 to 20 percent of the population—have been marked by strife. This, however, is a taboo subject in Egypt because it is internally explosive and provokes anger in the West.

A crisis in relations unfolded in August 1998, when two Copts were found murdered in Al Kosheh and Coptic spokesmen pointed their fingers at a gang of Muslims. They were questioned, but the authorities preferred that the perpetrators turn out to be Copts. When Copts protested the direction and brutality of the inquiry, officials retaliated by indicting the Coptic bishop and other community leaders for fomenting sectarian conflict and endangering national security.[11]

An investigation was undertaken by the Egyptian Organization for Human Rights which estimated that 1,200 Copts had been arrested. The *Cairo Times* was one of three Egyptian papers that dared to cover the story. Hisham managed to evade the censors but soon after the issue hit the newsstands he got a call from his distribution company telling him that it had received an order "prohibiting circulation." This was a level of censorship unknown since Nasser's day. Normally, the only one subject to penalty if a banned issue saw the light of day was the publisher. In this case, the order made it illegal for anyone to *possess* a copy. Worse still, the braver of the two printers in the Free Zone, the one who was now putting out the *Cairo Times*, called Hisham to say that he had been warned to desist. And, without explanation, the next issue was also banned. Hisham began to despair that the constant banning would put him out of business.

But in an odd twist the events at Al Kosheh taught the regime a lesson about the value of the *Cairo Times*. Perhaps due to the stories published in Egypt, more likely to links between Copts in Egypt and in the west, the story of Al Kosheh got abroad. The London *Telegraph* carried a particularly lurid version. It said Christians had been subjected to "horrific crucifixion rituals." Moreover, it continued, they had been

> raped and tortured by the security forces .... many were nailed to crosses ... then beaten and tortured with electric shocks to their genitals, while police denounced them as "infidels." Young girls were raped and mothers were forced to lay their babies on the floor of police stations and watch police beat them with sticks.[12]

Naturally, this account—which contained substantial exaggeration—stoked outrage. The International Coptic Federation took full page ads in the *New York Times,* the *Washington Post,* and other papers around the world. Twenty-eight members of the U.S. Congress sent a letter of protest to the Egyptian government, and a bill was passed, directing the State Department to combat religious persecution abroad.

Ironically, although the government had banned the *Cairo Times* for reporting on police abuses at Al Kosheh, now it very much preferred the paper's version to what was appearing in the Western press. An official in the foreign ministry asked Hisham to join him in a meeting with a leading overseas Coptic hierarch to present his take on what had happened in Al Kosheh because as a known government critic, Hisham would have more credibility than any official.

In Al Kosheh, a Christian was finally convicted of the murders, although Copts continued to believe he had been framed, and tensions in the village continued to simmer. Within a year they burst forth again in rioting that, according to reports in the *Cairo Times*, took 23 lives, almost all of them Copts.[13] This galvanized the government which responded by decreeing that the name of the village be changed from Al Kosheh, which can mean "enmity" in classical Arabic, to Al Salaam, which means "peace."

Even though Hisham had cooperated with the foreign ministry in presenting an objective account to the foreign visitor, he was deeply angry over the entire incident. When the director of the Egyptian Organization for Human Rights (EOHR) took refuge abroad from an arrest order issued because of his investigations in Al Kosheh, Hisham stepped in to replace him temporarily. And he decided to run a special edition of the *Cairo Times* devoted to the Coptic question. The tone of the nine articles that it comprised was low-key, not sensational or muck-raking. They were glossed with an introduction by Hisham that struck a painstakingly mild note: "Egypt doesn't have a Coptic 'crisis,' it might not even have a Coptic 'problem,' but it certainly has a Coptic something."[14] Further to soothe the authorities, the issue contained considerable criticism of militant Coptic activists in Egypt and the U.S. But the thrust of its analysis was conveyed in two passages. The first said:

> So how does one define the situation so unique to Egypt and so sensitive that it can't be discussed publicly without trepidation? Most definitions come down to "second-class citizenship," resulting from social prejudice on both sides, Muslim ignorance of the Coptic religion, and a glass ceiling that keeps Copts out of positions of authority.[15]

The second passage discussed a more recent suffering inflicted on the Copts:

> [T]he war between the extremists and the state intensified and came out into the open in 1992. Attacks on Copts by Islamist extremists were alarming—dozens were killed, commercial property was attacked, and churches burned—but the government interfered quite late, many claim. "The government knows full well that [attacks on] Copts were an experimental balloon used by the fundamentalists to measure the ability of the state to respond," says [a Copt leader]. "Stupidly, the state did not realize early enough that they were after grabbing power—and it's their necks, not the Copts', they're after."[16]

Gentle though its tenor, the publisher and staff knew that they were crossing one of the regime's "red lines." Hisham recalls that once the issue was put to bed as the staff waited for it to hit the streets, they nervously teased one another with salutes of "it's been a pleasure working with you." But the censor let the issue pass unmolested. "The taboo on discussing the Coptic question has ended," reported *Le Monde Diplomatique*, thanks to this "ground-breaking" edition of the *Cairo Times*.[17]

The incident at Al Kosheh became a landmark not only for Hisham's work as a newspaperman but also his role in the country's human rights movement. In 2000, new elections to the board of the EOHR were held amidst a crackdown on independent human rights organizations. The new board unanimously asked Hisham to become chairman. So now on two fronts, Hisham, the gradualist who once considered joining the NDP to work for reform from within, found himself in the vanguard of resistance to the regime: as chairman of the main human rights organization and publisher of the leading independent-minded periodical.

In addition to opening up the Coptic question, the *Cairo Times* took on such other controversial subjects as official corruption, the treatment of Islamist prisoners, and anti-regime protests.

The spirit of the *Cairo Times*—independent, iconoclastic, with a sense of journalistic integrity—was not to be found in other Egyptian publications.

His former partner in the translation business, Roland Trafford-Roberts, put it:

> Hisham's publishing philosophy is just to be more daring than the others, and to tell things how they are. No pictures of Mubarak sitting in a gilt chair, and plenty of quite dangerous stories about other stuff. Nothing that's ever got him locked up, ... but enough for foreigners and, increasingly, Egyptians to think—crikey, this guy isn't scared of telling the truth.

As the paper gained readers and advertisers, Hisham was able to bring it out weekly instead of fortnightly. And gradually he grew more adept at dodging the censor. Altogether, ten issues of the *Cairo Times* were banned. But many of these reached newsstands anyway, as he learned to circumvent the official distribution system. So confident did Hisham and his aides become at outwitting the regime's interference, they began to jest about the "virtual censor."

But just when it seemed that the paper's revenue might exceed its costs, enabling Hisham to begin to recoup his initial investment, he once again fell victim to the tides of Middle East politics. The Palestinian *intifada* which erupted late in 2000 put a serious crimp in Egypt's leading industry, tourism. The violence did not touch Egypt itself but depressed tourism across the region. This effect intensified as America invaded Iraq in 2003. Egypt's economy sank into recession. "We lost 45 percent of our advertising revenue," recalls Hisham, "and there was nothing to be done about it because it was across the market."

In 2002, with the paper about to go under, Hisham met Emma Bonino, a Radical Party member of the European parliament and the sparkplug in Italy of campaigns for freedom of abortion, women's rights, banning the death penalty, and numerous other causes. She told Hisham that it was vain to play by market rules in a country where market rules don't apply. She used her connections to the American philanthropist George Soros to secure a grant for the *Cairo Times* from a charity he sponsors called the Media Development Loan Fund. One hundred thousand dollars enabled the paper to get through another year, but when Hisham turned to the fund a second time, he was turned down.

Although, as its name suggests, this organization ordinarily gives loans, and this in all likelihood contributed to its refusal to renew its grant, Hisham also believes that ideology might have turned Soros against him. Soros was among the most militant opponents of U.S. policies in the Middle East. In contrast, Hisham was one of the very few non-Iraqi Arabs who had good words to say in public about the American invasion of Iraq. Insofar as the Bush doctrine meant pressing for democracy in the Middle East, Hisham endorsed it. As he was to put it a few years later in a special feature of *Time* magazine that asked a variety of international figures whether the war had been worth it:

> Sadly, I have to say yes.... There had to be a military intervention. You have a bloc of 22 countries in the Arab world dominated by authoritarianism and dictatorship. It is not a bloc you could engage politically and pressure for reform. By military intervention, the U.S. is able to pressure the region into adopting the reforms we are beginning to see across the region that might avert many countries from becoming failed states.[18]

Despite his support for American policy, which opened up to a torrent of accusations that he was an American "agent" or puppet, Hisham received no help from the United States. U.S. Ambassador David Welch, according to Hisham, told him that the plight of the *Cairo Times* "breaks my heart. I wish I could do something." But neither North Americans nor Europeans came to the rescue of this rare independent publication even while their governments proclaimed the goal of democratization in the region.

Finally, in July 2004, the *Cairo Times* found itself unable to continue publishing. Hisham was devastated. "It was like losing a child," he says. "The day I gave up the offices, I broke down completely. I thought I'd be stronger." In addition to the heartbreak there was also financial ruin. Hisham had sunk his inheritance into the paper. He came away worse than empty-handed, bearing substantial debts. "I think it makes me the only person who got into the press business in Egypt and impoverished himself," he jests. "Others made buckets of money."

Despite his sense of loss and financial travails, Hisham came away with an international reputation and unmatched experience at running an independent paper in Egypt. So, when Salah Diab, one of the country's most prosperous entrepreneurs, came up with a plan for a new Egyptian daily he turned to Hisham. Diab's base was in the oil business, but his grandfather had owned a newspaper, and he longed to have one, too. He had taken a run at it before, but the effort had fallen flat. Now he had gathered a group of investors behind the idea of launching a new daily.

Egypt had nine dailies in 2003: the three majors—*Al-Ahram, Al Akhbar,* and *Al Gamhouriya,* all of them government-controlled—and five smaller ones affiliated with various opposition parties, as well as one financial paper. Diab's idea was to launch the first daily owned by a joint stock company, beholden neither to the government nor to a party. He and his partners settled on the name *Al-Masry Al Youm,* which means *The Egyptian Today.*

When Diab first approached him, Hisham's reaction was mixed. Much about the proposal was alluring. An Arabic daily could reach more readers than an English weekly. It would be a luxury to have wealthy backers rather than facing a daily struggle to keep afloat. And it would be a relief not to have to duel with the censor since the proposed paper would be published in Egypt and therefore not subject to advance censorship.

However, Hisham wanted reassurance that the paper was not designed to serve the business interests of its major investors. Cushy relationships between news outlets and private interests had become an all too common feature of Egyptian journalism. Even after Diab convinced him that his goal was to create a newspaper of integrity, free of conflicts of interest, there were still other issues that kept the two men apart. For one thing, Hisham was not happy with the proposed name of the paper, with its faintly nationalistic resonance. For another, Hisham had strong ideas about the editorial stance that the paper should take. As he put it, there were three issues that should define the paper's political visage: "One, it should be pro open market. Two, it should accept Security Council resolution 242 rather than wanting to annihilate Israel. Three, it should welcome globalization and internationalism rather than taking the posture that 'it's the Arabs versus the world.'" Diab accepted all Hisham's terms except for the name of the new paper.

A launch date for *Al-Masry* was set for May 3, 2004. But when the day came, *Al-Masry Al Youm* had not yet received its license. Fortunately, the paper's backers included some of the country's most important businessmen, and so the authorities relented and granted the license after a month's delay. *Al-Masry Al Youm* hit the street on June 7. It was a month later that *Cairo Times* published its last. "It was like having a birth and a death at the same time," recalls Hisham.

Hisham's goal was to make *Al-Masry* Egypt's "newspaper of record" like the *New York Times*. This meant to practice journalism in a different way than was common in Egypt.

Although *Al-Masry* was not subject to formal censorship, the state security service would nonetheless try to suborn members of the staff to report its goings on, or perhaps to work for them in other ways, using their journalistic cover to collect information for the state. These are standard practices in a country whose *mukhabarat* is ubiquitous, albeit somewhat less secretive, brutal and omnipotent than in Communist countries.

Hisham had no hope that he could insulate *Al-Masry Al Youm* entirely from the tentacles of State Security, but he tried to diminish the pull of its two main forms of subornation: bribes and threats. He persuaded Diab and the board of directors to pay *Al-Masry*'s reporters wages higher than the going rates in order to lessen their need for supplemental income. And he told his reporters that he would back them to the hilt if they refused to answer inquiries from State Security agents. "Tell them to speak to me," he enjoined.

He also made it a policy to put all the paper's staff on one year renewable contracts. At the end of each year they could get hefty raises or be let go, a merit system that cut against the grain of employment practice in Egypt where pay is low, jobs are secure, and little is expected, so employees use their positions to maneuver for other kinds of emoluments. Hisham's goal was to develop a reportorial staff that was energetic and resistant to manipulation by the security service.

He also wanted his reporters to embody standards of journalistic objectivity, which was far from the norm in Egypt where papers typically weave their editorial voice into their news stories. Much to his consternation, Hisham discovered after a few months that the man he had hired as editor, Anwar Alhawary, was not in harmony with him on this principle. Hisham steamed when he picked up copies of the paper and found stories filled with value-laden terms on Egypt's hot button subjects. For example, he saw Israel referred to as "the

Zionist entity," standard practice in the Arab world. Hisham admonished him: "The place is called 'Israel,' and your job is to report. If it is called 'the Zionist entity' by the UN, then, fine, call it that. But as long as it is officially known as 'Israel,' that's what you are to call it." On another occasion, suicide bombers were referred to as "martyrs." "Suppose a Christian blows himself up in Tel Aviv," scolded Hisham. "Do you call him a martyr? That is not press language."

A proposed editorial caused another flare-up between the two men. Hisham says Alhawary showed it to him at the last minute when it was virtually too late to change. It was critical of government performance but written in the voice of a direct appeal to President Mubarak, telling him that some of his ministers were pursuing wrong-headed policies. The assumption was that the wise president would not approve such policies if he were in the know. Hisham exploded: "Everyone knows that the problem is not the ministers but Mubarak, himself." He felt that the paper would only embarrass itself by implicitly exonerating the man at the top.

The deepest problem between Hisham and his editor was simply that the other man simply could not grasp the style of journalism that Hisham envisioned. For example, Hisham wanted *Al-Masry* to run corrections of its own errors just inside the front page, in the manner of the *New York Times*. Once, when he noticed that no correction appeared when he knew a mistake had been made, he queried Alhawary. To Hisham's exasperation, the editor replied that the paper was poised to run something flattering about the same individual injured in its mistaken report. This, he said, would balance it, as if it were a matter of compensating for an insult rather than correcting the record. By doing it this way, *Al-Masry* would avoid the loss of face of admitting error. Such a reaction expressed the very cultural mores that Hisham wanted his paper to transcend.

The final showdown came neither over a news story nor an editorial, but over Alhawary's objection to Hisham's decision to accept an ad for Auld Stag blended whiskey, Egypt's own brew. The editor argued that since alcohol is forbidden by Islam it should not be advertised in Egypt whose constitution proclaims its Islamic character. Hisham saw the subject as a part of a larger issue. Although he was known in his human rights work for having defended Muslim Brotherhood members who suffered wrongful prosecution or mistreatment at the hands of the state, he was passionately opposed to the Islamist agenda. As he saw it, he was "defending the civil law. Nobody is going to impose *sharia* on us or blackmail me into it."

By now, the split between the two men had opened into a full-bore power struggle. Alhawary hoped to swing the board of directors to his side, thereby trumping Hisham, perhaps even forcing his ouster. Hisham knew that his adversary's argument about Islamic rules and sensitivities carried real weight and that he was on thin ice. He did not know if the newspaper's board would back him. But in the end, Hisham won out and he was able to replace Alhawary with a more compatible editor.

Alhawary was not the only executive whom Hisham regretted hiring because of the man's inability to transcend the traditional way of doing things. Early in the paper's life, the advertising manager brought Hisham copy for some articles. "What's this?" asked Hisham, and the man explained that they were stories flattering to potential advertisers. "I don't operate that way," explained Hisham. But the advertising manager persisted, pointing out that these could be lucrative clients and that this was the normal way of securing such business.

When Hisham was unmoved, the man sent him e-mail messages warning that his self-righteous policies would bankrupt the paper. Hisham inferred that the real purpose of putting this argument into writing was to leak it to the board so that it might overturn Hisham's policy. Hisham also believed that the ad man was not acting merely out of concern for the paper's bottom line. Just as the advertisers were in effect paying bribes for favorable coverage with their ads, they would also often grease the palms of advertising managers—part of the crony capitalism that was replacing Nasser's socialism—to serve as their spokesmen within the papers. Again, the board lined up behind Hisham, and the ad manager was sacked.

Banishing such graft involved not only the advertising department but also its reporters, for it was common practice for reporters also to become conduits for deals with advertisers. When a team of *Al-Masry* journalists investigated allegations that a pharmaceutical company had been making medicines from ingredients beyond their expiration dates, they secured an interview with the firm's chairman. When they entered his office he asked "where's your rate card?"—assuming they wanted to be bought off by advertising. Reporters covering a strike at an industrial plant had a similar experience. Egypt's Higher Press Council issues a periodic report on ethical practices in the news media. Among other scores, it counts the number of instances of ads in the guise of journalism. Under Hisham's management, only *Al-Masry* had none.

Publishing corrections; using non-loaded terminology; resisting government intimidation and subornation by private interests—these were only some of the tenets of journalism with which Hisham strove to imbue *Al-Masry*. I got a bird's eye view of another as I sat in his office one afternoon in the spring of 2005. The paper's new editor interrupted us for an urgent whispered conversation with Hisham. In the course of it, he showed Hisham some contact sheets of photographs. Hisham looked, listened, and then issued some instructions that I could not hear.

The photos, as it turned out, illustrated one of the other issues that had to be faced in creating an Egyptian "newspaper of record." They had been shot by a free lance photographer and showed a prominent Egyptian footballer (soccer player) in a café with a movie starlet in what seemed to be a tryst. Was either married? I asked. No, replied Hisham, but still this romantic moment between two celebrities in public would be as sizzling a story as similar photos in supermarket tabloids in America or Britain. The difference is that in Egypt's culture, with its fierce emphasis on premarital modesty, the sting of such exposure for the two lovebirds would be much sharper. The photos would surely sell papers, a godsend for a newspaper then only ten months old and still trying to attract attention, but Hisham instructed the editor to tell the enterprising photographer to ply his wares elsewhere. A "newspaper of record" cannot traffic in sensationalism.

Al-Masry's first two years of publication seemed to prove that Hisham's vision of a newspaper aspiring to high standards of independence and objectivity could succeed. Starting with just a few thousand copies, its circulation rose steadily to 80,000 with some issues hitting 100,000. This made it Egypt's fourth largest daily, surpassing all of the party-sponsored papers, trailing only the big three state-run dailies which claim a million readers apiece, although Hisham is sure that this is a five-fold exaggeration. Despite its refusal to guarantee advertisers favorable news coverage, its advertising revenue leapt from a few thousand Egyptian pounds per month to a profitable 1.4 million, and it had been operating in the black since its twentieth month. (An Egyptian pound is worth about one-sixth of a U.S. dollar.)

More important, *Al-Masry* began to make an impact on Egyptian political life, regarded by educated readers as a prime source of trustworthy information. And people with information to leak—political stories, not photos of lovers—increasingly thought of *Al-Masry* as the best venue to get their information out to the public.

For example, early in 2005, the government sponsored a "national dialogue" between Mubarak's ruling National Democratic Party (NDP) and the opposition. This was heralded by the regime as a landmark on the path of political reform. But the opposition groups that took part were not vibrant critics; they were the officially designated opposition parties that had long since been hollowed out by the rulers. Dutifully, the participants in the dialogue agreed that constitutional reform could wait until after Mubarak's fifth six-year term had been confirmed by referendum later that year.

No sooner had the assemblage put its imprimatur on the status quo than Mubarak, reacting to pressure from Washington, announced that Egypt would amend its constitution immediately to provide for a contested presidential election instead of the traditional one-man referendum. The embarrassment of the official "oppositionists" redoubled when someone leaked the minutes of the dialogue to *Al-Masry* which splashed them across its front page. They showed Noman Gomaa, the head of the once mighty but now tame Wafd party, declaring the NDP to be a "very clean" party.

Nothing could have more perfectly exemplified the Wafd leader's toadying to the rulers. Almost everyone in Egypt, even NDP supporters, knows that the party is deeply compromised by corruption. Gomaa's predecessor, who led the Wafd for years when it wielded far more influence, and who struck a much higher profile than Gomaa, was Fuad Serageldin. His niece, Samia Serageldin, wrote a *roman à clef* which contained this snippet of life under Mubarak:

> You've heard the rumor about Wassif Sirry, of course. After all these years of running the Audi concession—then as soon as he started to expand into parts assembly, he ran into stumbling blocks. He realized it had to be coming from the top—the son himself. Sirry asked for an audience with the president . . . met him personally . . . explained the situation.

Imagine this: he was asked: How many sons do you have? Four, Sirry answered. Well, he was told, now you have five! You understand what that meant, of course? A 20 percent cut. It was too much for the old man; he went home and had a heart attack![19]

Gomaa, an elder statesman, honored in his position of docile opposition figure, was unused to the disrespect of having his servility exposed in public. His embarrassment in the pages of *Al-Masry* was the first in a series of events that within a year were to lead to his ouster as leader of Al-Wafd.

To confirm the amendment to Egypt's constitution to hold a multicandidate presidential election, the government called a national referendum on May 25, 2005. Although the direct election of a president would be a first, the country regularly voted for the members of its legislature, consisting of the People's Assembly and a weaker upper house, the Shura Council. Since the ruling party ran the elections, the playing field was never level. In 2000, Hisham experienced this first hand when he ran as an independent for the Peoples' Assembly from a district in Cairo. For weeks he begged local authorities for a list of registered voters so that he might contact them to make his pitch. Finally, he was given the names, apparently, of every voter in the district, but nothing more. No addresses. No phone numbers. It was, in short, utterly useless. Needless to say, he did not win the election.

The 2005 referendum became a landmark in the rebellion of Egypt's judges, a significant development in the struggle for democracy in the Arab world. In 2000 a new law had given the judges responsibility for monitoring that year's election. Although the officially backed candidates lost many seats to independents, nonetheless, the proceedings were not appreciably more fair and honest than in the past, as Hisham's handicapped campaign had illustrated. The judges were present in polling places but were able to observe only a small slice of the proceedings. Much of the hanky-panky took place beforehand or outside the buildings. In the end many judges felt that their honor had been compromised: they were seen as sanctifying results of crooked proceedings.

When Mubarak announced his proposed electoral change in 2005, the judges saw both a danger and an opportunity. The danger was that they would once again be humiliated as they had been in 2000. The opportunity was that the elections offered them some new leverage. The Judges Club— a kind of guild—declared that the judges would monitor the elections only if they were given full authority both inside and outside the polling places.

The first vote that the judges were called upon to monitor in 2005 was the referendum on the new election law. In preparation, the Judges Club named a five-member commission to examine the conduct of the election and the judges' role in it. Their report was leaked to *Al-Masry Al Youm*, which gave a detailed account of it that was devastating. The paper reported:

> The [polling] stations that were headed by judges witnessed low voter turnout—some had no voters whatsoever, while others had a turnout that did not exceed 3%. One judge quoted a police officer as telling him jokingly: "We do not want to tire out your excellencies. We are satisfied with the [turnout at] other stations." The turnout at stations that were not supervised by judges reached 90% and in some cases 100%. The latter percentage would mean that none of the voters on the lists had died or moved since the lists were prepared or was even sick or unable to vote on that day for whatever reason. Moreover, many of such heads of branch stations were done with their work and submitted the ballot boxes to the main stations long before the closing time.[20]

The *Al-Masry* story continued:

There are pictures taken of open boxes in an open field with people sitting next to it, taking some [ballots] out and throwing [them] away. Also, there were pictures taken of a non-judicial head of a branch station who was filling out the ballots himself and then handing them to someone else to put them in the box.[21]

Despite discomfiting the regime with such stories, by the time of the presidential election period, *Al-Masry's* stature was such that Mubarak favored it with an exclusive interview, one of only two he gave to newspapers during the brief campaign, the other being with the leading government daily, *Al-Ahram.*

Few observers doubted that Mubarak would win a fifth six-year term, but the election impelled him to campaign for the first time and also made it possible for Egyptians to criticize their president more freely than ever before. Still, little of the spirit of democracy seemed to have infected the government and ruling party. By all signs it regarded a mere victory even by a landslide as insufficient. Mubarak wanted to win a nearly unanimous vote. He even wanted to control the outcome for second place.

His goal in this respect, apparently, was to block Ayman Nour from establishing himself as the leading voice of opposition. Born in 1964, Nour was the scion of a political family and became the leader of the national organization of high school students. Speaking out in that capacity against the regime of Anwar Sadat, Nour was arrested in 1981 and became at the time, so he believes, the country's youngest political prisoner.

In prison he was taken under the wing of Fuad Serageldin, then the leader of the Wafd Party. The country's dominant force in the decades before Nasser's revolution, the Wafd continued to win some seats in parliament and usually constituted the official opposition.

Nour ran on the Wafd ticket for the People's Assembly in 1995 and won, making him one of the youngest members of the body. After being reelected in 2000, he ran for deputy speaker and, although he did not win, he polled a surprising 161 votes (out of 454). Since there were only a few dozen opposition members, this meant that, on a secret ballot, he had drawn roughly 130 votes from legislators of the ruling NDP against that party's own nominee. It marked Nour as a man to be reckoned with and apparently in Mubarak's eyes as a threat to his wish to pass the presidency to his son, Gamal.

It also marked him as a rival to the man who had succeeded his mentor Serageldin as head of the Wafd Party, Noman Gomaa (the same man who was so embarrassed in 2005 when *Al-Masry* revealed his servile comments in the "national dialogue"). The split between the two men deepened until Gomaa expelled Nour from the party.

Nour then gathered a handful of like-minded legislators and founded Al-Ghad (Tomorrow), a new party taking the name of a liberal movement that had flourished in Egypt from the beginning of the twentieth century until it was suppressed by Nasser. Like all independent parties, the new Al-Ghad was denied a license, but Nour kept reapplying and appealed to the courts. Although Egypt's system is repressive, the government does not exercise absolute control. With the State Council poised to rule in Nour's favor, the licensing authority granted its approval to Al-Ghad on its fifth application, late in 2004.

No sooner had Nour won this victory than he was suddenly stripped of his parliamentary immunity and arrested. He was charged with forging some of the signatures on the petitions used in the license application. He was held for 45 days, a standard term of interrogation, some of it in solitary confinement, and he says he was beaten. Yet he remained defiant. Trying to prove that he was involved in some kind of plot against Egypt in collaboration with the United States, the interrogator asked Nour how he knew Madeleine Albright. "We went to high school together," Nour replied. To a similar question about Condoleezza Rice, he said they were college classmates—all with a deadpan that briefly masked the intended mockery.

The offense with which Nour was charged was implausible. The law requires one-hundred signatures for a party to qualify for a license. Al-Ghad had submitted over two thousand. Only half were alleged to have been forged. Why would he, a lawyer, have run the risk of violating the law when the extra signatures were of no consequence? Equally implausible were Nour's accusers. They were four men, all with shady pasts, who had turned up at Al-Ghad headquarters as volunteers and who then claimed that Nour had instructed them to create the falsifications. In reality, if Nour had intended to commit forgery, it stands to reason that he would have done it himself or entrusted the dangerous deed to his closest aides.

Nour shared Hisham's liberal convictions, but he was able to express them with a populist touch that reached beyond the educated elite to the average voter. Finally, Hisham had found a party in which he felt comfortable and joined Al-Ghad soon after its founding. In the face of persecution, Hisham's was the leading voice within the party for an uncompromising stand toward the regime. He was chosen to be one of the party's vice chairmen, in charge of foreign policy, and became one of Nour's closest associates.

So now Hisham was wearing three hats: publisher, chairman of the main human rights organization, and party leader. For the most part, these roles were mutually compatible, but at times there were tensions between them. He earned Nour's annoyance through *Al-Masry*'s straightforward coverage of turmoil within Al-Ghad, and there was some sense of competition between *Al-Masry* and Al-Ghad's own party newspaper. On another occasion, he was chided by EOHR executive director, Hafez Abu Saada, for comments supportive of the U.S. war in Iraq quoted in *Time* magazine.

When the case against Nour first came to court in May 2005, one of his accusers recanted on the witness stand. He said that agents of state security had fed him the story he had recited and had threatened harm to his two nieces if he refused to collaborate in framing Nour. Like the other accusers, this man had a history of run-ins with the law that made him especially vulnerable to police pressure.

In the United States, such a revelation of prosecutorial misconduct would have led at once to the dismissal of the charges, but in Egypt, the trial was merely held over for several months. The hiatus gave Nour the chance to campaign for president, which he did with aplomb unfamiliar in Egyptian politics. But the obstacles he confronted were overwhelming. To be eligible to vote in the September presidential balloting a citizen needed to have registered by January, a month before Mubarak's surprise announcement that a presidential election would be held. Campaigning was limited to nineteen days. The state-owned news media gave all candidates equal time slots during those days, but throughout the balance of the pre-election period they focused relentlessly on President Mubarak.

Nour's campaign encountered constant harassment. His posters were torn down and his tires slashed. Moreover, the natural constituency for Nour's liberal ideology was divided when Noman Gomaa, the compromised leader of the Wafd Party, declared his candidacy. When asked why he had entered the race, the 71-year-old Gomaa replied with disarming frankness that he had been asked to do so by the government.

According to the official results, Nour received just over 7 percent of the vote while Mubarak garnered over eighty. Al-Ghad claimed that Nour's true count was two or three times larger than reported, which may be true since Egypt's election "results" are often doctored. Even if accurate, 7 percent put Nour in second place with more than twice as many votes as Gomaa. It positioned Nour to assume the role of leader of the opposition if Al-Ghad could make a respectable showing in the legislative races that were scheduled for November and December, following the September presidential vote.

Nour had approached Hisham about running for the People's Assembly. Hisham's frustrating experience as an independent candidate five years earlier had not dampened his appetite for electoral politics. A U.S. Senator had once told him that in weighing a career in electoral politics the most important consideration was to discover whether you enjoyed campaigning. Hisham, whose life had been lived mostly among the privileged, found that he liked mixing with common Cairenes and, as he had done as a teen with his mates in the Alexandria boxing club, he conversed with them easily without talking down.

But when Hisham learned of the depleted state of Al-Ghad's resources after the presidential race, he decided against running. Not only was Al-Ghad drained, but the regime was far from finished with its efforts to cripple the upstart party. Dissidents within Al-Ghad broke away and formed a new party that they declared to be the true Al-Ghad, using the same name. The new Al-Ghad's founding convention was broadcast live on state television, which had never been done for other parties. This was only one sure sign that state security was deeply involved in orchestrating the split.

A newspaper, looking just like the Al-Ghad party paper and calling itself by the same name appeared on newsstands. The only way to tell it apart from Nour's Al-Ghad party paper was the content. Whereas Nour's version lambasted the government, the alternative Al-Ghad took a very different tack. One article waxed eloquent on the virtues of the President's son: "I would not exaggerate if I said that the Egyptian citizen Gamal Mubarak enjoys popularity that many ministers do not have. The simple people are closely attached to him." It also praised Gamal's "commitment to democracy."[22]

This whole stratagem seems juvenile and absurd, but it was ingeniously debilitating to Nour. How could his new party hope to present itself effectively to an inexperienced electorate when another party paraded about using the same name?

In the race for the People's Assembly, the breakaway Al-Ghad ran scores of candidates as did the original Al-Ghad. Undoubtedly, voters must have been confused. The result was a wipe-out for the original Al-Ghad. Nour, himself, lost his parliamentary seat, although he had been immensely popular in his district. He alleged that thousands of voters who did not live within the district had been bused in by the government to cast ballots there, an election practice not unknown in Egypt and not so difficult to arrange, since most Egyptian employees work for the state.

Adding to Nour's torments, he was subjected to attacks that extended beyond the political realm. Rumors were spread that he had made his money through corrupt dealings, although no specific details were provided. And, in an especially bizarre twist, shortly after the election he reported receiving a package of audio tapes in the mail containing the sounds of a couple in the throes of sexual intercourse. The tape was labeled "The scandal of Ayman Nour and his wife," and, according to the Nours, it was accompanied by a letter warning: "This time it is in audio. Next time, it will be video."[23]

The regime's vindictiveness did not cease with the completion of the legislative elections. Despite the recantation by one of the accusers, and his revelation of a conspiracy by state security to frame Nour, the case against him resumed. Although Egypt has some 8,000 judges, the one chosen to preside happened to be the very same one who had convicted and sentenced the dissident sociologist Saad Edin Ibrahim on spurious charges in 2001. Ibrahim's conviction was eventually reversed on appeal, but not before he had spent two years in prison resulting in permanent impairment of his health. To the surprise of no one, the court found Nour guilty. He was sentenced to five years at hard labor.

Although the regime was able for the most part to manipulate the outcomes to its liking, it ran into trouble over the conduct of the elections. Judges bristled at the regime's expectation that they would serve as its docile instruments. After its scathing report on the May 2005 referendum, the Judges Club had intensified its demands about the administration of the presidential and legislative balloting. But it settled for concessions that were paltry.

This only set the stage for a bigger confrontation during the legislative elections. Following the surprisingly strong showing by the Muslim Brotherhood in the first round, the process grew increasingly tendentious and distorted. A few days after the second round was completed, a drama unfolded in the offices of *Al-Masry Al Youm*. Hisham recalls:

> It wasn't a very good day for me, and around 4 o'clock in the afternoon, I started to pack, getting ready to take the rest of the day off. The editor walked in and closed the doors. He had papers in his hands, and he said he didn't even want my assistant in on this. She is in on ninety percent of what I do. So I knew this was serious. He handed me the papers and asked: what should we do with this? I read them and saw that it was a judge's testimony about how the election in the district she was superintending was rigged.

The judge was Noha El-Zeini. She had been assigned to supervise polling in the governorate of Damanhour, north of Cairo near Alexandria. Her statement began: "I was there. I was part of the whole thing. This is a testament for truth's sake. If I do not record it, I will be held accountable before

God on the day of judgment."[24] She went on to describe the perquisites of her Election Day role.

> The Supreme Committee for Elections ... provided us with all expenses including travel fares, top level accommodation, per diem, private transportation (our own cars with our own drivers), in addition to a couple of thousand Egyptian Pounds as a bonus for our supervisory efforts.... All of the aforementioned were to be covered by the state's budget; in other words, financed by the taxpayer's money.

"The voting," she said, "went as smoothly as planned." Then, each of the several polling places in the district brought its results to a central counting station. "The almost final results ... pointed to at least 25,000 votes going to Gamal Heshmat [the candidate of the Muslim Brotherhood] while only 7,000, at best estimate, voted for [Mustapha] Al Fikki, [the government candidate]," wrote El-Zeini. But then the officers of the General Committee, in charge of the entire district, ordered the overseers of the various individual polling places, such as El-Zeini, to leave the premises, although El-Zeini noticed some officials from the Ministry of the Interior remained inside as did someone identified to her as a member of State Security. El-Zeini went on: "The president of the General Committee asked me to leave after a long time, so I left while I was sure about the results. That is why I was surprised about the screams of suspicions coming out of the supporters of Heshmat outside the room.... The victory of their candidate was almost a foregone conclusion for all who took part in the process." But, to El-Zeini's astonishment, Al Fikki was declared the winner. It was "fraud" and "rigging," she declared boldly.

When Hisham finished reading, he told his editor, Magdy El-Galad, to phone El-Zeini and ask her if she would sign the statement. She had had it delivered to *Al-Masry* with her name on it but no signature. Hisham instructed his assistant to fax a copy to the newspaper's lawyer, and then Hisham got the man on the phone and told him that he needed a legal opinion within ten minutes. Was there danger in publishing this statement, he needed to know. Hisham was eager to get it into the next morning's edition, lest State Security try to mobilize the paper's shareholders against him.

On the telephone, El-Zeini agreed unflinchingly to add her signature. Any Egyptian, even a judge, might have trembled to expose official misconduct so dramatically. She, however, seemed indifferent to all considerations other than getting her story out fully and clearly—something she might not have been able to do were it not for *Al-Masry*. In the phone call she began to demand that the paper not change the title she had put on it: "Rigging Elections Under the Supervision of the Judiciary." The editor quickly cut her off to prevent her from pronouncing it on the phone, since he knew that State Security eavesdropped on calls and feared that the title would clue them in to what was going on.

El-Galad ordered an employee to collect El-Zeini's signature, but Hisham overruled him. Extremely concerned about secrecy, he insisted that the two of them go themselves. While they were gone, he had the statement set in type. "I'm going to keep the car engine running, and you go up and watch her sign it," he instructed El-Galad. "No coffee, no tea, right back down," he added in contravention of *de rigueur* Egyptian courtesies. In the car on the way back, *Al-Masry*'s lawyer called, and reassured Hisham that the paper was safe from legal liability so long as the statement was signed. The last thing left to do was to order the masthead lowered on the morning's edition so this piece could be placed right at the top of the page. Then, anticipating correctly that the story would be announced on a popular late night television program that previews items in the next morning's papers, Hisham turned off his cell phone so that State Security could not order him to take the paper off the market.

In the morning when he turned his phone back on, the first call he received was from his mother, Samia, who told him that there were no copies on the street in her Alexandria neighborhood. Hisham suspected that State Security had confiscated the issue. He called the distribution company and made a threat of his own to be conveyed to State Security. "If they interfere with the circulation of today's edition, I'm going to run El-Zeini's story ten days in a row." Whether he would have made good on this threat remains unknowable because the blockage that had kept the paper from Samia's neighborhood disappeared as mysteriously as it had appeared. The full print run was distributed.

Because the fraud El-Zeini described was perpetrated against the Muslim Brotherhood's candidate, *Roz El Yousef,* once known as a liberal daily but in recent years identified with Gamal Mubarak's wing of the NDP, began baiting *Al-Masry,* referring to it as *Al Ikhwan Al Youm,* meaning *The Brotherhood Today.*

In truth, Hisham's relations with the Muslim Brotherhood were nuanced. He had earned their appreciation in the course of his human rights work for having defended them against persecution. Hisham still alternates between indignation and mirth in describing one case on which he worked in which a Brotherhood member was accused of trying to overthrow the regime with an air rifle. On the other hand, Hisham has been more skeptical than some other liberal intellectuals of the Brotherhood's declarations of democratic intent. For them, the idea of alliance with the Brotherhood is tempting, because it commands a strong grassroots constituency that they lack. But Hisham notes that "they [the Brotherhood] have already once shown bad faith back in 1984 [when they formed an electoral alliance of convenience with the liberal Wafd Party].... The positions they have taken against secular thinkers make it difficult to trust the Brotherhood."

The published accusations linking Hisham to the Brotherhood exemplify some of the defects of Arab journalism that

Hisham's mission is to eradicate. Apart from government control and censorship, there is little sense of obligation to be sure something is true before printing it. Hisham has been hit by this from many directions. In 2007 the U.S. National Endowment for Democracy conferred its annual award on Hisham and three other embattled journalists from different corners of the world. The next day, President Bush hosted the recipients at the White House. Hisham returned home to a flurry of abuse. One scandal sheet ran his photo above the caption "apostate." *Al-Usboa* newspaper ran an exposé by its editor. Its headline repeated the canard linking Hisham to the Muslim Brotherhood, but the body attacked him from the opposite direction. "Hisham Kassem ... is loyal to American policy and supports normalizing relations between Egypt and Israel," it charged. Reaching back, it said that "Kassem established human rights as the main interest of the *Cairo Times*, which led to conflict between the magazine and state security and to attacks on Islam." "Kassem's honor for promoting democracy," it concluded, "reflects a plan by the U.S. administration ... to repeat the Iraqi model."[25]

Hisham does not back down to the accusation that he is soft on Israel, baiting his critics: "You think that you can wipe out four or five million people. OK, I'm listening. Tell me how. Put aside that somebody thinks that exterminating four or five million people is a good thing to do. Give me the scenario." He says he is tired of irredentism: "If the Austro-Hungarian Empire was still trying to get its borders back, I think humanity would have a headache."[26] He lauds Sadat for having tried to end the Israel-Arab conflict.

As for his ties with the U.S., Hisham retorted: "I am pro-Egyptian, not pro-American." During the visit to Washington when he met Bush, Hisham pilloried the president in the press for backing away from advocating democracy. "You can feel Egypt is on the back burner now," he told the *Washington Post*. "Everyone is in despair about the situation." Earlier,

Egyptian liberals "were getting air cover from the Bush administration," he added, but in 2007 "when the fighting started . . . they effectively said, 'you're on your own.'"[27]

In late 2006, Hisham resigned from *Al-Masry*. Despite its success, he had locked horns too many times with Salah Diab who owned a controlling share of the company. Hisham was particularly unhappy over Diab's penchant for communicating directly with the newsroom staff, fearing that this opened the door to the common Egyptian practice of using the news columns to serve business interests. Such issues aside, these were two strong-willed men, and there may not have been room for both in a single enterprise.

Based on his experience steering *Al-Masry*, Hisham plans to launch a new paper in 2009 that can complete the transformation of the Egyptian media that he initiated with the *Cairo Times* and *Al-Masry*. He says he is confident that his next venture will eclipse the state-run media. He wants to have enough investors so that none will own a dominant part. Meanwhile, he writes a column for another liberal paper, *al-Dostur*, a weekly that went daily after the example of *Al-Masry*, and in 2008 he was elected to another term as chairman of the EOHR.

As for his third hat, he turned down requests to fill in for Ayman Nour as chairman of Al-Ghad, although he hopes that Nour's political fortunes will revive when his prison term ends in 2010. But disappointment of the soaring hopes of 2005 has left Hisham sobered. He scoffs at those "who . . . take the position that it is either Westminster democracy or nothing. [They] are not serious, . . . just . . . narcissistic," adding, "Reform is a long process that requires stamina, patience, and modesty."[28]

He recalls that following a visit to Egypt by Secretary of State Condoleezza Rice in the spring of 2006 Mubarak had pronounced that she and he were in agreement that democracy in Egypt would require a generation. "I agree, too," says Hisham, "but when do we begin?"[29]

In truth, while Mubarak has remained immobile as the sphinx, Hisham has already begun to democratize Egypt.

The Activist

Palestine: Bassem Eid

In 1988, during the first Palestinian *intifada,* some prominent left-wing Israelis founded the human rights organization *B'Tselem* ("In the Image") to combat abuses of Palestinians. Since it was unlikely that *B'Tselem*'s members would witness many of the violent confrontations between Palestinian rock-throwers and Israeli soldiers, the organization would have to gather and investigate complaints. But how many Palestinians would open up to Israelis knocking at their doors, claiming to want to help them, even if the Israelis spoke Arabic, which most did not? And how many Israelis would credit stories of misbehavior by their army, when they knew that Palestinians not infrequently resorted to hyperbole? *B'Tselem* needed an investigator who could command trust on both sides, someone to whom the Palestinians would talk freely but who would at the same time vet their stories with a critical eye.

B'Tselem's search led to a thirty-year-old Palestinian journalist who worked mostly as a free-lancer or stringer. Bassem Eid wrote sometimes in Arabic for Palestinian papers, but he was fluent in Hebrew as well, and *B'Tselem*'s founders knew his byline from *Kol Ha'ir,* a Jerusalem weekly published by the leading national daily, *Ha'aretz.*

Over five years, Eid had established a reputation for gritty and careful investigative journalism. For example, there was the ugly incident in the village of Salem, near Nablus in early 1988. Residents alleged that an Israeli army unit, after apprehending some young men for throwing stones, took them to a spot near the village entrance and used a bulldozer to teach them a lesson by burying them up to their chests in sand. By the time Bassem reached the scene, the youths had been extricated. All that he could see was a mound of sand. True, the spot was not naturally sandy, so it seemed clear that the sand had been brought there. But Bassem demanded stronger proof of the villagers' tale. When one of the alleged victims claimed he had lost a shoe under the sand as he was pulled free, Bassem urged the people to take shovels and dig for it. Lo and behold, the sand yielded a shoe, and like Cinderella's glass slipper, it matched the one that the young man produced. On the strength of this evidence, the army investigated and confirmed the incident. When Bassem wrote it up for *Kol Ha'ir,* it raised a small scandal.

Like any good investigative journalist, Bassem followed his stories wherever they led. Once he received a complaint from a blind newspaper vendor in the Balata refugee camp that his 14-year-old son had been arrested by the Israeli army for stone-throwing and held for almost a year without the hearing to which he was entitled. Bassem secured permission to visit the offices of the military court in Nablus to examine the files on the case.

The boy's defense was being handled by a famous Israeli Arab lawyer, Jawad Boulos, whose clientele included the leaders of the PLO and later the Palestinian National Authority, itself. Bassem dug through the files and found sixteen instances in which the presiding judge had signed a note saying he had received a phone call from Boulos, asking for postponement. Perhaps Boulos thought it would serve the boy's interest; more likely he was just too busy for such a small fish. *Kol Ha'ir* published Bassem's story, "The Tactics of Boulos." The upshot was that the court decided to consider the boy's case without the presence of his lawyer, who was out of the country at the next scheduled court date, and it decided to release the youngster on the grounds that he had already served a long incarceration. Bassem's work embarrassed Boulos but got his client freed.

On another occasion, a woman approached Bassem with a story about her difficulty in obtaining a divorce. As a Palestinian Jerusalemite, like Bassem, she held both an Israeli identity card and Jordanian citizenship. Matters like divorce fall within the purview of religious courts in both countries. Typically, according to Bassem, Jerusalemite women prefer to go to the Israeli Muslim court because "it protects the rights of the woman much more than the Jordanian Muslim court." In this case, however, the woman was not receiving justice. Bassem recalls: "The judge was a sheikh. The woman told me that each time she went to court, the judge postponed her case because he was interested in her sexually." The story made Bassem, who is no prude, indignant. As far as Bassem is concerned, "Everybody can allow himself to practice sexual acts outside of marriage, except a Muslim judge. This is like prostitution."[1]

Bassem explained that to help her, he needed proof. The woman proposed that he accompany her to the court, but Bassem nixed this idea. Instead he proposed that she call the judge that very moment from his office and record the conversation on his answering machine. So she did. Bassem reconstructs the interlude:

> She said, "Mr. Sheikh, why you are postponing my case all the time?" And he said, "Until you come to my home."
> And she said, "I do not know where your home is."
> He asked, "From where are you calling?"
> She said, "From a public telephone."
> And he said, "Can you come now?"
> And she said, "Yes, I can, in half an hour."
> And then he described a place. He said, "There is a public telephone there. Stop beside it. I will come and pick you up."

She agreed and rang off. Bassem took the phone and called his editor at *Kol Ha'ir* who immediately dispatched a team of photographers to stake out the rendezvous. Then, as Bassem continues the saga:

> We went. I hid myself. She stood near the public telephone and he came in pajamas. It was around four o'clock in the

afternoon. He was in pajamas and with a friend. And he came to the public telephone. He took her arm, and started walking. He was around sixty-five years old. Then, two photographers jumped in front of him and took pictures, and he started running. He escaped from the place, leaving his friend and the woman.

We went back to the newspaper and we showed the pictures to the editor. And the editor said, "Go ahead with the story." Of course, we had recorded him, which was another proof against him. And we published the story. We called somebody from the Israeli Ministry of Religion for comment because this court is under its authority, and we got the response, "We are going to investigate."

Except for the woman, nobody was happy with this story. The judge was humiliated, and the Muslim authorities were embarrassed. Israeli officials were on the spot. Such a serious case of extortion demanded action, but to intervene against a Muslim cleric could only be a headache for Israel. Someone from the ministry even complained aloud that the woman had gone to the press rather than the police. But she may have made a wise choice. She got her divorce. As for the judge, he ended up merely being transferred from the Islamic Court in Jerusalem to the one in Haifa.

Bassem's utter indifference to whom he displeased in pursuit of a story is rare anywhere, but especially in a part of the world where connections count for so much. It was this quality that caught the eye of *B'Tselem*.

Who was this extraordinary journalist? What was his background? Unlike most other liberal thinkers in the Middle East, Bassem Eid did not come from the educated middle class. His father, Mohammed, eked out a living as a tailor, working alone with his sewing machine in a tiny stall in the shouk in the old city of Jerusalem. Before the birth of the state of Israel, Mohammed's family had raised oranges in a tiny village, now vanished, called Salameh, located near the beach between Tel Aviv and Jaffa. Anyone who has made the 5-10 minute trip from Tel Aviv to Jaffa can imagine just how small Salameh must have been.

The family fled for Ramallah during the 1948 war and from there to Amman, where most have remained to this day. But Mohammed moved to East Jerusalem, which was then part of Jordan, and established his tailoring shop. There, he met Mahdiyah, also a refugee from the war, the daughter of a poor cobbler-turned-imam in Lod, the town outside Tel Aviv where Ben Gurion airport is located today.

In 1951, Mohammed married Mahdiyah who bore four sons in rapid succession, Bassem being the fourth, and then a daughter. Early in the marriage the young family had moved from a home in the Muslim Quarter of the Old City to one in the Jewish Quarter. Although Yasser Arafat later denied the historical connection of Jews to Jerusalem, the Arab residents of this part of the city always called it the "Jewish Quarter" in Arabic, even when no Jews lived there.

Although the flat in the Jewish Quarter was more attractive, it nonetheless consisted of just a single room plus a small kitchen and a toilet. In that room, the seven Eids ate and slept and studied and baked bread. There was a public school nearby which Bassem and his siblings attended. The building is still there, although today it is a yeshiva, the Sephardic Learning Center.

Bassem remembers feeling crowded, but not unhappy. "I knew people who were 12 in one room. We were considered a small family," he says. When the crush bothered him, Bassem found refuge with his mother's sister. Unusual though it was in their culture, this aunt was a spinster who lived alone in the Cardo, the remains of the central street of the city in the Byzantine era, which was just a minute's walk from Bassem's home.

In 1966, the Jordanian government decided, for reasons unknown, to empty that part of the Jewish Quarter of its inhabitants. No force was used, simply an enticement. The United Nations Relief and Works Agency (UNRWA) had just built a new refugee camp, called Shuafat, on the northern edge of Jerusalem along the road to Ramallah. Each family was offered a home and plot of land free of charge. Families of 6 and fewer were entitled to one room and 60 square meters; larger families, like the Eids, got two rooms and 80 meters. They were also at liberty to build additions onto these new homes. For the Eids, it was a big increase in space, as well as saving them the rent they had been paying for their single room in the Jewish Quarter.

In consequence of the move, the Eids were not displaced by the war of 1967 as were many other denizens of East Jerusalem. They were not, however, spared all trauma.

Bassem had kept a close tie with his spinster aunt in whose house he used to find refuge from his own home's crowding. As it happens, he had gone to visit her the day that the battle for Jerusalem began. Bassem was nine, and he recalls huddling with his aunt in her one room apartment in the Cardo:

> When the war started there was a small radio at my aunt's. And they started saying "Yahud, Yahud, Yahud" [Jew, in Arabic.] I had no idea what it meant. So I asked my aunt, "What does it mean, Yahud? Are they human beings like us?"
> And she said, "No, they eat human beings."
> "Oh, goodness! They might come here and eat us."
> "No, do not worry. I locked the outside door."

For five days they lived on whatever provisions were on hand. The radio gave them some news, of dubious reliability, but it was their only link to the outside. The home had no phone; nor did that of Bassem's parents. Mohammed and Mahdiyah could only pray to Allah to preserve their young son isolated in the midst of some of the most intense fighting. On the sixth day, Bassem recalls:

Somebody knocked at the door, and immediately I ran towards my aunt and I said, "The Jews have come to eat us."

She said, "No, no, it is not the Jews. Go and open the door."

I said, "No, you are older than I am. You have to open it."

Then she said, "Do not worry. This may be your uncle."

Then I went and I opened it. And I saw soldiers, and immediately I ran inside the house. Then they entered. They spoke Arabic well. They asked if there were men in the home, and my aunt she said, "No one, except me and this child."

And then one soldier said, "If you need some food you can go outside. There is a point here which is distributing food—some tomatoes, some bread and milk."

And then my aunt looked at me and she said, "Do you want to bring some?"

And I said, "No."

Then the soldier looked at me, saying, "Why not?" in Arabic. "You can go. It is safe. Nobody will bother you."

And I said, "No."

When the soldiers had left, Bassem asked his aunt: "Do you believe him that they are distributing bread and tomatoes and milk?" And she said, "Yes." Bassem challenged her: "You told me the Jews eat human beings. Why should they feed us?" Then she said, "This is what your grandfather told me," but she confessed she did not know the truth of it, herself. So Bassem ventured out, and he found "all of the neighborhood people were there, bringing tomatoes, bread and milk. They gave it to everybody."

The next day, the radio reported that all fighting had ceased, and that the Israeli military authorities said that civilians were free to travel. So he walked the four kilometers, through the war's damage including dead soldiers whose nationality he could not tell, back to his much-relieved family.

That the Jewish soldiers were so much kinder than he had been led to expect may have contributed to Bassem's attitude toward Israel, which, even when he was acting as its most irritating hair shirt, never was marked by the least hint of hatred. Even more, discovering in such vivid fashion the utter falsehood of the tale of Jewish cannibalism that his aunt passed down to him from his grandfather seems to have imprinted young Bassem with the strong sense of the difference between fact and rumor that was to become the trademark of his career.

Another thing he learned early was resourcefulness. The two-bedroom home in Shuafat had seemed spacious when the Eids and their five children moved into it. But in the next years, Mahdiyah bore five more sons. Although Mohammed got various breaks on taxes and services, due to his refugee status, and despite landing a menial job at Hadassah Hospital, paying more than he had brought home from the shouk, the family's finances could not keep pace with its growth. The oldest son, Hatem, dropped out of high school and took up barbering to help make ends meet, but still the family struggled.

So nine-year-old Bassem took matters into his own hands. From some of the other boys in the camp, he learned about the newspaper business. He would get a bundle of *Maariv* or *Yediot Aharanot* or other popular Hebrew dailies, venture out in Jerusalem traffic in the Jewish areas, and hawk papers at stop lights or even at security checkpoints.

Bassem's enterprise benefited from the fortuitous juxtaposition of Muslim and Jewish traditions. Friday is the Muslim holy day and therefore Bassem's school was closed, meaning he could put in longer hours. Saturday is the Jewish Sabbath, and in Israel this means that the thick weekend editions of newspapers, like those that appear on Sundays in America, appear on Fridays. Naturally, they cost several times more than the daily editions, and this means that the seller earns several times more on each paper. Fridays were good to Bassem.

This weekly infusion of cash gave him a range of opportunities. "I could play something much better than football in the street," Bassem recalls. "I could go to a coffee shop to play on a machine because I had money." In addition to playing pinball, he "could run to the store and order a sandwich." Coming from the kind of poverty in which food was not always available on demand, this freedom from hunger made him feel "rich and independent." Having his own money stoked his pride. Unlike his brothers, Bassem did not have to settle for hand-me-downs. "I could buy the best school bag at the beginning of the year, the best shoes, the best shirt," he recalls with pleasure. "We used to dress in a beige uniform. I had everything."

In addition to the material and psychological rewards of his work, Bassem gained yet another benefit. He began to learn Hebrew which was unaccountably not taught by the UNRWA school. Oddly, too, his high school, run by the municipal authorities, offered only cursory instruction in the language. But by then, Bassem had already grown fluent in Hebrew through his daily dealings with Israeli vendors and customers.

Meanwhile, he kept his grades up and formed plans to go to college, perhaps to learn journalism. He studied hard for the nationwide comprehensive exam that, in the Israeli school system, marks the completion of high school and qualification for college. Bassem was delighted, although not surprised, to learn that he had passed. But he was still in for a shock. Unbeknownst to anyone else in the family, eldest brother Hatem, who longed to continue his own education, had taken the same exam. He had been studying on his own, in secret, during the hours he was not cutting hair. He, too, had passed.

It did not take long for Mohammed to decide what to do. He had put aside a little money to help pay college tuition for

Bassem. But even that was a stretch; he could not possibly help both boys. Hatem had already sacrificed for the family. He deserved the chance now. Bassem was deeply disappointed, but he did not fault the justice of his father's reasoning. Instead, he set out to pay his own way. He was a good earner, and he had already discovered that there was even more money in waiting tables than hawking newspapers:

> I worked in most of the restaurants in West Jerusalem. Whoever was paying most, I would go to. When I work, I want to work. I will wash dishes. I have no problem. I will clean the restaurant, even. I have no problem. I'm not a person that came from a high-class society. My father was not born in the United States. I am not one who would say, "How could it be that I, the son of Mohammad, clean a restaurant?" Come on. We came from a very simple family. So whatever you want, I will do and I will even be proud to do it.

While he saved for college, he stumbled into an additional activity that influenced his development. In high school, with no definite purpose, he had bought a Hebrew typewriter. Then one day, walking through a section of the shouk in the old city where butcher shops were concentrated, he was offended by what he saw and smelled. The butchers in the shouk had no refrigeration. Sides of meat hung from hooks; slabs were laid out on counters. This is the norm in poorer parts of the world, but upkeep was poor. "The streets smelled so bad and were so dirty," Bassem recalls. He went home and typed a letter in fluent Hebrew to the mayor of Jerusalem, Teddy Kolek, complaining of the conditions. Two weeks later the post brought a reply. Kolek thanked him for bringing the problem to his attention, praised him as a good citizen, and promised to clean up the butchers' row.

That was exciting; so next, he sent a letter to Prime Minister Shimon Peres. Bassem can no longer remember the subject, just that once again he got a reply—signed by the Prime

Minister. Bassem told others of his correspondence and word began to circulate that he had the power to communicate with the Israeli authorities. Bassem recalls:

> Then people started coming to me, saying things like, "Listen, I have problem with the national insurance. Can you write me a letter to explain to them that in this year I never worked, I was sick? I have the medical reports here with me."

After about a year, Bassem made a small business of this. He rented a stall near his home, got a post office box, and even installed a telephone—something the Eid household had never been able to afford. The residents of Shuafat would bring him their disputes with various government offices or utility companies, and Bassem would type letters in Hebrew, pleading their cases. They would pay him a few shekels, and sometimes when he saved someone a bundle, they would give him a tip. He expanded his activity by developing a relationship with a Jewish lawyer. When a client needed legal help, Bassem would call this friend to see if he would take the case. When he did, Bassem received a fee.

He developed confidence in his own talents as an advocate. He also learned something about the nature of democracy. "For each letter I sent, I received a response in a written letter," he says. "This is not common in the Arab world, at all. In Israel it is. Any letter you send—sometimes it takes time to check the case—but in the end you will receive a written answer."

This sense of how democratic government work was reinforced, he recalls, by stories he read in the Israeli press:

> I used to read Israeli newspapers every day, and I found interesting stories. For example, a supermarket charged one agora [one-hundredth of a shekel] more than it should have. And he [the customer] received 3,000 shekels from the judge's decision. Interesting! So I can do the same because there is no

difference between me and him. He approached a lawyer; I can approach a lawyer.

After four years of working restaurants by day and writing advocacy letters by night—or vice versa—Bassem had saved enough money to enroll in Hebrew University to study journalism, convinced by his success as a professional letter-writer that this was his calling. "Journalism requires someone who is able to speak out and who is able to write," he says. He was confident he possessed both qualities.

He soaked up what the university had to offer, enjoying "relationships with professors, students, students from abroad—it was really very good." Relations between Arab and Jewish students were relaxed, "much better than today, unfortunately," he observes. But after two years his funds ran out, and without any place to turn, he was forced to abandon his studies. He resumed working in restaurants and writing letters for members of his community, but he also he began to write as a free-lancer for Arab and Hebrew papers, and soon he caught on with *Kol Ha'ir*. His connection remained free-lance, but for the next five years, his contributions were regular.

In 1985, Bassem married a Palestinian woman from the al Amaari refugee camp. The marriage was arranged in the traditional way, and she was a traditional woman who never became the least involved in his professional life. She moved into the Eid family home. The original two rooms that the family had been given in Shuafat had expanded sideways within its allocated 80 meters and upward without limit, some additions cantilevered above others. As each of the sons married, his bride moved in with him, and two additional rooms were constructed to accommodate each new family. Eventually seven of the married sons were to live there with their families, including Bassem. The responsibilities of marriage—and in time four children—closed the door on Bassem's hopes to return to school. However, the pleasure he got as an investigative reporter subdued his disappointment.

It was from his growing reputation in that role that he was discovered and recruited by the founders of *B'Tselem*. Initially, the organization had a staff of six, of which Bassem was the only Arab and the only fulltime field worker. He was the heart of the operation. "For me, Bassem Eid is *B'Tselem*," said Gideon Levy, a columnist of the newspaper *Ha'aretz* who covered Palestinian affairs. "He brings them their hard information, their raw material."[2] In time, Bassem occasionally would take other staff members along on his investigations, translating for them. Later, the group hired an Israeli who was fluent in Arabic who also did field work, but this was after *B'Tselem* had won the trust of the Palestinians, thanks largely to Bassem.

On his early missions for *B'Tselem* Bassem was greeted with skepticism. Typically, he would begin by explaining that he had come "on behalf of an Israeli organization to investigate the killing of 'Muhammed' by the Israeli army." The usual response, he recalls was: "What you are talking about? Are the Israelis really so concerned about 'Muhammad' as to investigate his death? Why didn't they protect his life before he was dead?"

To break through this, Bassem decided to write a weekly story for *Al Quds*, the main Palestinian newspaper, relating cases he had investigated. Each time the Israeli army was accused of misbehavior, *B'Tselem* would send it a report based on the testimony Bassem had taken. The army would then investigate and either deny or admit the accusation. In his articles, Bassem stressed the toughness of *B'Tselem*, and he frequently mentioned cases in which the army confessed fault and offered apologies or restitution. He also wanted to show the Palestinians "how much *B'Tselem* really cared about human rights, not because you are Palestinians but because we care about human rights."

In addition to investigating cases, Bassem would escort Israelis or foreigners who wanted a firsthand view of the issues he was publicizing. Once, he brought the gadfly leftist legislator, Shulamit Aloni, to observe some home demolitions. This is a punishment that the Israeli army borrowed from the British colonial administration intended to convince would-be terrorists that "martyrdom" will not benefit their families. The three homes targeted that day were on a street in a refugee camp too narrow for bulldozers, so explosives were used, the force of which collapsed ten additional houses. Having been an eye-witness, Aloni addressed angry complaints to Yitzhak Rabin, who was then the Defense Minister, with even more than her usual abundant zeal and with the authority of being an eye-witness. The owners of the accidentally destroyed homes received full compensation.

That Bassem was in fact a sympathetic listener did not mean that he believed everything he heard. On the contrary he made it a practice to probe the accuracy of the testimony he received before telling his colleagues in the *B'Tselem* headquarters to send a formal letter to the army asking its version of the events alleged to him. It was not uncommon for him to discover distortion.

Once, for example, a five-year-old girl was shot in her family's car by Israeli soldiers manning a checkpoint near Hebron. According to the girl's father, he was driving, stopped at the checkpoint, and the soldiers opened fire without provocation. Bassem took down this account, typed it up at the *B'Tselem* office, but asked his colleagues to hold onto it for a day while he investigated further. "It was an amazing story," said Bassem. "I wanted to sell it to the Israeli media." But it did not ring true. After a day of asking questions, he elicited a different version. While the father slept, his fifteen-year-old son took the keys to the car to go for a joy ride. Apparently feeling his oats, he invited his three younger sisters along, promising to buy them a sweet. He made a turn that brought him by surprise to a checkpoint. Perhaps frightened because he had no driver's license, he turned and tried to race away. The soldiers ordered him to stop, and when he did not, they fired two rounds, one of which killed the five-year-old. The army eventually confirmed Bassem's version, and the shooter was punished. Although the truth was nothing like the original Palestinian account, Israeli orders instruct soldiers to shoot to disable a fleeing vehicle, not to kill.

Another time, a six-year-old girl died from a gunshot wound to the head that her father, a member of the Palestinian security forces, said an Israeli settler fired into his car as he drove the girl somewhere. In this case, it only took some phone calls to neighbors for Bassem to learn that in truth, the bullet came from the father's own gun as he was cleaning it in his home.

Even well-respected figures sometimes took part in dissimulation. In the first days of the second *intifada,* Palestinian doctors at Ramallah hospital held a press conference together with Moustapha Barghouti, a minister in the Palestinian cabinet and a noted democracy advocate. They displayed a dead body with injuries that they said were inflicted by Israelis who had kidnapped, tortured and murdered the man. They pointed to burns they said had been caused by cigarettes. A few days later, when two sympathetic forensic doctors arrived from Chicago, Bassem told them he was skeptical. What had become of the man's clothes, he asked, and, even more important, where was his car, since he was known to own one? When foreign human rights organizations investigated, they concluded that the victim had died in a one-car auto accident far from any Israeli. Indeed his body had been found next to his smashed vehicle.

Such deception by Palestinians reinforced Israeli skepticism toward their complaints, so Bassem tried to teach his countrymen how to prove a case. Once, for example, he heard that a Jewish settler had killed a Palestinian in the village of

Der Sharaf, outside Nablus. He rushed to investigate, but found that the body had already been buried. He told the family, "I can do nothing unless you will allow us to take it for an autopsy." They countered that they would agree to the exhumation if allowed to make a "public nationalist funeral."

Bassem says he challenged them on whether their goal was to foment violence. When he was assured that the family sought nothing other than an opportunity to celebrate the dead man's martyrdom, Bassem phoned left-wing Knesset member Yossi Sarid, who in turn contacted the general in charge of the Nablus district, and an agreement was struck. The body would be paraded with a Palestinian flag. The Israeli army would keep its distance. Then the body would be loaded into a Palestinian ambulance, driven to a checkpoint where it would be transferred to an Israeli ambulance, thence taken to a forensic clinic in Jaffa connected to the Israeli Justice Ministry. This complicated plan came off without a hitch, and the autopsy's results lent credence to the locals' account of the man's murder. Ultimately, an Israeli settler was arrested for the crime.

His ability to discover the fraudulence of some stories just by working the phone reflected his knowledge of the territories and wide range of connections. These were at the center of another celebrated case. A 13-year-old shepherd was grazing his flock in the Jordan valley and accidentally detonated some ordnance apparently left from Israeli military exercises, blowing off his leg. The boy was taken by the Israelis to Hadassah hospital where surgeons performed a heroic procedure to reattach the leg or what part of it they could. While he was recovering, the hospital's billing department informed his father that he would be facing a charge of about 100,000 shekels, or $25,000—an impossible sum. That night, the father carried the son from his hospital bed and stole him away.

A year and a half later, Bassem received a call from an Israeli journalist. He was working on a medical story, and the surgeons at Hadassah hospital had told him about the boy, apparently because the surgery was so unusual. The journalist wanted to find him. He had spoken to Israeli President Ezer Weisman who had in turn contacted Palestinian Authority chairman Yasser Arafat. Arafat promised that his security forces would find the boy, but nothing came of it. The journalist wondered if Bassem, who had investigated the case at the time of the explosion, could help. Bassem knew exactly where to locate father and son, and he persuaded them to accompany him to Hadassah, assuring the father that this was all under the aegis of President Weisman.

The leg had successfully taken hold, but the foot had been severed from the leg in the blast and either lost or damaged beyond salvation. Sometime after his flight from the hospital, the father had taken the boy to doctors in Nablus who had fashioned an artificial foot of rubber, far below the standards of western prosthesis. The surgeons at Hadassah were happy to see that their operation had worked and wanted to make the boy a better foot. But once again, the matter of the bill intruded, and so a televised appeal asked viewers to call Bassem's cell phone to pledge help. The donations amounted to twenty times the cost of the new procedure.

Israeli commentators of the center and right were often highly critical of B'Tselem, accusing it of playing into the hands of Israel's enemies. The *Jerusalem Post* editorialized that although the group "calls itself a human rights organization .... its leaders are all super-doves ... with a transparent political agenda."[3] Bassem, however, was neither an Israeli nor a player in Israeli politics. He has always insisted that his work has no ulterior motive. "I never try to document violations of human rights in order to achieve a political goal," he says, "never in my life, although I'm quite sure that there are some Palestinians who do it."

Bassem sometimes drove Israeli military officials crazy. Once, for example, the army arrested a 16-year-old resident of a West Bank village, Beir Nabala, who confessed to blocking a road overnight with stones. When asked how he had traveled the considerable distance from his home to the spot of the blockage, the lad said he had taken his father's donkey. The next day, soldiers arrived with a truck and confiscated the donkey. When the family told Bassem what had happened, he dashed off a letter to the legal advisor to the military. He inquired about the whereabouts of the donkey, asking: "I want to know if you have a prison for donkeys. I want to know how you are treating the donkeys. And I want to know if the owners have a right to visit their donkeys." The legal advisor replied in humorless bureaucratese, explaining that he needed a case number and asking whether the donkey in question had any distinguishing characteristics. Bassem released the exchange to the press which he knew would appreciate its drollness. When it made the front pages of three Israeli papers, the donkey was returned.

But although he was a thorn in its side, the army came grudgingly to respect Bassem. It recognized that his reports were free from the fancy and exaggeration that is all too common in Palestinian discourse. Soon after *B'Tselem* was founded, a Palestinian magazine decided to highlight the first anniversary of the *intifada*. Bassem recalls: "They decided to publish statistics. How many Palestinians had been killed. How many injured. How many houses demolished. They collected data from several Palestinian organizations and sent it to the censor," as was required at the time before the Oslo accords of 1993, when the Palestinian territories were still under Israeli military rule.

When the censor barred the material, the editor turned to Bassem whose pieces in *Al Quds* had always gotten through. After examining the banned article, Bassem told the editor that the casualty statistics it contained were higher than his own. "I know every case," he said. "Ask me where 'Mohammed' was killed, I will tell you Ramallah. Ask me where 'Ahmed' was killed, I will tell you Hebron." The editor asked Bassem to take another crack at the story. Bassem agreed, with a caveat: "I will write it, but only according to B'Tselem's statistics, not these statistics." In this manner it cleared the censor. "Why exaggerate?" asks Bassem. "For example, if 2,000 houses have been demolished, why make it 10,000? If the Israelis killed four, why say it was forty?"

Sometimes Israeli soldiers troubled by misbehavior by their fellows made use of Bassem. In 1990 a reservist contacted him to report that his unit had rounded up a bunch of youths in the village of Aboud, near Ramallah, who were suspected of having thrown stones at some Jewish settlers. The soldiers beat them and humiliated them. It happened to be the Jewish holiday of Purim when costumes are donned, and some soldiers forced the lads to put paint on their faces and repeat a Purim song. Bassem gathered corroborating testimony, and several other soldiers eventually confessed and were punished.

In addition to his deep knowledge of the area, his objectivity, and his ability to relate both to his own people and to the Israelis, Bassem brought remarkable courage to his work. He was unafraid of the Israeli army and of Palestinian radicals. Hagai Tsoref, an Israeli historian who went into the field with Bassem as a volunteer with B'Tselem, describes him:

> He is a brave man. Nothing frightened him. If the army is there, he says, "Okay, let us walk through the field. Let us find a way between the checkpoints. Let us hide, etc." If I get caught, so what? I'm Israeli; nothing will happen. But if he gets caught, it is a completely different story. I got the impression that he never thinks of his own welfare. He had a mission, and he would do it, no matter what it takes.[4]

Nor did the danger that Bassem courted come only from one direction. Tsoref recalls:

Bassem lives in Jerusalem so his car has a yellow [license plate]—an Israeli one. So it was quite risky because the people [in the territories], they see a car with a yellow [plate], they do not know that the guy driving it is an Arab; they think it is an Israeli car. There were a few incidents in which we were nearly attacked.

These were not the toughest scrapes that Bassem got himself into on the Palestinian side. Once during the first *intifada*, his friend, Gideon Levy, told Bassem that he would like to do a story for *Ha'aretz* about Palestinians wanted by the Israeli army. Bassem contacted some people he knew were in touch with the radicals, and they agreed to set up a meeting. Bassem took Levy to a house in Tulkarm where one of the fugitives was living. With proper Arab hospitality, the man provided them a fine lunch and gave Levy an interview, even allowing his photo to be taken. This was a Sunday, and Levy said the feature would run in the next weekend edition, to appear on Friday. Their host told them with bravado, "I hope I will live until Friday to see my picture in *Ha'aretz*."

He did not get his wish. On Wednesday the army found him, and he was killed. The rumor quickly spread throughout the village that Bassem and Levy had given him away. The fact that they had taken photos of the man seemed especially suspicious. Bassem says he was "totally out of my mind" with distress at the accusation. But rather than fleeing, he decided to visit the village alone the very day after the killing. He met with the politically active people of Tulkarm and challenged their suspicions head on. "Yes, we met with him, but don't say that we gave anyone his picture," he said. "I don't think that the army did not know his face and other details and were just waiting for us to submit his picture." Even more convincing than his words was his behavior, coming to the village immediately of his own volition to address the accusations. He walked away unscathed.

In 1993, in his column in *Al Quds*, Bassem denounced a lynching in the Balata refugee camp near Nablus. The victim was a pregnant woman accused of being a "collaborator" with Israel, and the killer was one of the leaders of Fatah in that camp. The *"shabiba,"* a term designating young toughs who constitute the shock troops of the various uprisings and militant groups, distributed a flyer threatening Bassem with death if he returned to the city. His bravery does not extend to recklessness, so he stayed away. But after a few weeks, they had second thoughts. Bassem was a tribune on whom they relied, and it was often he who accompanied Western correspondents to such places as Balata to report the Palestinian side of the conflict. "I'm the one who can make trouble" for the Israelis, he said.[5] So a delegation of *shabiba* paid a call on him in his home in Shuafat, to ask him to resume his visits to Nablus, guaranteeing his safety.

In one of Bassem's more celebrated cases, he brushed up against danger from many directions. This involved radical Islamist activists whom Israel deported to southern Lebanon in December 1992. When Hamas kidnapped and murdered an Israeli border guard, the fifth or sixth such killing in a short spell, the government of Yitzhak Rabin, who was now Prime Minister, rounded up 415 Hamas and Islamic Jihad members whom it regarded as instigators, and took them by bus to Lebanon. At that time the southern band of Lebanon was controlled by a largely Christian militia, the South Lebanon Army (SLA), that was backed by Israel. Israel dumped these prisoners as deep into Lebanon as the writ of its allies reached.

It is hard to see how these expulsions—which were in each case for a prescribed duration of one or two years—could be considered severe punishment in light of the brutal crimes committed by the groups that the men belonged to. But the problem was that the punishment was collective without any due process in which each of the individuals could defend himself against specific charges. To underscore the reality that the Israelis, however formidable their intelligence apparatus, were fallible and therefore that some of those caught in this net might be innocent, the government was soon forced by Israeli courts to rescind the deportation orders against a handful of the men.

Many foreign organizations criticized the deportations, as did *B'Tselem*. In addition to the legal issues, there was also concern about the circumstances of the deportees. The Lebanese government did not want them. They certainly were not likely to get along with the Israel-allied Lebanese militia in the south. Israel had left them with food and blankets, but they were isolated from the world, somewhere in the wilderness of Lebanon. *B'Tselem* asked Bassem to try to visit the deportees to report on their condition.

To reach the men, Bassem needed to enter Lebanon via Syria whose regime sympathized with them but would not cooperate with Bassem because he worked for an Israeli organization. After abortive efforts to sneak into Syria via Jordan, Bassem secured a Syrian visa from the PLO representative in Cyprus and flew directly to Damascus. His next hurdle was customs, since the material he was carrying would give away his affiliation. When he reached the border officer who was searching bags, he leaned close and said softly: "Listen carefully. My sick mother is waiting for me outside. Please take this fifty dollars and keep it." "No problem," said the officer, passing Bassem's bag through unexamined.

Bassem found a ride to the border and entered Lebanon, where he applied to the Lebanese government for permission to go see the deportees. When this was denied, he made his way to the southern Lebanese town of Shtura where the Al Quds Military Hospital was a hub of Palestinian activity. Explaining his mission, he was welcomed warmly and promised that everything would be arranged the next day.

Upon rising, he was taken to an office outside the hospital, presided over by an outsized sheikh to whom all of the others deferred. They explained Bassem's purpose, and the sheikh replied somewhat in the manner of the Wizard of Oz, "Come back tomorrow morning." Bassem protested that he needed to proceed that day, but the sheikh insisted: "Not today. There is no transportation. Tomorrow." At eight the next morning, Bassem was back in the sheikh's office. "Come back in four hours," he was told. Bassem argued in vain that time was precious since his visa would expire. At noon, the sheikh told Bassem to return at 6 PM.

At last, then, the sheikh got in his car and drove Bassem four kilometers. He stopped at a private house and told Bassem, "I will come back for you in an hour and a half." Bassem did as told. The homeowners had laid out a nice meal that he bolted down impatiently. The sheikh returned as scheduled, and the two resumed the journey—but only for five minutes. At that point they reached a mountain. Some men appeared with donkeys. "Go with those guys," said the sheikh, turning back to his car. Bassem protested: "There is no car." The sheikh took the measure of Bassem's naivety: "There is no way to go there by car. You have to walk."

After four-and-a-half hours, they reached a tent colony and were taken at once to Abdel Aziz Rantisi, the man who later became head of Hamas before being assassinated by Israel. Rantisi served him dates, the traditional hospitality with which guests are greeted, and checked him out. After Rantisi satisfied himself that Bassem was who he said he was, he was led to a place where he could sleep.

Hours later, around four in the morning, he was wakened for the pre-dawn prayer. "No, thank you," he said. "So they began to suspect I was a Christian, not a Muslim," recalls Bassem. "But I was okay with that."

He awoke again later that morning and circulated questionnaires that *B'Tselem* had prepared. He also told the men, who had no access to postal service, that he would convey their correspondence. But he also cautioned them:

I would like to take letters from you to your families but please be careful. Ask about the children, ask about the house; do not ask about weapons, do not ask about money because then I will face troubles. If your pistol is under the bed, do not tell your wife in the letter that I am carrying that the pistol is there.

His primary fear was not of the Israelis, but rather the Jordanians. He planned to return via Jordan, and he had already been given a hard time by Jordanian security when he first tried to reach Syria. "You know what the Jordanian *mukhabarat* is like," he said. After 26 hours he trudged back through the mountains carrying the questionnaires and letters, as well as photos and video cassettes. Then he made his way directly to Jordan. He was not surprised by what greeted him:

> The whole *mukhabarat* was waiting there. They started carrying my bags, which they did not hand back, and they said, "Bassem, tomorrow you know where to come." And I said, "Yeah, of course." Next day, I went [to mukhabarat headquarters where he had been interrogated upon his first, abortive effort to reach the deportees]. I found that they copied everything; even the letters they opened, and they copied the letter itself and the envelope. They made slides of the pictures.

Having gotten what they wanted, they returned the material to Bassem. To avoid having to repeat this experience on the Israeli side, he bundled it into a package and sent it by Federal Express from Amman to the office of Human Rights Watch in New York with a request that they forward it to *B'Tselem*. Then he made his way to Allenby Bridge and crossed back into Israel without any documents or other material in his possession except his toiletries and change of clothes. Israeli officials did not detain him for a moment.

As if Bassem did not court enough danger in his work between Israelis and Palestinians, in 1994 he accepted another assignment entailing its own horrific risks. The French organization, *Reporters Sans Frontières*, retained him to make a visit to Iraq to prepare a report on press freedom (or its absence) under Saddam Hussein. Bassem traveled to Amman and thence to the Iraqi frontier where a hefty bribe to an officer of the border guard got him inside the country. According to an account in the *Jerusalem Post,* Bassem held a series of surreptitious meetings with Iraqi reporters who affirmed what he already knew, "that all they were allowed to run was praise of Saddam."[6] He asked for a meeting at the Ministry of Information, but after a testy exchange with a low-ranking employee, he was advised by friends to make a hasty departure from Baghdad. A bribe of cigarettes enabled him to exit back into Jordan, and he returned home to file his report.

1994 was a pivotal year for Bassem, as for his countrymen. In July, ten months after the awkward handshake between Rabin and Arafat on the White House lawn, the PLO leadership made its triumphant return to Palestine to set up a government. All Palestinians longed for a state of their own, but Bassem, like many others, had reservations about the long-exiled PLO leadership. Rabin had once publicly justified doing a deal with a man he openly despised by observing that Arafat would control the Palestinians and "deal with them as they need to be dealt with, without … interference by *B'Tselem.*"

Bassem had already had his run-ins with some of the Fatah toughs within the territories, such as the threats he had received from the *shabiba* of Nablus. He also had been instrumental in a *B'Tselem* report issued early in 1994 on the subject of the killing by Palestinians of other Palestinians suspected of "collaborating" with Israel. Its findings were stark:

> Many hundreds of individuals were tortured and killed by Palestinians because they were said to be collaborating with the Israeli authorities. Those responsible included not only

the perpetrators themselves, but the Palestinian political organizations, with whom the perpetrators were identified, and on whose political, ideological and fiscal support they relied.... [M]ost of the attacks on suspected collaborators were carried out by cells closely connected with the various factions of the PLO.[7]

These findings were compounded by a further damning observation:

The broad definition placed on the term "collaborator" by Palestinian organizations and their activists and their *modus operandi* led to the killing of hundreds of Palestinians who did not operate in the service of the security authorities. Many were killed because their behavior was perceived as immoral or because they were considered "negative elements" in the society, or for other reasons. Some killings were carried out within the framework of internal disputes, or to settle personal rivalries, and were then portrayed as punishment for collaboration.[8]

Would Arafat and his well-armed crew tamp down this violence, wondered Bassem, or add to it? It was not long before his apprehensions were confirmed. Arafat created a variety of armed agencies of which the best known was the eerily-named Preventive Security Service (PSS) commanded by Jibril Rajoub, who had spent a long stretch in Israeli prison for tossing a hand grenade at some soldiers before joining Arafat in Tunis. Soon, Palestinians began to come to Bassem with stories of abuse at the hands of Rajoub's minions. "I started receiving telephone calls from people who had been arrested and tortured and then released," recalls Bassem. "Some of them were really afraid." Because there were so many such complaints, Bassem concluded that these were not isolated incidents, but "a phenomenon."

"Terrible as Israel's guidelines [for handling prisoners] are, at least they exist," Bassem told an interviewer at the time. "When Israel kept people for 18 days without a court ruling, the Palestinians went mad and filled the High Court. Now a detainee can go for 70 days or a hundred. It's a disaster."[9] He added, "It's like Syria or Iraq. We're still in the Arab mind-set, which has no idea of the meaning of the word democracy."

Bassem urged his superiors at *B'Tselem* to open an investigation into abuses by the new Palestinian National Authority, but they said that as an Israeli organization, it was their mission to criticize misdeeds by Israel, not by the nascent Palestinian government. So Bassem began to keep his own records. As these files thickened Bassem appealed to *B'Tselem* to reverse its policy and allow him to prepare an official report on the abuses. He collected sample testimonies, translated them into Hebrew, and distributed them to the members of the board which then voted to authorize the report. It was published in August 1995, and it cited cases of:

> extra-judicial punishment, abduction of residents, illegal arrests, prolonged detention without any judicial scrutiny, refusal to allow legal representation, refusal to allow regular family visits, and use of torture techniques such as beatings, painful tying-up, threats, humiliation, sleep deprivation, and withholding of medical treatment. The refusal of most of those who gave testimony to *B'Tselem,* and many others who have been interviewed by the media on these matters, to have their names published indicates that many West Bank residents refrain from publicly criticizing the PSS out of fear of a severe and violent reaction by the PSS.[10]

These were "not rare occurrences committed by a few individuals; they result from PA policy." This was proved, it said, not only by the volume of cases, but also by the fact that "despite repeated complaints about these acts, not one case exists in which the PA in Jericho took legal measures against any of those responsible."

Before making its report public, *B'Tselem* followed the same routine it used when criticizing the Israeli army: it sent the report to the Preventive Security Service for comment. A response arrived, signed by "Preventive Security Service Command/General Staff." It said: "All acts of the Preventive Security Service ... express the lofty moral behavior of the Palestinian people, its vanguard warrior force, the tolerance of the Service, and its humane and civilized values." In particular, "detainee[s] benefit ... from all human rights under international conventions" and "it is absolutely forbidden to mistreat detainees, torture them or harm their dignity in any way." The many Palestinians who claimed to have been mistreated were dismissed as "nonobjective sources," mostly "persons with criminal backgrounds, criminals, drug dealers, thieves, and perverts in the national and moral sense."[11]

The official response was less interesting than the unofficial one. Rajoub instructed Bassem's oldest brother, Hatem, who had become a Fatah activist and leader of the *intifada*, to convey a warning that Rajoub would denounce Bassem as a "collaborator" if the report were published. When it appeared, Rajoub made good on his threat, adding the fillip that Bassem was an "Israeli police agent." This all but put a bounty on Bassem's head. Human Rights Watch reported: "Many rights groups protested this remark as a malicious and unsubstantiated allegation that could endanger Eid's personal safety. The PA gave assurances that human rights groups were free to work in the self-rule areas, but did not formally retract the accusation."[12]

The target Rajoub painted on his back forced Bassem to alter his methods. Now, when he visited dangerous areas, he would take along a colleague, particularly Israeli or foreign journalists, whose presence as potential witnesses would deter attacks. But he did not back down. A month later another report of his was published. This one was not by *B'Tselem* but by *Reporters Sans Frontières*, the same French group for which he had traveled to Iraq. It detailed the forced closings of newspapers as well as arrests and beatings of reporters whose writings were irksome to Palestinian officials.

This brought him into direct conflict with his brother, Hatem, who worked in the Palestinian Ministry of Information in charge of overseeing newspapers. "He's the Palestinian Authority's censor," said Bassem at the time.[13] Hatem, for his part, told an interviewer: "I do support bringing him [Bassem] to court on grounds of defamation and untrue statements."[14] Worse, still, for brotherly relations, Hatem seemed to echo Rajoub's menacing accusation. B'Tselem, he charged, "is directly connected with the Israeli police and intelligence services."[15]

On almost the same day that his report on the absence of press freedom was issued, Bassem was asked by the family of 52-year-old Azzam Mosleh to investigate his death in the custody of the Preventive Security Service. Bassem would have taken the case anyway, but it was especially important to him since it exemplified the charges he had recently made against the PSS in the B'Tselem report.

Mosleh held American citizenship and owned a grocery store in Dallas that made him a rich man in Palestine. He had been escorted from a café in the village of Ein Yabroud, near Ramallah, by men who identified themselves as being from the PSS. At that time in the West Bank, the Palestinian Authority ruled only Jericho, so Rajoub's men had no legal standing in Ramallah. Nonetheless, they had already begun to operate all over the territory, their authority flowing from their weapons rather than any law. In this case, they did not arrest Mosleh, but rather asked him to accompany them to their station in Jericho to help investigate the theft of some jewelry from his sister. When he did not return, the family made inquiries that led nowhere. The next night his body was delivered by ambulance to the head of the Ein Yabroud village council who refused to take it, so it was dumped in front of his home. The family arranged burial, and someone from the village called Bassem, who came at once, also alerting the *Washington Post*.

Bassem and a correspondent were told by family members that Mosleh's "forehead was bruised blue, his lip was torn, blood had flowed from one ear, and there were what appeared to be burn marks on his right foot."[16] The *Post* reported, "Palestinian security officials, speaking on condition of anonymity," said "Mosleh was overcome by the 98-degree weather in Jericho and had a heart attack." A source who also "did not want to be identified" claimed that Mosleh was a "collaborator" with Israel. The family was frightened and reluctant to approve an autopsy. Mosleh's brother-in-law said that they "did not want further trouble with Preventive Security," adding "anybody can have a heart attack."[17] But Bassem made representations to the American consulate since Mosleh was a U.S. citizen, and the consulate demanded an autopsy. The body was exhumed after twenty-one days and taken to Israel for forensic examination, with a Palestinian medical examiner present, as was Bassem. The unanimous interpretation of the doctors was that the man had been badly beaten and died of internal bleeding.

In January 1996, the Palestinians held elections for a president and a legislative council. In a public statement, Bassem criticized Arafat for the failure of Palestinian TV to give coverage to other candidates. That same night, as Bassem arrived home in Shuafat about 11PM, a man got out of a parked car and approached him. He identified himself as Abu Fuad Jneidi, an officer of Force Seventeen, a security service tasked with protecting Arafat among other special duties. He asked if Bassem would accompany him to his office in Ramallah for "a cup of coffee." Bassem laughed and said: "I know of many people invited to drink coffee with you who never returned."

Jneidi acted offended, acknowledging Bassem's eminence and assuring him that he would be treated as a guest.

Bassem calculated that if he refused, this would be put into the rumor mill as proof he was a "collaborator," so he assented. Jneidi asked him to come in his car, but Bassem said he would follow in his own. They took a circuitous route to avoid Israeli checkpoints, since Jneidi would have been arrested. En route, Bassem called some journalists from *Reporters Sans Frontières* to tell them his situation. Apparently they started at once making calls on his behalf.

At the office in Ramallah, Jneidi asked a soldier to bring them some coffee. Then he made a phone call. Bassem heard him say, "He is in my office." When he hung up Bassem asked, "Is this going to take long?"

"Probably until tomorrow," Jneidi answered.

"Am I under arrest?" asked Bassem.

"No," insisted Jneidi, "please do not misunderstand us."

"So what am I?" asked Bassem.

"You are a guest."

"May I leave?" said Bassem, making as if to rise.

"No," said Jneidi placing his hand on Bassem's.

Bassem asked if he might call his wife to tell her he was not coming home that night. Jneidi denied the request, and Bassem started shouting. A soldier heard the commotion and entered, and listened to Bassem's indignation. Then the soldier pleaded Bassem's case to his commander. As Bassem reconstructs his words, he said: "You know when the Israelis killed my brother in Kibiya, near Ramallah. He is the one who came and investigated. Why you are doing this to him?" Jneidi relented and allowed Bassem the call. Bassem asked the soldier for a cigarette, and the man went out and brought him four packs, sharing Bassem's expectation that he might be held for a protracted time.

Bassem and the sympathetic soldier assigned to watch over him passed the night on cots in Jneidi's office. In the morning, the soldier got them some hummus and falafel for breakfast. "So it wasn't really a prison; it was a five star hotel," jokes Bassem. At noon they listened to a report about Bassem's disappearance on Israeli radio news. It quoted a Palestinian commander claiming to have scoured Palestinian detention facilities for Eid, and arguing that it must be the Israelis who were holding him. Bassem quipped to Jneidi: "I have been sitting here, and I did not see anyone come searching for Bassem Eid." With tongue-in-cheek bravado he recalls his kid-gloves treatment: "Twenty-five hours passed like this—telling jokes, laughing, drinking coffee, smoking, eating kebab. Even if they would release me, I would refuse." But when Ahmed Tibi, an Arab member of the Israeli Knesset who was also a close advisor to Arafat, appeared and ordered his release, he did not refuse to go, knowing full well what danger he was in. Direct appeals to Arafat by U.S. Secretary of State Warren Christopher and Israeli Prime Minister Shimon Peres and widespread news coverage had saved him.

For all his jocularity, Bassem did not forgive Arafat for this experience, strengthening his resolve to monitor abuses by the Palestinian authorities. But the leadership of *B'Tselem* was divided about whether the group should make itself a watchdog on Palestinian authorities, as well as Israeli. Those who placed human rights above ideology wanted to do so, but there was another group, led by veteran leftist politician Uri Avnery, that sympathized with the PLO and wanted *B'Tselem* to keep its guns trained on Israel. In July 1996, at a meeting of the *B'Tselem* board called to resolve the issue, Bassem announced his resignation.

He joined Al Haq, a Palestinian human rights group connected to the Popular Front for the Liberation of Palestine. But he became disillusioned almost at once. Al Haq used the issue of Israeli violations of human rights to advance the national cause, but it was little interested in violations by Palestinian officials. For example, rather than criticize barbarities committed against alleged "collaborators," Al Haq turned its attention on what it called "human rights violations" *by* collaborators.

So Bassem created his own organization. "I feel I must protect my nation from any kind of authority, even its own authority," he said. "I want the Palestinians to build a democratic state, not just extend their authority."[18] He began from his home, writing letters seeking support. After a few months he secured his first grant—$15,000 from a Norwegian organization. It was enough to hire a hall in East Jerusalem's Ambassador Hotel, cookies included, for a press conference in December 1996, announcing the launch of the Palestinian Human Rights Monitoring Group.

Bassem rented a small office and hired two assistants, and the PHRMG set about doing what such groups do: collecting and assembling reliable data on abuses; publishing a stream of reports on specific issues (torture, deaths in custody, forced newspaper closings, persecution of Christians, violations of academic freedom, "honor killings," etc.), as well as an annual report with a comprehensive overview. The PHRMG focused primarily on Palestinian authorities, but it also kept a critical eye on Israel's actions, publishing reports on home demolitions, detention of Palestinian prisoners, violence by Israeli settlers against Palestinians, and the like.

Its first comprehensive report was issued in May 1997, six months after its founding. Its description of "torture on a large scale" and "norms of illegal behavior" by the Palestinian Authority "def[ied] a taboo," in the words of the *Washington Post*.[19] "In a political culture that has silenced many critics, the boldness of the organizers, who called a news conference at an Arab-owned hotel in East Jerusalem, stood out as much as their measured and critical report," said the paper. The *Post* also noted that no mention of the PHRMG appeared in the Palestinian media, supplying an anecdote from Bassem's press conference: "Eid, spotting a reporter from the *Al-Quds* daily [in whose pages Bassem had once exposed Israeli misdeeds on a weekly basis] ... laughed and asked why he had bothered to attend. The reporter said he had hoped that Eid's report would mention Israeli abuses, which he could publish." For much of the work of compiling data and organizing reports, Bassem relied on assistants. The largest share of his time continued to be devoted to investigating cases, at which he was nonpareil. His cell phone number remained the equivalent of 911 for Palestinians abused by the authorities.

In addition, he returned to the file of complaints of abuses by Palestinian officials that his superiors at *B'Tselem* had not allowed him to investigate. One was the case of Farouk Abu-Hassan, who had been arrested within months of the arrival of Arafat in Gaza and accused of being a collaborator. Soon after the creation of PHRMG, Bassem traveled to Gaza to meet his family.

Abu-Hassan had been a militant in the radical Popular Front for the Liberation of Palestine. In 1973, he had been arrested by Israeli authorities and sentenced to thirteen years. During his term, his thinking evolved. When President Anwar Sadat made his historic visit to Jerusalem in 1977 to bring to an end the state of war between Egypt and Israel, Arafat and other Palestinian leaders condemned him and supported the Arab League's decision to expel Egypt. But Abu-Hassan dissented. From the Ashkelon prison, he and several fellow inmates sent a letter to Sadat, "supporting and saluting" his initiative. Desperate for Palestinian support, Sadat read it aloud to the Egyptian People's Assembly. As a result of their stand, Abu-Hassan and his co-signers reported in a follow-up letter to Sadat, "we suffered a lot inside the detention prison, and we were accused of all kinds of charges," by other inmates. Despite this, they formed the Palestinian National Movement for Peace. "Our movement refuses wars and violence, and ... acts against them," they declared, endorsing instead "the method of negotiation and discussion," and adding that "a comprehensive peace in the region will put an end to the conflict between the two peoples." All of this was sharply at odds with Arafat's stance at the time.

The PLO in Tunis kept track of such apostasy, and once it set up its administration in Gaza, it settled scores with Abu-Hassan, notwithstanding that its own declared policy was now no different from what he had proclaimed in his prison manifesto. The entire basis of the charge of collaboration was his letter to Sadat. The evidence shown to Abu-Hassan by his interrogators was a clipping from an Egyptian magazine, reprinting it.

In 1997, when Bassem investigated the case, Abu-Hassan had already been held for nearly three years by the Palestinian military intelligence service in Gaza which was then headed by Musa Arafat, a cousin of Yasser's, and a man who grew notorious among Palestinians for his corruption. Bassem hired a lawyer to appeal to the Palestinian high court which six months later issued an order for Abu-Hassan's release. When Bassem received the news, he was jubilant. He asked the lawyer to bring the decision at once to military intelligence headquarters.

The lawyer was shown into Musa Arafat's office and explained why he had come. Arafat asked to see the court's decree, took out his pen and made a large X across the document. He handed it back to the lawyer, saying, "If you come here again on this matter, I'll put you next to Abu-Hassan." Despite the legal judgment, Abu-Hassan was not released for another nine years. This was six months after Musa Arafat got his just deserts, pulled from his home and killed by a caravan of eighty armed men who overwhelmed his bodyguards. So hated had he become among his own people that Israeli analysts could not agree whether the perpetrators were Hamas members, Fatah rivals, or competing racketeers.

Although the problem of corruption was not central to the PHRMG's agenda, sometimes it directly touched human rights issues. In 1998 Bassem received calls from some businessmen in Hebron complaining about extortion by the Preventive Security Services. Apparently the PSS was routinely arresting businessmen, accusing them of tax evasion, some-times torturing them or holding them for extensive durations, and releasing them only upon the payment of large sums of money. Whether these sums were putatively overdue taxes or fines, they went directly to the PSS rather than to tax authori-ties. Bassem collected 36 affidavits from victims as well as receipts that the PSS had issued to some of them. In addition to issuing a report, he shared the documents with the new human rights committee of the legislative council.

That night or one soon after, Bassem received a call from Ramzi Khoury, one of Arafat's advisors, who said that the president wanted to see him right away. It was around 11PM, and Bassem asked: "Right now? He can't wait until tomor-row?" Khoury persisted, and Bassem closed the matter. "Tell the president I am not interested," he said. A few moments later, the phone rang again. This time it was his brother, Hatem. You can't refuse to see the president of Palestine, he said, pointing out that Arafat could provide PHRMG with financial support. Bassem reminded him that in 1990 when Arafat made his first appearance before the UN Security Council, he bolstered his complaints against Israel by citing *B'Tselem*. Bassem ended the conversation: "I worked for *B'T-selem* eight years documenting Israeli violations. And you remember the prize that Arafat gave me? He arrested me for 25 hours. That is the award that I received. I do not want to talk to him."

Bassem's attitude towards Arafat was not only a matter of personal pique. He was determined to keep his distance from the PA because he believed that human rights organiza-tions must be independent. In an article that year he criti-cized other groups on this point:

> Three years after the arrival of the PA, our human rights com-munity has been transformed from brave leaders in the strug-gle against the Occupation into a group which is much more

sympathetic to the local authorities, if they are Palestinian. . . .
To date, twelve Palestinians have died in the hands of the PA.
Is it less patriotic to denounce their murderers? . . .

Three explanations for the current situation have been
presented: the Palestinians mustn't "air dirty laundry in public"; Arafat and the PA must be given time to establish themselves amid difficult political conditions; and there is genuine
(and well-based) fear of what the new regime will do to its
critics. . . .

Most political organizations in Palestine have a history
of supporting human rights only when it serves their purposes
. . . . [i]n particular when supporting human rights is part of
the struggle for national liberation.[20]

This stance was wrong, said Bassem, "because national
liberation without freedom and democracy is a hollow
prize. . . . Human rights and democracy are not incidental . . . .
They are a central part of the struggle . . . ignored at our own
risk."

Bassem received his rejoinder not from the other Palestinian organizations, but from his old nemesis on the board of
B'Tselem Uri Avnery. Within *B'Tselem* Avnery had opposed
criticizing abuses by Palestinians on the ground that this task
belonged to the Palestinians themselves. Now, however, he
objected to criticisms of Arafat's regime even by Palestinians.
Their president, he insisted, must be treated as above
reproach. Why? Because Arafat "needs massive support from
international public opinion and the enlightened Israeli public," in order to establish a Palestinian state. "Whoever
destroys his standing in the international arena is pulling the
carpet from under the feet of the Palestinian cause."[21]

Therefore, concluded Avnery in a thinly veiled reference
to Bassem, Palestinians who reveal abuses by Arafat and his
team are "the new collaborators." This echoed Rajoub's
charge and thus helped to set Bassem up for assassination.

Anyone wanting to do the deed could rationalize that even Israelis say he is a collaborator.

Bassem responded with remarkable restraint:

> If Avnery had a single example of unprofessional work, or false charges raised by a significant human right outfit, he would have presented it with relish.... [H]e knows all too well, that the difficult and often shocking facts we present are indeed an accurate reflection of reality under the PNA [Palestinian National Authority]. The difference between us is that Avnery feels that these facts should be hidden, whereas we argue that the reality of them must be vigorously fought. Avnery feels Arafat's pain, and is saddened because we do not allow political interests to divert the attention of the Palestinian people from what is happening on the ground.... [His] blind support for Arafat—at the expense of the many Palestinian victims of torture and unjust imprisonment—does not do much for the Palestinian people.[22]

The running battle between Bassem and the authorities continued into the next year. Bassem denounced a new tactic they employed:

> The PNA attempted to establish new human rights organizations with a view to replacing the old effective ones that had been critical of PNA violations. The new powerful organizations supported by the authority began criticizing genuine human rights organizations that were working efficiently in order to establish a democratic civil society. This situation resulted in the undermining of actual work in the field.[23]

He also chastised Israel and the United States for abetting abuses by the Palestinian authorities, on the theory that they needed a free hand to prevent radicals from subverting the peace process. "When President Arafat decided to establish the State Security Court in April 1995 by Presidential decree, Israel and the United States not only gave their blessing to its establishment but also supported the illegal way in which it has functioned since 1995," he wrote. He had made a similar complaint in his report on Palestinian abuses for *B'Tselem,* charging that Israeli officials had given explicit assurances to Arafat that they would countenance whatever measures he used to fulfill his obligation to protect Israelis from violence by Palestinian radicals.

Nonetheless, the authorities had little success in blunting Bassem's work. In 1999 he received a call from the father of a 35-year-old Gazan accused of rape by an Arab woman in the Israeli Arab town of Tira, where he worked. When Israeli authorities exonerated him based on DNA, the complainant took her accusation to the Gazan police who arrested him.

Bassem traveled to Nazareth, the site of the Israeli court, and copied the files containing the DNA evidence. He then held a press conference denouncing the Gazan police for holding a man who already had been exculpated. That evening, Bassem received a request from the Palestinian police chief, Ghazi Jabali, who was based in Gaza, to bring him the evidence.

> Bassem recalls the scene as he entered Jabali's office:
> He extended his hand to me; I extended mine to him. He kissed me; I kissed him. Then we sat. I said that the prisoner has been tortured. And he said, "Do you have evidence?" I said, "If you will show me the prisoner, I will show you the evidence."

Jabali led Bassem to an infirmary within the police headquarters where the accused lay, surrounded by his family whose members had told Bassem two days earlier that they had not been allowed to see him. Bassem approached one of the elder family members and asked how many times he had visited, and the man responded, "Only today." Then Jabali asked the prisoner to stand and shake Bassem's hand. The man had trouble standing, and once he stood, Bassem asked him to raise his gown. The man's body was covered with injuries.

Bassem looked at Jabali accusingly, and Jabali said that the prisoner would be released. "Please accept his release as our gift to you," he told Bassem, and Bassem replied, "I am not seeking gifts; I'm seeking justice." Jabali turned to one of his deputies and instructed him to take Bassem to lunch and then to drive him back to the Erez crossing. The accused rapist was released that day.

In September 2000, the second, or "Al Aqsa" *intifada* created a new context for Bassem's work. Initially Bassem's criticisms targeted the Israelis. "What has pushed the Palestinians toward violence is frustration," he told an American reporter. "The Israelis are still bulldozing Palestinian homes, still building settlements, still killing Palestinians."[24] One week into the new broils, the PHRMG issued a report on child fatalities among the Palestinians, detailing four cases and listing the names and ages of eleven other youngsters who had perished.[25] Another PHRMG statement protested Israel's closing of the Gaza airport, and demanded, at a minimum, landing rights for planes carrying medical assistance.[26]

In December, the PHRMG issued a 50-page report on the uprising, harshly critical of Israeli actions. Its key accusation was that: "Israeli soldiers have used excessive force to quell the demonstrations.... Lethal weapons have been used as a matter of routine even if the lives of Israeli soldiers were hardly at risk, and other—non-lethal—weapons could have achieved the same objective." In addition, it said: "Israeli settlers in the Palestinian territories have conducted numerous attacks on Palestinian property and civilians to which the Israeli security forces have responded with extraordinary leniency."[27]

Even while faulting the Israelis, Bassem tried to maintain his objectivity. For example, he blamed part of the violence on intra-Palestinian rivalries, telling a western reporter: "According to the street, there is a kind of revolt against Mr. Arafat from his own movement. [Marwan] Barghouti is challenging the Palestinian Authority. I think it is dangerous."[28] In addition to attacking the Israeli press for its lack of objectivity, he accused Palestinian news organizations of spreading "disinformation,"[29] and he was particularly tough on other Palestinian human rights groups that he thought were exploiting the events. He wrote:

> Since the eruption of the Al-Aqsa Uprising, these organizations have become press offices, issuing at times inaccurate reports at such rapid speed that international press agencies have lost trust in them.
>
> Are these organizations really serving the cause of human rights, or are they trying to gain publicity at the expense of human rights? Do we, as Palestinians, really need to exaggerate matters at this time when the Palestinian people are bleeding? The facts speak for themselves. The Palestinians are victims; overstatements and inaccurate reporting will only damage our credibility.[30]

As the violence dragged on, growing only more intense, Bassem grew increasingly critical of the Palestinian side. In February, he publicly called upon Arafat to "shift the focus of the uprising from armed resistance to unarmed, civil protest.... The future of the entire region will be determined not by the intifada but by the peace process," he added.[31] Over the next years he repeated this appeal. "The violent path chosen by the Palestinians in the al-Aqsa intifada has failed," he warned.[32]

His words fell on deaf ears, and the next years, his criticisms grew more acerbic. In a 2003 newspaper essay he went after his old nemesis, Arafat:

> The Palestinian president is still talking about shaheeds and he encouraged children to become martyrs by telling them

that one shaheed on earth is considered by God as great as 40 shaheeds in heaven. (This statement has not yet been condemned by any organizations for the protection of children.)

It seems Arafat is still encouraging Palestinians to victimize themselves, an attitude that is without logic or ethics. Instead of talking about peace and life, instead of supporting coexistence, instead of fulfilling the consciousness of human beings, Arafat is calling for death. It appears the nearly 2,500 Palestinians and more than 700 Israelis who were killed during this intifada are not enough to fulfill Arafat's political interests.[33]

A 2004 PHRMG report decried what it called "The Chaos of the Weapons" within the Palestinian territories.[34] And in a newspaper essay, Bassem angrily cited chapter and verse of Palestinian violence against Palestinians, which he had earlier dubbed the "Intra'fada." For example, he charged, "Nablus is ruled by two armed illiterate thugs. These two people are feared by the populations and control the civil life of the city." As for the Palestinian Authority, he scoffed, "There is someone called an interior minister, who has lost his function, mission, and jurisdiction." He offered a radical solution: "I recommend that the Palestinian government call upon the governments of Jordan, Egypt and perhaps Turkey [to] send ... their security forces to restore order in the Palestinian territories and to put an end to attacks against Palestinian citizens."[35]

Yet he knew that none of his proposals, radical or otherwise, was likely to be considered. He told an interviewer: "Arafat is the obstacle to any reforms within Palestinian society."[36]

Bassem had plenty of firsthand experience with the "chaos of the weapons," a state of affairs that outlasted Arafat. In 2006, Amnesty International asked him to observe a trial in Jericho, the West Bank's quietest city. Six brothers were accused of gunning down two members of Fatah who had murdered their father before their eyes years earlier when they were children, accusing him of being a "collaborator." No lawyer, says Bassem, had the courage to defend them. He attended several sessions that he says were packed with Fatah members. Upon adjournment one day, the Fatah members emerged from the court and opened fire on members of the defendants' family. Bassem fled. "In such circumstances, I disappear," he says. "I don't want to die." The six were convicted, and some months later, Fatah inmates got out of their cells in the same Palestinian prison where four of the brothers were serving their sentences and killed them. The other two survived because they were incarcerated elsewhere.

The long years of the second *intifada,* followed by the "intra'fada" and the Hamas seizure of Gaza, filled Bassem with discouragement. A Palestinian state, as he sees it, is "not close." Indeed, he believes "I'm probably not going to live to see it. The coming generation is going to have to work harder than we did to achieve it." He speaks of the millions of dollars poured into Palestine and asks ruefully, "What have we achieved?" Continuing his lament, he says:

> In the past 40 years the Palestinians always laid on others [the burden] of helping them, and they did not help themselves. Without helping yourself, others cannot really help. From '67 until today, so many changes have happened in the world. But in the Palestinian case, we are moving backward rather than forward.

Although he condemned Israel for not coordinating its withdrawal from Gaza with Palestinian leaders, he is unsparing in his criticism of what followed: "The conditions prevailing in Gaza after the Israeli withdrawal further indicate the Palestinian inability to achieve self-governance. Not a single greenhouse has been constructed—and we've destroyed those Israel left behind."[37]

He added, "Violence, it seems, has become endemic to the Palestinian mind-set and political culture.... Palestinian society suffers ... from an ethical chaos that no one dares address."[38]

He fears, too, that the "civil war" of Palestinian against Palestinian has not yet played itself out.

His disappointments in Palestine and his observations of events in Iraq have impelled him to probe for deeper causes. "It looks like it is very hard to build democracy in the Arab region," he says. One reason is that "in our culture there is no self-criticism," rather, "people feel so happy when you criticize 'the other.'"

Nor does he harbor much hope for a resolution of the conflict with Israel in the short run. "A permanent solution will be very difficult to reach in this period," he says. "The bridge of trust between the two sides has almost collapsed." He looks instead to interim measures that would improve the daily lives of Palestinians, improving economic conditions and "allowing people to breathe." He argues that numerous Israeli checkpoints could be removed without compromising Israel's security. "Why does Nablus have to be isolated from Tulkarm?" he asks. Nonetheless, he would not welcome unilateral Israeli withdrawal from the West Bank, as was done from Gaza, for fear that an all-out war between Hamas and Fatah would ensue.

A silver lining to the cloud of the last decade's disappointments is the healing of the breach between Bassem and his brother Hatem. Hatem had won a seat in the first Palestinian National Council (PNC) in 1996, losing it in 2006, when Hamas swept out Fatah. Growing into his responsibilities as a member of the PNC's human rights committee, he had parted ways with Arafat. In one street confrontation he was left beaten so badly by Palestinian security personnel that it fell to the Israelis to transport him to Augusta Victoria hospital in East Jerusalem, where he spent a week.[39]

Hatem has come to sound more like Bassem. "We need a civic community, not a military community," he says. "Democracy is democracy, and human rights are human rights. It's not important if you are Fatah or Hamas, Jewish or Palestinian. Blood is the same color for all people." Hatem speaks with admiration of Bassem's work, adding: "He is my brother."

Despite his pessimism, Bassem still dreams of peace and democracy—and still labors for them. The peace he envisions is not the chilly one that exists between Egypt and Israel, but something friendlier. While some speak of a possible confederation of Palestine and Jordan, Bassem says he would prefer one with Israel. "What can we Palestinians benefit from the Jordanians?" he asks. "We can benefit enormously from the Israelis." Better yet, and of course more unlikely, he would like to see a confederation of four peoples: Palestinians, Israelis, Jordanians, and Egyptians.

Of his twin goals, Bassem puts first emphasis on democracy. "Democracy will bring peace; but peace does not bring democracy," he notes, citing Egypt's continued authoritarianism thirty years after the Camp David agreements.

What does he mean by democracy? He has a model:

> The Israelis never practiced democracy on us, but they practice it among themselves, and this is how we learned. We would like to see the Palestinian parliament like the Israeli Knesset—everybody is shouting and everybody is suggesting laws.

Interestingly, Hatem makes the same point, notwithstanding his five terms in Israeli prisons. "We need democracy, and we have been learning our democracy from the Israelis," he says. "We need the same model to build our state."

During the twenty-odd years that Bassem has devoted to combating human rights abuses, some aspects of his life have changed and some have not. He divorced, and his wife moved back to her own family with their four children, whom he sees regularly. Once they left, Bassem moved out of his parents' home for the first time in his life. He found a quiet place in Jericho, the most peaceful of Palestinian towns, from which it is a short commute to the PHRMG office in East Jerusalem, barring hassles at checkpoints. He still visits his parents and brothers and nephews and nieces at the family home in Shuafat often, greeting his father, Mohammed, with the traditional gesture of respect, kissing his hand, touching it to his forehead, and kissing it again.

Despite his pessimism, should Bassem's vision of a democratic Palestine be realized before he becomes too old, what of his own future? Does he see himself as a leader of this new nation? No, he'll leave politics to Hatem. As for himself, his role would remain the same. "The world is full of politicians," he notes with a hint of disdain. "But there is a lack of human rights activists. This is what I do."

The Feminist

Kuwait: Rola Dashti

In 2007, the year after women won the vote and the right to run for office in Kuwait, Islamist MP Ahmad Baqer went on Kuwaiti television and swore, "No woman will be elected in Kuwait in 50 years time."[1] Most viewers recognized that he was whistling past the graveyard where male exclusivity in government will soon be buried. Its terminal state was largely the doing of Rola Dashti, a forty-something American-trained economist of mixed Kuwaiti and Lebanese blood, who had pressured and outmaneuvered the entire male establishment in forcing open the doors to politics.

Rola had trampled in male domains her whole life. Throughout her school-age years, she had lived in East Beirut in an apartment building where the children near to her in age were mostly boys, which suited Rola fine. She could more than hold her own at the various games and sports, especially soccer, that she played with her older brother, Saleh, and the others. Rola's boyish play sometimes brought boyish results. When she was four or five she challenged Saleh to a race in which each child perched atop a watermelon and tried to propel it forward. Rola fell off and broke her arm. And she broke it again a few years later, "trying to make her bike jump, like a boy," recalls her mother, Helal, laughing in retrospect although she was horrified at the time.[2] Rola, needless to say, had been unfazed.

In addition to physical games, Rola loved cerebral challenges. Saleh learned chess at school, and Rola figured out the rules by watching him play against his classmates. She also liked cards and the region's ubiquitous board game, backgammon. Her grandfather played that a lot, and Rola liked to tag along and tell him which of his moves she thought were wrong.

Rola made her mark in school, too, regularly receiving the highest grades although she was a year younger than her classmates. Helal recalls that she made a practice of helping Saleh with his homework. But Rola never needed the help or the encouragement to study. Sometimes, to Helal's delight, other adults took note of little Rola's precocity, and she never forgot when a respected Egyptian visitor remarked, "Someday that girl will be something."

Helal had more than the usual reasons to take pride in her impressive daughter. Helal had grown up in Kuwaiti society where females were subordinate, and she had experienced the consequences of this in a deeply personal way. At 15 she had married the 30-year-old Abdullah Ali Dashti, her father's business acquaintance, and within a year bore him Saleh. Out about town some months later, her belly swelling again, this time with Rola, she stopped unexpectedly at Abdullah's office and was surprised to see a little boy bouncing around and calling Abdullah, "daddy." Her husband confessed that when they married he already had another wife, in fact two of them, living across town. Devastated, Helal wanted to leave Abdullah, but her grandfather decreed, "Our family does not divorce." Dutifully, she returned to Abdullah, although her heart was now empty of him, and she filled it instead with her children, taking them back to her native Lebanon after a few years while Abdullah remained in Kuwait, although they visited periodically.

A third child, Jamal, was born in 1970 when Rola was 6, but if this signified some kind of reconciliation between Helal and Abdullah, it was short-lived. A few years later, she divorced him. There was no new development that led her to that decision, just the growing realization as she matured that she could defy her grandfather's insistence that she tolerate Abdullah's polygamy.

It was, however, of paramount importance to her that the divorce be friendly. By Muslim law, the children belong to the father. So she appealed to him to let her raise them: "I told him, 'If the kids turn out good, it will be good for both of us;

and if they turn out bad, they will be bad for both of us—
whether we are married or divorced.'" He assented. He had
by then not two but three other wives and eventually twenty
other children to absorb his attention, not to mention that he
remained active as a businessman and also became a member of parliament.

Beirut, however, was becoming an increasingly dicey
place to raise children. For thirty years, beginning in 1945,
Lebanon had been home to the Arab world's only successful
experience of democratic rule. It was an odd form of democracy, to be sure, based on a fixed allocation of offices to each
ethnic faction. By agreement, the president was a Maronite
Catholic; the prime minister, a Sunni; and the speaker of the
parliament, a Shiite. Lesser posts were allotted to the Druse,
the Greek Orthodox, and other sects. It was further agreed
that no new census would be taken lest it discredit the
arrangement by revealing that the country's true demograph-
ics contradicted its implicit hierarchy. But this "consocia-
tional" system worked to make the country an oasis of peace
and prosperity in poor and tumultuous surroundings.

But in 1975, the Lebanese system collapsed under the
weight of foreign forces. The Palestine Liberation Organization,
which had been expelled from Jordan after trying to take over
that country, had found refuge in Lebanon and then began to
treat parts of the country as a fiefdom. Civil war erupted,
largely on sectarian lines, and Lebanon's two mightier neighbors, Syria and then Israel, embroiled themselves in its politics.

The gunfire of urban warfare forced families to remain
indoors. Rola, who was 11 when the war began, recalls having to run to the basement in response to the bombardment
and having to make do with sandwiches of bread, butter, and
sugar, when other provisions ran out and it was too dangerous to shop.

Rola's school was located downtown, an area mostly
destroyed by the combat. Traveling there, or to many other

places, grew treacherous, as the so-called "green line," dividing the predominantly Christian east from the predominantly Muslim west, hardened, patrolled by trigger-happy militias on both sides. Fortunately, the militiamen were not after children, and they themselves were mostly locals who knew or came to know the families that were moving about in their neighborhoods. But when the fighting intensified, it grew perilous to be a Muslim family living on the Christian side. Rola explains:

> We had our [Christian] friends and some of them had relationships with the militias, so if there was an attack, we were protected. The danger was not that someone would come to our house and kill us. The danger was when we were crossing roads and sections, then the protection was lost, because [our friends] could not tell every single militiaman, "Do not kill these people."[3]

The fighting ebbed and flowed, and during intense periods, Helal tried to get the children away from it. For several months, they moved in with her parents on the Muslim side of town. At another hot moment, they all joined Abdullah in Shiraz, Iran, where he had business. They stayed six months, and even made preparations to enroll in school. But then the fighting subsided, and, as during other lulls, Helal gathered her children and returned home.

With the adults around them killing and increasingly hating one another, did Rola and her friends imitate their elders and take sides along sectarian lines? Not as far as she can remember. "The only thing you really think," she says, "is that you want to see peace so you can go out and play." The strains she remembers were not inter-communal but intergenerational. To the adolescents on both sides, the restrictions their parents placed on them amidst the gunfire were "overprotective," and they collaborated in evading them whenever possible.

In school, Rola seemed to have two sides. On the one hand she was competitive and ambitious. Helal recalls once going to Rola's room and finding her sobbing and tearing her hair. When she asked what was wrong, Rola replied, "I only got the second highest grade." But Rola also prized her friends and sometimes sacrificed her standing with teachers on their behalf.

Once, when Rola's desk was next to the teacher's, she caught sight of the upcoming Arabic language exam, and she quickly copied it. She then shared it not only with her two closest girlfriends but the rest of the class, as well. Unfortunately for Rola, one girl was too lazy to memorize the answers and instead wrote them out on a scrap of paper that the teacher noticed. The ensuing inquisition traced back to Rola. Not only was she punished by being denied recess for a week, but the teacher thereafter referred to Rola as "the thief."

This wounded Rola, and she convinced herself that she was innocent. It was not her fault that the teacher had left the exam in view. "I did not know that my eyes should not look at it," she recalls thinking, her self-righteousness fueled by the grandness of having surmounted her competitive instincts. "I'm not a thief," she reasoned. "I'm a good person who found something good and shared it with everybody."

"That word [thief] triggered me to become a social activist," says Rola. By "social activist" Rola does not mean that she took an interest in political affairs. That was to come later. Rather, she carved out a distinct role for herself for the balance of her junior high and high school years. She became what another teacher called, "the class lawyer," taking it on herself to argue the case of any classmate who received a low grade or was accused of misbehavior.

At sixteen, Rola entered the American University of Beirut. She and everyone around her had assumed that, smart as she was, she was destined to become a physician. On days when she had chemistry class in high school, she sometimes came home wearing her white lab coat, and the members of her family would say, "Here comes the doctor."

When she reached college, however, she had second thoughts. She had a penchant for math and also for language, but not for the hard science courses that constituted the pre-med curriculum. Also, admission to medical school was extremely competitive. Usually Rola thrived on competition, but making the heady leap from high school to college, she had other things on her mind. "I wanted to enjoy life," she recalls. "I thought freshman year comes just once, and it's supposed to be a fun year." So Rola sought a less taxing major.

Under the system at AUB, she had until the end of freshman year to reach a decision, but the answer did not come to her. Hanging out in the familiar manner of college students, she responded to inquiries about her major with "cafeteriology." As freshman year neared its end, this quip no longer would suffice. Several of her friends had decided to major in agriculture, which had the attraction of spending one year away from campus, doing field training in the Bekaa valley. Then came a fortuitous event:

> A movie about Africa was playing on campus where I saw poverty and people in need of help, and I thought, "This is good. Why not do agriculture and travel to Africa and help the people of Africa?" I was going to be a doctor to help people; I can do the same in agriculture.

There were also less grandiose reasons: "The fun part was that I was going to live for a year in the Bekaa area, and my friends were going. That was cool."

Rola's new major was received by her family without enthusiasm. When she went to Kuwait to visit her father and step-siblings, she recalls they made fun of her. "We have an agriculture person," she recalls them taunting. "We give him a hundred dollars and he takes care of the garden. Is that what you are going to do?"

This all became moot, however. In 1982, just at the conclusion of Rola's first year of agriculture studies, Israel invaded Lebanon to dislodge the PLO. As Israeli forces pushed up into Lebanon from the south, many thousands of Lebanese fled to Beirut. Here was a challenge that fit Rola's budding idealism. Final exams were canceled, and Rola, together with other students, threw herself into finding shelter and food for displaced people, recruiting blood donors, and undertaking other emergency tasks. As the front lines moved closer to Beirut, and as Rola's activities took her closer to the fighting, Helal's anxiety mounted. She determined that they would leave Lebanon.

This was no easy task, since the fighting had closed the airport and severed Beirut's other transportation links. However, Helal learned that boats were able to depart from the northern city of Junieh, a Christian stronghold. Through her Christian friends she managed to secure tickets to Cyprus. Seats were hard to come by, so she had gotten a ticket for Rola on the first available boat, and others for herself and the two boys on a later voyage. She was in a rush to get Rola out of harm's way.

Rola was reluctant to leave her humanitarian work, but she was 18, and some of the other interests natural to her age melted her resistance to Helal's plan. "They said that I would be going by boat," recalls Rola, who had never traveled by sea before. "I used to watch a lot of the program, *Love Boat*. I thought this would be a cruise like that, and I liked the idea."

She was in for a rude awakening. The vessel was a cargo ship, filled with sheep and other goods. The berths were sleeping bags on the floor, but there was limited floor space, so it was given to the children and elderly. Once out to sea, the ship was surrounded by Israeli gun boats. "Everybody was scared to death," Rola recalls. "A friend standing next to me said, 'It would take only a minute for them to hit us with fifty missiles.' And I said, 'A minute? It would take only five seconds.'"

The Israelis did not fire. The boat had sailed with their permission, but apparently the captain's radio was defective, and he had failed to respond to communications from the Israeli boats, arousing their suspicions. Perhaps waiting for the matter to be clarified, or perhaps as punishment, the Israelis held Rola's "love boat" for ten hours, prolonging the uncomfortable journey. But Rola made it to Cyprus and was followed by her mother and brothers, whence they proceeded to Kuwait.

There, plans were made for Saleh and Rola to continue their educations in the West. The royal family of Kuwait, like that of Saudi Arabia, uses the country's large oil revenues to provide a vast array of benefits to citizens. Because she was a good student, the ministry was prepared to underwrite the cost of Rola's study abroad. Rola told the counselor at the ministry that she wanted to find a school in America. When asked where in America, Rola responded with the two places she knew from TV. "California or Texas," she said. She was confounded when the counselor asked her *where* within those two states she had in mind. She had imagined these were discreet places. Having lived only in two small countries, she could not picture that Lebanon could fit into California fifteen times over, as could Kuwait into Texas.

The confusion was resolved when Saleh found the program he wanted at California State University at Chico. This settled the issue because Helal's fierce maternalism came into play. She was not going to have her children scattered hither and yon. If Saleh was going to Chico, then Rola should go to Chico, and she and twelve-year-old Jamal would go, too. Jamal would enroll in American schools, and Helal would keep house for her brood.

Settling into Chico naturally brought its share of culture shock. When Rola and Saleh went to a furniture store to outfit the unfurnished house they had rented they persisted in trying to negotiate over the prices until they were asked to leave. When Rola went to open an account at a local bank and pulled a wad of six-thousand dollars from her pocket that her father had given her, the female bank officer deposited the money but would allow Rola to have only one-hundred back as a withdrawal. Rola was indignant, but the woman was merely being protective after Rola told her that she had been keeping the cash in her pocket. There were surprises of a more pleasant kind, too. They found they could get water and electricity turned on without having personal connections, and that the utilities were willing to bill them and trust they would pay.

Still, Rola was homesick and a bit hostile, too. She ached for Beirut, which had suffered such a fierce pounding by Israeli bombs supplied by the United States. For the first five months of her stay, she refused to adjust her watch, keeping it set to Beirut time. And, unlike Saleh who quickly melded into his surroundings, she found her friends among fellow Arabs or other foreign students, not mingling much with Americans. But eventually, Rola lowered her guard and found more things to like about America.

One was that "you are treated as an individual and not an extension of a family." She liked the American way of calling people by first names, a habit she acquired. What pleased her was not the informality, but the contrast with the information that people inevitably seek to tease out of a name in the Arab world. This includes, as she puts it:

> where the person comes from and sometimes the family's economic status. Then you can decide to associate or network. If so, you ask 300 questions until you find some tie, like a cousin of a cousin married to his brother, or the sort. In the U.S., you just say "Hi, how are you?" and you move on. You judge a person by the person's identity and character. Who was the ancestor of his father's ancestors is irrelevant.

Other things that appealed to her were encapsuled by an experience when she went to take a summer course at Washington State University in Pullman. At its end, she had a ticket for a flight back to Chico, but she was fascinated by a bulletin board where students posted notices for sharing rides. She saw one for a place in a car headed to San Francisco and figured that she could be dropped off at Chico on the way. She calculated that the ride would get her home ahead of the flight she was supposed to take, so she could keep her adventure from Helal. "I thought that if I told my mother she would freak out and convince me not to do it."

She loved the ride, the conversation with the other students, the stops at McDonald's along the way. Her only anxious moment came when she was told it was her turn to take the wheel. This was part of the purpose of the ride-share, but it had not occurred to her. She had no license and did not know how to drive. The others were forgiving and picked up her slack.

When Rola walked into the house, it was Helal who was surprised. She had called the airport and learned that Rola's flight was canceled. Confronted, Rola confessed her alternative transport, and, sure enough, Helal freaked out: "You could have been killed. They could have kidnapped you. Why didn't you tell me?"

Despite Helal's anguish, Rola cherished the experience and what it represented to her: "independence—the freedom to take decisions and learn from your mistakes." She embraced the American idea of privacy and personal "space." This term, she says, is

missing from our dictionary. Your problem is everybody else's problem. Your concern is everybody else's concern, [including] internal matters that others do not have to know. There is no line on space and privacy and independence. To us, you will be protected maybe until you get married and maybe until you have a child.

The problem, as Rola sees it, is not only that extremely tight family bonds can be stifling, but also that they act as a brake on political change. "Our opinions always have an extension," she puts it, "how it will impact someone else: my father, my uncle, my family." Thus, a dissident, contemplating defying the authorities, must calculate not only what price he or she may pay but also what retaliation may be taken against the extended family.

She also was making discoveries on the academic side. To her horror, she found that the college had listed her as an economics major and had assigned her to some classes accordingly. But since she knew that her agriculture major required a couple of courses in economics, she swallowed her anger and decided to get basic micro and macro courses out of the way and to straighten out her major later. Amazingly she "fell in love with economics."

She switched to a double major, agriculture and economics. Although this meant she had to take extra courses, nonetheless she graduated after three semesters, taking as many as 30 credits in one. The college would not allow a student to register for that many, but Rola took the maximum that it allowed, and then took some other courses evenings at another nearby school, persuading Chico to honor those credits, too. This was the old Rola, who had wept and torn her hair over getting only the second best grade. Graduating in the spring of 1984, she enrolled at once in graduate school at Sacramento State, not far from Chico, and after getting a head start by taking summer courses at Georgetown University, she received her master's in the spring of 1985, with a concentration in banking and finance.

MA in hand, Rola returned home to Kuwait. It was not only the degree that Rola brought with her, it was also some of the things she favored about American ways. She instructed her father and other family members that she did not want them to employ any "wasta," that is, connections. "I want to apply for a job and get it on my own merit," she explained.

She turned her back on one job interview when the receptionist slighted her, assuming, because of her sex, age, and Lebanese accent, that she was seeking a menial or secretary position. She turned down a position at a bank when the CEO, upon learning she was Abdullah Dashti's daughter, welcomed her too effusively. "It just pissed me off," recalls Rola. "People would have said that anything I accomplished in my work was because of my father. I would never be recognized as an individual."

Finally she took a position with a research firm, enjoying a niche as the country's only agricultural economist. Nonetheless, after a couple of years she decided to pursue a doctorate, towards which she won admission to Baltimore's Johns Hopkins University. It was 1987, and her older brother, Saleh, who seemed to know more about having fun than Rola, was getting ready to head home to Kuwait, finally having completed his meander through undergraduate education. Younger brother Jamal had just graduated from high school, and he got admitted to JHU for undergraduate study. Helal, now five years into her motherly U.S. sojourn, moved to Baltimore to look after Rola and Jamal.

By 1990 Rola had completed her class work, passed her comprehensive exams, and started in on her dissertation, while moonlighting as a consultant to the World Bank. Then, one day that summer, she arrived home in Baltimore from the Bank, and Helal told her the news: "Iraq invaded Kuwait."

At first, Rola brushed it aside, assuming that Saddam Hussein wanted to seize a few kilometers of territory in order to ransom it. Then what she saw on the television news "shocked and paralyzed" her: a complete conquest of the country was underway. She made urgent calls home, including to some of her step-brothers who were in the army, but the Kuwaitis knew less about what was going on than what she was getting from CNN.

Rola was devastated. Even though she had spent more of her years in Lebanon, she felt deeply Kuwaiti for reasons that she had trouble explaining. She puts it:

> It was always the centrifuge of my life. It was the magnet. You go away, but you know every other place is temporary, transient. And here is the core. This is why it was shocking to me. That center was not there. Saddam Hussein had wiped Kuwait from the map and said there was nothing called Kuwait.

Rola dropped out of school. Helal and her academic advisor tried to dissuade her, but Rola was inconsolable and obstinate. "If you do not have an identity, nothing else means anything," she says. "What is a Ph.D. without an identity? Nothing was important to me aside from having Kuwait back."

She and other Kuwaiti students moved into the Kuwaiti embassy in Washington and began to organize any activity they could think of to restore their homeland. Rola did not believe that Kuwait could be rescued by diplomacy. "Every time [Secretary of State James] Baker met with [Iraqi Foreign Minister] Tariq Aziz, we were hoping they would not come to a deal, because the Iraqis will maneuver and tell stories." As a result, she feared, Kuwait would be in permanent limbo, "like Palestine."

She was equally pessimistic about the path advocated by many Senators as an alternative to war, the application of economic sanctions. Rola and her compatriots lobbied against this idea, reminding Senators that "South Africa has been under sanctions for 15 years, and nothing has happened."

Rola felt certain that only military action would restore her country:

> War is not popular, not something one wants to aspire to, but sometimes you feel that war will bring peace and liberty to people. So it was with us. This is where our liberty and freedom lay: it was only through war with Saddam. You could not deal with him aside from war because he is unpredictable, ruthless, a big maneuverer, full of hatred, and full of arrogance and autocratic ways.

Nor did she wish to leave the fighting to the Americans. When a male friend decided to sneak back into Kuwait to participate in resistance, Rola decided to go with him. But Helal reacted with such alarm that Rola dropped the idea. This was good not only for Helal's peace of mind, but also for the cause of Kuwait, because, as one of the leading activists, Rola performed a prodigious service from Washington.

Rola and her compatriots formed the Free Kuwait Movement. In addition to lobbying on Capitol Hill, they staged protests in front of the Iraqi embassy, bombarded the American news media with stories about the plight of their homeland, and circulated thousands of postcards for mailing to legislators and distributed t-shirts emblazoned with their slogans. Like others, Rola lost the source of her tuition, which had been paid by the Kuwaiti government, but this was a moot point because she had no interest in school work for the moment, only the national cause.

Americans may have been divided about going to war, but their outpouring of sympathy for Kuwaitis touched Rola. "We had thousands of phone calls from American families, saying, for example, 'I have a spare room for a Kuwaiti student who cannot pay rent,'" she recalls. Other Americans mailed them checks which they had no way of cashing or depositing. When the group shopped for supplies or provisions sporting "Free Kuwait" t-shirts, merchants who discovered their identity refused to charge them.

In addition to lobbying for war to liberate Kuwait and succoring stranded Kuwaiti students, Rola threw herself into planning her country's restoration. An Emergency Recovery Program was set up by the Kuwaiti embassy in Washington, and Rola was recruited to serve as one of its economists. Technical teams were created to represent every major ministry in the Kuwaiti government—health, education, public works, oil, defense, agriculture, etc. Since the country was damaged in combat and looted by the Iraqis, detailed plans were laid for rebuilding infrastructure in each of these areas. Rola, a 27-year-old Ph.D. candidate who had never held government office, was charged with negotiating with contractors to provide the various needs. Kuwait's funds were held by Chemical Bank, and when the project was over, one of its officers tried to lure Rola to a position at the bank. She had issued more letters of credit in those months than he had done in his career, he said.

Before Kuwait could be rebuilt, however, it had first to be liberated. Rola chafed as the U.S. Senate debated, and even after the bombs began to fall on January 15th she was impatient for the ground invasion. Finally the troops moved and quickly expelled the Iraqi occupiers. February 26th is sealed in her memory as the date of "freedom and liberty. It brought back your identity, brought back your life, brought back your existence. It was a day of joy."

She yearned to head directly to Kuwait. Among other things, her brothers were there. The younger, Jamal, had dropped out of Johns Hopkins and enlisted in the U.S. Marines under a special program through which several hundred Kuwaiti students were recruited for emergency duty. They were given a compressed six-week basic training and sent to the front, on the assumption that what they lacked in military experience would be made up for by their knowledge of their homeland. Jamal was assigned to a unit that fought its way into Kuwait from Saudi Arabia and captured the airport.

Once the Iraqis fled, Jamal got leave to go to the family home in search of his older brother, Saleh, who had been in Kuwait at the time of the Iraqi takeover. Saleh had joined the opposition, been detained for some days, then released. But of course, Jamal had little word of his situation, just as Saleh had little of Jamal's. Although Saleh was not at home, a neighbor told Jamal where he might be found. Jamal set off, trailed by a camera team from CNN, and succeeded in finding Saleh. A world of TV viewers saw their happy, tearful embrace.

Rola would have loved to have been there, but by now her responsibilities were too heavy to leave. The work of executing contracts for Kuwait's reconstruction was urgent, and it could not be moved to Kuwait because the country was in ruins. Basic equipment and services necessary to run an office were not available. For the time being, Kuwait's Emergency Recovery Program had to remain in Washington in order to function effectively, and Rola could not leave her desk.

It was not for another six months, until August, that the pace of Rola's work slowed enough for her to make a trip to Kuwait. For ten days she drove around the country, from border to border, just soaking in her homeland. Nights, she kept Saleh up late, making him recount in extreme detail the six months of occupation and its eery aftermath when smoke from the oil fires blocked all sunlight, making it pitch dark in midday.

She returned to DC, spent two more months wrapping up the affairs of the contract office, and then plunged back into her dissertation. Now, she was desperate to finish so she could return to Kuwait to stay. Less than a year later, she successfully defended the dissertation, and late in 1992 headed home.

Rola returned to Kuwait transformed. To make a living, she spent a few months managing a small construction company that Saleh had started, then returned to her old research position before moving on to jobs in banking and finance. But she invested her passion in the two causes she now made her own.

The first of these was the status of some six hundred Kuwaiti POWs who had been taken to Iraq and never accounted for. This issue was close to Rola's heart because one of her half-brothers had been taken although he had been released after four months. Rola toured the world, speaking to civil and parliamentary groups, begging intercession on behalf of these POWs.

The second issue that seized Rola was the status of women in Kuwait. Until the 1950s, Kuwaiti women were "secluded, veiled and overwhelmingly illiterate."[4] The influx of wealth from oil exportation, which commenced in 1946, began to strengthen the winds of modernization. By the 1960s educational opportunities for girls expanded significantly and women were freed from having to wear the *abbaya*, the tent-like black gown that covers the person from neck to toe, and is usually complemented by a headscarf and sometimes a face veil. Despite the formation of some women's advocacy organizations in the next decades, the cause of equal rights made little progress, swimming as it was against a rising tide of Islamic fundamentalism.

But the Iraqi occupation changed everything, somewhat as World War Two's Rosie the Riveter had spurred women's rights in America. In addition to the work that Rola did in the proto-government in exile, many women inside Kuwait took part in the resistance. According to one account:

> Many Kuwaitis consider women to have been the backbone of the Resistance.... At first, the Iraqis tended to treat Kuwaiti women driving alone with respect and restraint. Most of the troops had obviously been given orders to behave with women. Recognizing this, the Kuwaiti women played the

Iraqis for all they were worth by carrying concealed weapons and ammunition through checkpoints where men would have been searched.[5]

Among several women who were executed in the resistance, Asrar Qabani, a short, stout, bespectacled thirty-year-old who helped smuggle the children of the royal family out of the country as well as committing countless other acts of resistance, gained national renown. Fifteen years later, American researchers reported that in a focus group in Kuwait, a Bedouin woman, presumably of little formal education, recounted the legend of "women martyrs who laid down their lives for the country during the invasion."[6]

The Kuwait to which Rola returned was a country where women still required a male "guardian" for many things. Granted, this rule was less restrictive than in Saudi Arabia, where a woman could scarcely go outside without a guardian. But still in Kuwait, a woman could not marry, open a bank account, or get a passport without the formal approval of her guardian. As in Saudi Arabia, if she were widowed her "guardian" might even be her son.

And, of course, women had no political rights. In Saudi Arabia, this was a moot point, since it is an absolute monarchy, and until recent small reforms no one outside the royal family, male or female, had any political rights. Kuwait, in contrast, has never been an absolutist state. To be sure, it is a monarchy: much power rests with the royal family, and the press is not free to criticize it. But there is a constitution and a parliament to which the monarch is accountable. In 2006, it even replaced the monarch when the succession fell to a sickly royal whom the MPs regarded as unfit to discharge the duties of the throne. But while Kuwaiti citizens have long had a role in politics, participation was limited to men.

"When I came back at the end of 1992," recalls Rola, "I realized that I cannot have a voice. Yes, I'm a citizen, but I'm not a citizen. I'm just a number in the census." Moreover, as she saw it, the lack of a right to vote ramified into every other area of life:

> I will always hit a glass ceiling because I do not have a voice. People who have a voice will have networks that reach where we cannot reach because we do not have rights. We do not elect so officials will not listen. Okay, they will hear you but at the end of the day they will give you a cup of tea and hear you and thank you, and they will go on about their business.

She joined several women's groups, organized rallies and lobbied parliamentarians for political rights for women. A special project of Rola's focused on the UN's fourth World Conference on Women held in Beijing in 1995. The official Kuwaiti delegation was led by the wife of the crown prince who was in fact a public *opponent* of political rights for women. Her motif was that Kuwaiti women were content with the status quo. Rola and some colleagues raised funds to send an alternative delegation of some 40-45 women activists to dispute this.

Rola was approached by the Kuwaiti government and asked to join the official delegation. The government was eager that the sore issue of Kuwait's unaccounted-for POWs be raised at the Beijing conference, and it recognized that Rola was Kuwait's most eloquent female advocate on this subject. Rola was more than happy to represent Kuwait on this issue which remained dear to her, but she refused to join the official delegation, made up of the female analog of Uncle Toms. After a brief standoff, the government agreed that Rola would be Kuwait's representative on the POW issue but only as a member of the alternative women's delegation. The effect was to give that delegation a certain formal standing, thus humiliating the official delegation.

As the women's movement gained momentum in the 1990s, it gained a critical ally, none other than the emir, Kuwait's ruler. According to the constitution, when the parliament is dissolved, the emir may make laws by decree, subject to subsequent ratification by parliament. In 1999, the aging emir, Sheikh Jaber al-Ahmad al-Sabah, issued a decree granting women full political rights, meaning both to vote and to run for office.

This, however, was not the final word. The decree still needed to be ratified by the new parliament which was elected by the old rules, meaning only men could run or vote. When it was seated, a sharp struggle began. Legislators resented the package of 63 decrees issued by the emir after dissolving parliament and were eager to reassert their authority. Thus they viewed these measures with jaundiced eyes, including the decree on women's rights, even though it was different from the others. It did not emanate from the government, but was expressed as a personal "wish" of the emir, the first in Kuwaiti history.

Nonetheless, the opposition was formidable. Extreme Islamists were the most vitriolic, but, says Rola, "Even the moderate Islamists were not moderate toward women with political rights." The Islamists were joined on this issue by other traditionalists, and the government failed to put its muscle behind the measure. The motion to ratify the emir's decree failed, by a vote of 32 to 30. "Hundreds of men cheered in the streets," reported the *Guardian*.[7] Rola and her colleagues were devastated.

In the wake of defeat in the legislature, Rola hit on the idea of turning to the courts, much as the U.S. civil rights movement had done in the 1950s. Article 29 of Kuwait's Constitution prohibited discrimination by race or gender. Oddly, the official English translation of the Constitution omits the reference to gender, but the Arabic is clear. Her goal was to secure a ruling from the Constitutional Court, striking down the current election law because it excluded female participation.

However, individual appellants had no standing before that court. According to its statute, it was empowered to hear only cases brought by the government, the parliament, or a lower court. Since Rola could count neither the government nor the parliament as reliable allies, she and her colleagues contrived to get a lower court to bring the matter forward. Again like U.S. civil rights advocates, their strategy was to create a case in a lower court that would compel it to ask the higher court to pass on the election law's constitutionality.

They had to wait until the period for voter registration opened. Then Rola, and a few colleagues in other districts, went to the appointed officials and attempted to register. When the registrars turned them down, they went to the police station and filed complaints. Rola's case unfolded first. Her lawyer went to court, asking the court to order the registrar to enroll Rola on the voting books. In response, as the women had calculated, the lower court asked the Constitutional Court to render a judgment on the law.

The case made members of parliament uneasy. They would be embarrassed if the court ruled that their decision had been unconstitutional, and, to boot, they did not want to encourage the practice of judicial review, which was not routine in Kuwait. Some MPs offered Rola a deal: withdrawal of her case in exchange for reconsideration of the bill on women's rights. Rola countered that if the bill were reconsidered first, then she would drop her case. No deal was struck.

Rola's legal maneuver failed. The Constitutional Court refused to hear the case. It commented that the brief Rola's lawyers had filed revealed that she had intended all along to elicit a constitutional ruling, thereby circumscribing the normal purposes of that court. Rola tried again, this time with a brief written to avoid the points used against her. She waited a year until the next voter registration period and repeated her effort to register. Alas, the lower court refused to refer the case this time, citing the Constitutional Court's previous ruling against her.

Stymied in the courts, Rola returned to political agitation. Her strategy was to frame the issue as a matter of the national interest. Failure to include women as full citizens would limit the country's human resources, which it could ill afford, given its tiny native population. She portrayed the struggle for women's rights as a continuation of earlier battles that had secured an elected parliament in 1938 (before independence), a partially democratic constitution in 1961, and other barriers against autocracy. "The same way that our fathers fought so that Kuwait would have a constitution and democratization in order to sustain its existence and the relationship between the people and the ruler, so I felt Kuwait's development and prosperity needed women to be an integral element," she says.

In addition, she argued that Kuwait could not hold itself out as a leader in democratization within the region as long as it continued to exclude women. To give force to this point, she attempted to build foreign pressure by talking up the issue relentlessly at international forums and by cultivating foreign news organizations.

While this was going on, she also moved to make herself more independent professionally. She left her job at an investment firm in 1999 and opened her own financial consultant and investment business. As one of the country's leading economists, she found no shortage of consultancy work. She invested the proceeds in small businesses. This focus was influenced by her social vision, but it was not charity. She chose small ventures that she judged could flourish, and she succeeded well enough that she was able to reduce the amount of time she devoted to business, so that she could use the other hours for pet causes.

She also built a base for herself outside of the women's movement. In Kuwait, as throughout the region, government keeps a tight grip on private organizations. Thus, private business is the strongest force independent of state and mosque. For this reason the Kuwait Economic Society is one of the weightiest organizations in the country. One-third of the publicly traded companies in Kuwait belong, as do about 500 individuals, mostly professionals, managers and businessmen. Relative to population, this is equivalent to one hundred thousand members in a U.S. organization. In addition to offering a venue for networking, the KES advocates policies for a more free economy, and it offers a variety of technical services and training programs.

The organization had been founded in 1970, and, as is common with such establishmentarian groups, it had grown staid and sluggish. That was until Rola, who was already a member, took it in mind to transform KES. She envisioned its playing a more dynamic role in the development of the country and as an engine for "reform in the region." So in anticipation of the general membership meeting of 2004, she put together a slate of young people to challenge incumbents for seats on the board. The officers are chosen by the board, and she raised the stakes by announcing that if she were elected, she would seek the chairmanship.

Rola's slate captured six of the ten seats. During the ensuing 48 hours before the board met to choose officers, influential Kuwaitis lobbied to deny her the chairmanship. They argued that she would turn the organization into a platform for women's rights, deflecting it from its mission in economic development. Rola, herself, was beseeched to defer, to accept any position other than the chairmanship. Never in Kuwait, and perhaps not elsewhere in the region, had a woman been chosen to head such an important, predominantly male organization. But Rola stood firm, and so did the five other members of her slate.

To Rola,

> It was an experience that reinforced a belief in me that a woman, irrespective of how good she is, irrespective of how capable she is, how respected she is, if she crosses a certain aspiration line, then the fight will come, a fierce fight—irre-

spective of ideological group. We are talking about an organization that is liberal; most of its members are moderate liberal thinkers. We are talking about an old guard who are liberal in their ideology. It is amazing the fight that I got.

But if Rola was on the receiving end of some fights, she was on the giving end of others, especially her ceaseless agitation for political rights. Early in 2005 several MPs agreed to pick up the torch of Rola's defeated legal strategy by asking the Constitutional Court for a ruling on women's political exclusion. Their standing before the court was different than hers. But the government intervened, asking the MPs to hold off and promising to introduce new legislation and proposing to allow women to vote in municipal elections that were scheduled that year. Parliamentary elections were scheduled for 2007, two years down the road, and they suggested that if women voted first in municipalities, this could establish a precedent for including them in the national vote.

Rola swung into action, spending full-time lobbying the members of parliament. She organized the largest demonstration for women's rights in Kuwaiti history. She recruited a variety of groups to participate, not only women's groups, to underscore her point that women's role was "a barometer of Kuwait's future, moving toward openness and away from extremism."

The bill passed, but with less than a majority in favor, nearly half of the parliamentarians abstaining or absenting themselves, which triggered a constitutional crisis. There was no precedent to make it clear whether a mere plurality was sufficient to enact a law. After a tussle, it was agreed to schedule another vote. But now it was May, and the government had set a date for the municipal elections in July.

Rola was furious. Due to the procedures for voter registration, a July election meant that even if the bill now passed with an indisputable majority, it could not take effect in time for the vote. So, in practice, it would apply only to the next municipal election, to be held in 2009. Worse, still, if it confirmed the compromise under which women would vote in a municipal election before voting in a parliamentary ballot, then that would delay their most important gain until 2011 or beyond.

Rola was convinced that people within the government were maneuvering to delay women's rights. The next day she invited two colleagues to her home and drafted a statement. In language that was uncommonly harsh for Kuwaiti political discourse, it made three points. First, it accused the government of dissembling, pretending to favor women's political rights while actually sabotaging them. Second, it called on MPs who supported women's rights to vote *against* the bill that would let women vote in municipal elections. Third, it demanded that at the legislative session scheduled a few days later the government put forward a law granting full political rights to women rather than merely participation in municipal elections.

Rola's position divided the women's movement. Some, more moderate than she, did not want to reject the bill for municipal election rights even if it would not take effect until 2009. But others followed Rola's militancy, and within a day she gathered 130 signatures on her statement. Then she took it to every one of the country's daily newspapers in time to make the Saturday paper. Saturday is the beginning of the work week in the region, and Rola was hoping to set the agenda. She knew many of the journalists and editors, and she lobbied them shamelessly. "I need a favor," she recalls saying. "I need this published, and I need it put in a good place."

Her declaration hit the front page of several of the papers, causing a stir. Building on the publicity, Rola decided that same day to request a meeting with the prime minister. She enlisted Souhad al-Sabah, a female member of the royal family who supported the cause, asking her to secure the meeting and to lead the delegation that would take part. Later that day, huddling with other women activists and nine MPs who were their most stalwart supporters, Rola implored the MPs not to vote for the municipal rights law. She explained her reasoning. The Prime Minister was nominally supporting them, but he was not really swinging his weight. Since the municipal-vote bill was the government's bill, he had a prestige stake in getting it through. If those nine withheld their votes, he would have to twist arms or trade favors to win nine other votes. She had no doubt he could succeed at that, but if he did she believed that it would prove he had enough clout to pass a law on full political rights for women, giving the lie to his pretense not to have enough votes.

Rola also gave an interview that appeared in the next day's papers in which she accused the Deputy Prime Minister of sabotaging the effort. "The people who are handling the fight for women's political rights in the cabinet are against those rights," she said. "Behind doors they are doing things to damage the cause." After reading the interview, the official confronted Rola on the floor of the Parliament. She said, "If you are supporting us you are not working very hard. Try to work harder." He replied, "Give us some time."

Next, Rola secured legal advice on how to get the issue of full political rights for women, which had repeatedly been buried in committee, to the floor of the National Assembly for a vote. This was complicated by the fact that there was only one item on the docket for the coming session: a second reading of the bill concerning solely the municipal vote. She wanted to parry any claims by the government that constitutional rules precluded a vote on full rights in that session. The procedure, she learned, would be tortuous, but it was doable.

The meeting with the Prime Minister—who, under Kuwaiti tradition, is the crown prince—was held exactly one week before the scheduled National Assembly meeting of

May 16. The date was special because it was the sixth anniversary of the emir's 1999 decree granting women rights that had been overridden by parliament. Rola and Souhad al-Sabah and about fifteen others made up the delegation. Rola recalls, "As usual, the women were very nice, saying, 'Your Highness, we know you support women's political rights, and we need your assistance.'" The Prime Minister replied that he was already working hard on the issue, but each MP had his own opinion, and "I cannot push every one of them."

Rola recalls she "did not like what I was hearing, so I intervened." She reconstructs what she said: "Your Highness, you are for women's political rights; I do not question this. But the problem is the file is not in your hands. It is in the hands of people in your Cabinet who do not believe in it."

It is likely the other women were squirming at the audacity with which Rola confronted the Prime Minister, who was in line to be the next emir, but she was just warming up. She continued:

> You can indeed push MPs because I saw you during the first hearing of the municipal-vote issue, how you let some of the MPs go. When the vote happened they left the room, so as not to be embarrassed, and you got it passed, and then they came back. I was there and I saw you: you looked at them and then they left. So if you were able to do that at the municipality level, I'm sure you will be able to do it for national women's rights.

Although she had all but called him a liar, their exchange continued. He challenged her version of the earlier event and said that the issue of full women's rights was not so easy. Rola kept pressing: "Next week is the session. We want women's rights on the agenda. I know you can do it if you want to." The Prime Minister replied by calling her a trouble-maker, and asking her to back off her attacks in the domestic and international media. "Give me my rights, and then I'll back off," she retorted, then softened her tone. "You believe in it, so let's work together," she said. "Inshallah," he replied.

As the group said its good-byes to the Prime Minister, he and Rola exchanged a few words to the side. "Are you going to keep being a trouble-maker?" she recalls him asking. She replied, "I'm like your daughter. You have to tolerate me."

After the meeting, the women sat together to assess it. The Prime Minister had promised to try to meet their demands, but asked them not to speak to the press about it and to tone down the rhetoric. As she had already made clear in the meeting, Rola was disinclined to honor this request because she did not trust the government. But the other members of the delegation wanted to go along with the Prime Minister, and Rola felt herself bound by the group's wishes.

Biting her tongue, she deflected reporters' questions, claiming nothing important had transpired at the meeting. One Western journalist was perplexed by Rola's unwonted nonchalance. "This is not you," he said. When she persisted in the same evasive vein, he thought he had uncovered a big story. "Were you threatened?" he asked excitedly. And ignoring Rola's denials he urged her to let him expose to the world whatever was being done to her.

As the days until May 16 ticked away, Rola chafed at the reticence that she felt bound to keep due to her agreement with the other women. Happily, a group of students contacted her to say that they were planning a rally to support the women on May 15, a day before the parliamentary session. Rola felt that her commitment to the women barred her from speaking at the rally, but she busied herself helping the students to organize it. She also had a critical task in persuading them to shift their direction. The rally had been intended to support the bill for women's rights at the municipal level. Rola met with the student leaders to explain to them her view that the municipal election law had become a snare and that what the women really needed was a vote now to give them full rights. The students were at first touchy about allowing any older person to reshape their demands, and Rola, who had already passed forty, was of their parents' generation. She stayed and argued with them until 1:30 in the morning, finally leaving them to make their decision, which they did not want to do in her presence. Within the hour they called to say they would rally for "women's political rights," without specifying details of legislation. The rally brought a large and enthusiastic turnout, including students from all of Kuwait City's schools, giving the cause momentum on the eve of the parliamentary showdown.

That evening, she received a call from an official, informing her that the government had decided to bring the issue of full political rights for women to the floor the next day. "I could not believe it," she recalls. "I could not sleep all night."

Some of the students had decided to resume their rally that next morning in front of the National Assembly, so Rola met them there at 7AM to help with the logistics. When it was time for the body to convene, she went inside.

The government put forward the measure, to the shock of some MPs. Aside from the substance, the procedure was irregular, since the bill had not previously been announced. The government, however, was following the parliamentary gymnastics that Rola had earlier figured out, bringing the issue under an "order of urgency." It was referred for immediate action to the Interior Committee, which was charged to report back that same day. Opponents of women's rights reacted quickly to this stratagem. They demanded that the committee also consider giving voting rights to soldiers, who were barred from it under existing law, and reducing the voting age from 21 to 18. Each of these measures was controversial in itself, and the tactic was designed to produce a bill that would draw opposition from many quarters.

With the government and the women working in tandem, however, the Interior Committee was persuaded to bring back a bill dealing only with women's rights. With elegant simplicity, it consisted of the deletion of a single word—"men"—from the election law.

Now, the chamber was near pandemonium. Debate was much more heated than usual in this parliament, and several recesses were called to calm things. The interruptions frightened Rola. The bill needed to be voted on twice because it had had no previous hearing. She feared that if the recesses forced the issue to be carried over to another day, the momentum would be lost. The government had done its part, twisting arms of reluctant legislators. Those arms could be twisted in reverse if the Islamists and other opponents of women's rights were given time to throw their weight at the legislators.

At last, at 6PM, the final vote was taken. After an amendment to appease Islamists, decreeing that females who participate in politics must "abide by Islamic law," the vote was 35 to 23. The chamber went silent for a moment, and then, on signal from Rola, the women who had packed the gallery broke into the national anthem.

Rola's leadership was widely recognized. The *Kuwait Times* wrote that her name had "become synonymous with the Kuwaiti women's fight for their political rights." And the regional magazine, *Arabian Business,* put her face on its cover, with the headline "The Kuwaiti Liberator." For Rola, however, this was just the beginning. Peering across Kuwait's borders she expressed hope for a "domino effect," encouraging women's victories in other Gulf countries.[8] And in Kuwait, she saw this triumph as a springboard to others. As she left the legislative chambers after the May 16 vote, she told the gathered reporters that she was running for parliament.

The parliamentary election was scheduled for 2007, giving Rola plenty of time to plan her campaign. First she went to work organizing education and publicity to inform women of their new rights and to encourage them to register to vote. Her task was vastly simplified when the National Assembly passed a bill late in 2005 automatically registering the female electorate.

Her campaign plans, however, became ensnarled in another issue roiling Kuwaiti politics. Reformers, including both liberals and Islamists, and led by young people, agitated for redrawing the electoral districts. The National Assembly included 50 elected members (in addition to the appointed members of the cabinet who were automatically given seats in parliament). These 50 were elected two apiece from twenty-five districts. The reformers complained that these very small electoral districts were easily manipulated by the royal family through tribal networking and outright vote-buying. They demanded that the number of districts be reduced to five with ten MPs elected from each.

The reformers quickly won the support of a majority in parliament (thereby perhaps disproving their own argument). The government countered by proposing a compromise of ten districts. The assembly rejected this, to which the emir responded by dissolving parliament. This forced new elections, which were held on the old 25-district basis. More to the point, it moved the elections forward a year into 2006. Rola had planned to work her district, whatever its boundaries, retail. With more than a year until the election she had hoped to knock on thousands of doors, introducing herself to the voters. The abbreviation of the campaign period crippled this plan.

Some other political maneuvers put her at a further disadvantage. Political parties are not legal in Kuwait, but there are informal groupings that in effect function as parties. In Rola's district, two incumbents were running for reelection, but they were at odds. One was a loyalist of the regime's whom Rola describes as a notorious vote-buyer. The other was a liberal reformer. Each of these men chose to form a slate with a second candidate. The regime loyalist found a second like himself. Rola would have made a natural running mate for the reformer, but the liberal bloc, fearing for its chances, decided instead to forge an alliance with conservative Islamists, who had a candidate of their own, a former MP. Counting these four and Rola, a total of 27 candidates ran for the two seats from that district.

Left as an independent, Rola mounted a spirited campaign. Younger brother Jamal served as campaign manager, and Saleh and Helal worked for her, as did some of her half-siblings. In her stump speech she began:

> Who is Rola Dashti, and what will she do for you? I am your sister and your daughter. I will improve your standard of living. I will ask the government to give its small contracts to young Kuwaitis to increase their income. I will set up a housing fund for widows, divorcees and unmarried women who lack financial support. I offer you bills of law, not slogans.[9]

Rola took her message to women, but equally to men, making the rounds of *diwaniyyas*, drawing rooms, often in courtyards, where men gather for tea and talk. Sometimes at these, if she suspected the crowd was old or socially conservative, she would pull an *abbaya* over her clothes, but she did not alter her bare-headed style. "If I just put [on] a *hijab* today, I'll gain six or seven hundred votes," she said. "But I'm not going to do this."[10]

She also stirred up opposition. A text message sent to hundreds of cell phones disparaged Rola's Iranian ancestry and her Lebanese accent, and accused her of being in the pay of the American embassy.[11]

Despite such shenanigans, Rola ran well, polling the largest vote of any of the 28 women who ran among the twenty-five districts. She did not, however, draw enough to win. She ran fifth in her district, trailing the two two-man slates, but polling better than any of the other 22 independents. The liberals' opportunistic alliance with the Islamists backfired. The Islamist won, as did the incumbent regime loyalist, while the incumbent liberal lost. He might have done better to have formed a slate with Rola.

In the nation as a whole, reformers scored well, as measured by the stance on the electoral district issue. A firm majority of those elected favored the shift to fewer, larger districts, although the fact that so many advocates of change won under this rerun of the old arrangement again called into question the belief that the 25-district system put them at a disadvantage.

The race for parliament was not the only election Rola contested in 2006. Six months later, she had a second one on her hands. The Kuwait Economic Society elects its board and officers every two years. Rola's insurgent slate had triumphed in 2004; in 2006 the "old guard" mobilized for a comeback. The slate it offered was seeded with some younger people, so as to deflect the generational issue. Once again, the charge was raised that Rola intended to turn the group into a platform for women's issues. The showdown was intensified because it coincided with new milestones in the fight for women's rights in the political arena. Both sides worked feverishly to get their supporters to turn out. The government watched the contest closely, as a straw in the political wind.

Amazingly, 85 percent of the society's members showed up for the meeting and elected Rola's entire slate—7 men and 3 women—by a landslide. She boasts that even if the absent 15 percent had all voted for the old guard, her slate would have won, nonetheless. Since then, she has encouraged women to run for the boards of other professional associations.

Also, Rola and her close colleagues, who had previously worked together ad hoc, founded a formal NGO, the Women's Partnership Organization, to push the issue of equal rights. It lobbies the parliament, encourages young women toward activism, and maintains a data base of women with various professional qualifications to aid their advancement.

In 2008, the emir dissolved parliament, and snap elections were held under the new districting system in which the top ten vote-getters were elected in each of the five districts. Rola ran again as an independent and again fell short, coming in thirteenth among scores of candidates in the Third district. Once again, not a single woman was elected, but they came closer than the year before. In addition to Rola's thirteenth-place finish for ten seats, Aseel Al-Awadhi, who was included in the liberal slate, came even closer, running eleventh.

Little wonder, then, that the likes of Islamist MP Ahmad Baqer are so desperate to stave off the inevitable. In the same broadcast in which he swore that women would never be elected, he invoked the life of the Prophet, whom he said "sent male governors, judges, and ambassadors, but he never sent women ... even though the most perfect women lived in his time."

Rola calls this tactic "psychological terrorism," explaining:

Women were terrorized in the name of Islam as being anti-religious to the extent of being blasphemous, anti-patriotic agents of the West, destroyers of the social fabric, anti-family, and promoters of homosexuality and adultery.... just because we wanted women to be involved in politics ... and become active participants in public life.[12]

Such attacks bring out Helal's maternal protectiveness and something of the horror she felt when Rola fell off that watermelon or her bike. For all her pride in Rola's accomplishments, she wishes her daughter had found a gentler calling and urges her to "Leave this life. Look after yourself." Rola, however, is bent on giving the lie to Ahmad Baqer and his like. "I will keep on running," she vows, "until we see a woman in parliament, me or someone else." She has reason to be confident it will not be much longer.

The Dissident

Syria: Ammar Abdulhamid

The older man made a show of courtesy, coming around from behind his desk to sit side-by-side with his guest, so that each had to turn his head sideways to face the other. They sipped tea as they spoke. The leather armchairs were comfortable. But neither man relaxed. Their words were angry, and there was a lot at stake. The younger man was about to learn just how much.

He was in his late 30s, about 6 feet 2 inches, trim of build and longhaired. He was dressed in jeans and a sport jacket. The older man, about 55, was even taller and much thicker. A heavy bar of a black moustache set off his square features, making him look something like Saddam Hussein. There was a hardness about him that his plush Italian suit did not soften.

The host was Assef Shawkat, and he was the son-in-law of the late dictator, Hafez Al-Assad. Marrying the boss's daughter is a time-honored shortcut to success, but in the Assad family things were not so simple. The other Assad men folk competed fiercely among themselves, and Shawkat had advanced by traversing an internecine minefield. He had escaped a car bomb, attributed to his wife's uncle, Rifaat. He had endured four terms of imprisonment ordered by his brother-in-law, Basil, trying to block the marriage. And he had survived a bullet through his gut, fired by another brother-in-law, Maher, during an altercation in the family drawing room.

Still standing after all of this, Shawkat had tied his fortunes to those of his third brother-in-law, Bashar, who eventually was crowned successor to Hafez Al-Assad. Once in power, Bashar appointed Shawkat chief of military intelligence, and by most reckonings, Shawkat was now the second most powerful man in Syria.

The young visitor in Shawkat's office that afternoon in June of 2005 was Ammar Abdulhamid, Syria's most outspoken dissident. The number of public dissidents in Syria was small, their heresies mild, their punishments severe. But Abdulhamid benefited from a measure of protection that others did not enjoy. His mother was Muna Wassef, Syria's Greta Garbo, and Shawkat had paid her a visit before summoning Abdulhamid. In a respectful manner, he had told her to shut the boy up for his own sake, and she in response had threatened to use all her fame and popularity against the regime if it harmed her only child. His special standing had emboldened Abdulhamid, and he had done things that other dissidents had not: giving interviews to Israeli reporters, publishing blistering critiques of the regime in Lebanese newspapers, and allowing himself to be quoted in the American press in ways that no one else did.

Just a few weeks before this fateful sit-down, he had commented to the *Washington Post* about the upcoming congress of the ruling Baath Party that "we are looking [at] a very, very dismal future for this country." The regime, he added, was trying to pull "a rabbit out of a hat. But the hat is bottomless, the rabbit is long dead, and the president is not a magician."[1] No one in Syria got away with such *lèse majesté*.

Shawkat riffled a stack of black file folders on his desk and pulled out one. Making a display of reading some of its contents, he said: "Ammar, you are calling for demonstrations now and for civil disobedience. You're even defending the Islamists," adding sarcastically, "What's this new line? I thought you were a secular liberal?" Without waiting for an answer, he continued: "Apparently the people who are paying you are sending you in a new direction."

Abdulhamid heard out the larger man and then tried to explain his position reasonably. All he had done, said Abdulhamid, was to protest the closure of the Atassi Forum. The Jamal Atassi Forum for Democratic Dialogue had been licensed by the state during the "Damascus spring," a period of liberalization that had followed Bashar Assad's accession to power. It was a salon, meeting in the home of the Atassis, one of Syria's most prominent families, and it had become a singular oasis of free speech in one of the world's most closed polities. The month before, one of its leaders, Ali Abdullah, a secular human rights activist, had read aloud a letter to the forum from Ali Sadreddin Bayanouni, the head of the Syrian Muslim Brotherhood. In response, or on this pretext, the regime had imprisoned Abdullah, detained briefly the other members of the Atassi Forum's board, and forbidden the organization from continuing to operate. Abdulhamid had taken to the pages of Lebanon's *Daily Star* to protest the closure.[2]

"I am not defending the Islamists' point of view, but their right to voice it," he tried to explain, but Shawkat was deaf to such logic, and he renewed his attack until Abdulhamid asked: "What do you want?" His host replied: "Work with us. We're looking for brilliant people like you."

Abdulhamid understood at once that this could mean spying on other dissidents or feeding false information to Western journalists or changing the tenor of his own writings. He refused, and Shawkat came back at him more angrily this time. This ignited the younger man's temper, and he recalls barely avoiding the dangerous mistake of responding with invective.

Then Shawkat turned to him and said: "Look, Ammar. We are not going to make a hero of you. We're not going to put you in prison." Ammar understood this for what it was: a death threat. Better from the regime's point of view, apparently, to withstand a single outburst of suspicion or protest if he turned up dead, than to have his illustrious mother leading a "free Ammar" campaign for months on end.

Abdulhamid had reached a Rubicon. His first impulse was defiance. But then he thought about his loved ones. If they did kill him, his mother would hurl herself at the regime in full fury. Given her popularity, she might damage the rulers, but they would hurt her in return. His two stepchildren with whom he was closely bonded had already lost one father to illness. And his wife, Khawla, had already lost her father at the hands of the authorities.

"I knew I needed to get out of this. It took only a second to make all these calculations," recalled Ammar. "It was one of those instances where you don't sort out until later what happened." He would bow before Shawkat's threats, but he would not work for the authorities. Instead, he offered a compromise. He had previously spent a year as a visiting fellow at the Brookings Institution in Washington, DC. "What if I make my presence scarce in this country?" he proposed. "I could move back to Washington for a while. I think Brookings would take me back."

On hearing this, Shawkat relaxed perceptibly. Although he had the upper hand, acting on his threat would not have been without a price for the regime. Ammar had some international visibility, so his death would not have gone unnoticed, not to mention the ruckus his mother would have raised. This was cleaner. "That's a good idea," he said. They finished their tea, and Ammar was shown out, but not before Shawkat wrapped him in an embrace, resuming the pretense of comity with which he had begun.[3]

In a few months, Ammar and his wife and the children did indeed leave Syria. But this did not get him out of the hair of Shawkat and his master. Rather than return to Brookings and assume the role of quiescent scholar, he made himself a linchpin of anti-regime activism among Syrians abroad.

Perhaps this restlessness owes something to his complex genealogy. His father, Muhammad Chahine, was the twelfth-born child of a Damascene family. They were of Kurdish stock, but their forebears had migrated from Kurdistan and become "Arabized." The eleven siblings who preceded Muhammad had each died in infancy. With Muhammad, finally, the family's fate changed. After him came two more sons, and these three boys lived into adulthood.

As a young teen, Muhammad joined other boys in throwing stones at French occupation soldiers, even apparently with the approval of his mother who recalled fondly her own teenage high jinks at the expense of Turkish soldiers during the First World War. But there was no more time for such frivolity once Muhammad's father, an officer in the local gendarmerie, failed to awake one morning. One of the younger brothers held a mirror to the old man's lips and confirmed that there was no breath. Muhammad, then 17, took on responsibility for supporting the family. Rather than forsake higher education, he won admission to military academy, where a stipend enabled him to continue as breadwinner.

At the academy, like many of the idealistic youth of his generation, he joined the Baath party. Although he graduated at the top of his class as an artillery engineer, Muhammad's interests were less martial than artistic. He sang, played the oud, and composed songs. At the time, there was no theater in Syria because religious conservatives frowned upon such entertainment. As in many "Third World" countries, the Syrian military played a pervasive role in society, so Muhammad persuaded his superiors to allow him to create a theater within the armed forces. Muhammad served both as chief officer and as the director of individual productions, mostly translations of Western dramas.

The 1950s was a time of ferment in Syria, as elsewhere in the Arab world, which had just roller-coastered from the euphoria of decolonization to the depression of defeat by the newborn state of Israel in 1948. In 1958, under the spell of Gamal Abdel Nasser, the avatar of pan-Arabism, Syria merged with Egypt to form a single country, the United Arab Republic. Like many Syrians, Muhammad quickly came to resent the Egyptians' superciliousness toward their new Syrian countrymen, and he took part in the 1961 coup that precipitated Syria's withdrawal from the short-lived union.

That year of disunion for the UAR was a year of union for Muhammad. He was then 29 years old and had been married briefly before divorcing a few years before. Now he found himself enchanted by the verve and beauty of an actress eleven years his junior.

That was Muna Wassef, not yet a star. Her mother, Helaneh, was a Christian, half Maronite Catholic and half Orthodox, and her father, Moustapha, was an Iraqi Kurd from Mosul. Displaying an early theatrical temperament, she dropped out of school after failing ninth grade math and entered the workplace, where few women ventured. She sold candy at the fair before making her way into fashion modeling. At 18, she turned to the stage and supplemented this by landing a job as secretary to Muhammad Chahine, director of the Armed Forces Theater. Decades later she summarized their courtship to her son by saying that Muhammad always liked the way she served him coffee.

Upon their wedding Muna was forced to give up acting. Looked upon as a dubious occupation for a woman, it was forbidden to the wife of an officer. When a national Syrian television network was created, Muhammad became its director. He resigned his military commission, but did not tell Muna, apparently preferring that she not perform.

Muna, however, learned of his changed circumstance from a friend. She went home, packed her bags, and then told her husband she would return to her parents unless he allowed her to resume acting. Muhammad capitulated.

Within a few years, boosted by an acclaimed portrayal of Jocasta in *Oedipus Rex*, she came to be regarded as the leading lady of the Syrian stage. In the late 1960s, an Arab filmmaking industry took hold, and she turned to the silver screen. Private investment in Syrian films was scarce, so the most well-funded and professional productions were made by the governmental Syrian Foundation for Cinema. Muhammad directed some of its productions, but Muna was a stronger presence. In its first 25 years, the Foundation produced some thirty films, and she appeared in two-thirds of them.

It was a private commercial production, however, that propelled her fame beyond Syria's borders to the rest of the Arab world. In the mid 1970s, the Hollywood director Moustapha Akkad hit upon the idea of a film about the prophet Mohammed, telling the story of Islam in the form of an epic, much as Hollywood had done with the Jewish and Christian bibles.

Because it is a sacrilege to depict the prophet, Akkad devised a script in which people talk and listen to Mohammed, but he is never seen. Another unusual feature of Akkad's production was that he shot two separate versions back to back on the same sets, an English and an Arabic. The former starred Anthony Quinn and Irene Pappas. Muna played the female lead in the Arabic version. In a poignant footnote to Akkad's endeavor to present a sympathetic understanding of his faith through a popular medium, he died violently in 2005 in an Amman hotel blown up by suicide bombers. Muna became a fixture at events across the Arab world commemorating his work.

In 1966 Muna gave birth to Ammar Abdulhamid.[4] For a year she stayed home to breast feed the child. But then, it was back to her calling. Muna's mother helped with Ammar, and the family could afford servants, but when the lad was three, they decided he would be best off in a boarding school. The one that seemed most suitable was run by Maronite nuns in Lebanon. Ammar's earliest memories are of *Soeur* Danielle, one of the nuns who was especially attentive to him. "I remember the taste of the candy she used to give me every now and then, which was really sweet," he says. "And when I was sick I slept in her room, and she threw me candy over the curtain that separated us." There were such moments of kindness but also much loneliness, and the nuns "beat the heck out of me whenever I misbehaved," recalls Ammar.[5]

In one way, the nuns did their job too well, resulting in an early termination of his stint at boarding school. Ammar would come home on holidays to be with his family, and by the time he was five, his father's mother, Bahiya, observed a shocking development. The boy was crossing himself and reciting Hail Mary. Bahiyah was accepting of Muna and did not object if she considered herself Christian. But the child's religion, in their culture, comes from the father. Ammar, the son of her son, was a Muslim and had to remain a Muslim. It was unacceptable for him to be turned into something else.

She prevailed upon Muna and Muhammad to bring the boy home from boarding school to live with her. The parents could see him frequently without the burden of attending to his quotidian needs. And he would be raised a proper Muslim.

Although he was very relieved to return to the bosom of his family, Ammar found himself even more torn between worlds. He already felt the rift between his Christian and Muslim parts. He now experienced an additional, subtler divide. He lived with his grandmother in Muhajireen (a word meaning "immigrants"), a poor Damascus neighborhood climbing the southern face of Mount Qasayoun that was highly traditional in its values and practices. He also spent considerable time in his parents' home in al-Jisr al-Abyad (White Bridge), below the mountain, only fifteen minutes away by car, but a century apart in its mores. In those years, Al-Jisr al-Abyad was a mixed neighborhood of Muslims and Christians, with a cosmopolitan feel, home to an affluent, secular, artistic crowd. The French and Lebanese accents in Ammar's Arabic passed easily in Al-Jisr al-Abyad but made him feel out of place in Muhajireen until their traces faded away.

In grammar school, he also failed to fit in. Its official name was the Brothers' Private School—Taken Over, which signified that it had been a Franciscan school that was nationalized when the Baath Party seized power. Not only were the Brothers run off, but in a further revolutionary thrust against colonial memories, the study of French was abolished, depriving Ammar of what would have been his best subject, since at the Maronite boarding school, French had been the principal language.

The other children were aware that Ammar's mother was the famous movie star. It was the kind of circumstance that could make a child either a hero or a target. Ammar, moody and bookish, was helpless to turn it to his advantage. He had already been bounced around a lot, and his lack of sense of belonging bred insecurity. From hanging around the stage with his mother, he developed the habit of speaking in classical Arabic. This was the language of the theater, not the streets, and it sounded to his schoolmates like a snobbish affectation. They would tease and torment him, and during recesses, when the others would play, he would seek out quiet places to be alone with his thoughts and fantasies.

The worst part of the day was the ride back and forth in the school bus. There was no escape from the bullies for whom he made easy prey. When he complained, his parents made other arrangements: a local blacksmith would transport Ammar on his motorcycle for a small fee. But this meant passing time before or after at the blacksmith's home, and Ammar felt the same unease with the blacksmith's rough-hewn children that he did with his classmates. At last, in fourth grade, Ammar won parental permission to commute to school by foot. This was a relief, but brought its own dangers. Once, walking along in short pants, Ammar felt a sharp sting as a man riding past on a motorcycle slapped his bare calf to punish him for violating Islamic modesty.

Cared for mostly by nuns and grandmothers, Ammar longed for the gentleness of female company. There were girls in the grammar school, but the sexes were kept apart, and he had little chance to cross the barrier.

Junior high school was even worse. There were no girls at all, except the principal's daughter, and among Ammar's classmates was a boy named Bashar, the son of the president, Hafez Al-Assad. Another son, Maher, the same fellow who was later to shoot Assef Shawkat in the stomach, also attended in a different grade.

Bashar and Maher and their roughneck bodyguards were a law unto themselves, with whom no one could tangle, not even the principal. Once, a male teacher missed several weeks of school after having said something in class to which young Bashar took exception. The word went around that he took sick leave to nurse the injuries inflicted by the youth's guards. It was not uncommon for students to get manhandled by these toughs for the least pretext. They knocked around Ammar a few times. Once he protested when one of them cut ahead of him in line and was rewarded with some humiliating slaps in the face. "I hated their guts from that point on," he says, meaning the ruling family.

His quest for belonging led him to religious exploration. When he was twelve he read a book on Buddhism. Its emphasis on life's pains resonated with his lonesome sadness, so he tried to concoct an olio of Buddhism and Islam, but the task was beyond him. At thirteen, he discovered a fellow sufferer from teenage insomnia, so the two began to meet in the wee hours to attend *fajr*, the first mandatory prayer of the Muslim day, which is held before dawn. "The morning prayer in that part of Damascus in those days was less crowded than it is today, and there was a sort of serenity in the air that I enjoyed," he recalls. But after a few days, one of the sheikhs noticed that these two boys were coming to morning prayers but not to the other four obligatory daily prayers. Rather than trying to draw them in, he responded sternly. Either do it right or not at all, he admonished. So they stopped coming.

With the arrival of adolescence came thoughts of dating, courtship and sex. Due to his mother's celebrity (and probably, although he doesn't seem to have been aware of it, also to his own good looks), Ammar did not lack for attention from girls. But his social awkwardness was paralyzing. "I was too shy to go after the girls I wanted," he remembers, "and at the same time I had to put up with girls I didn't want. It was ridiculous, but I didn't know how to deal with it."

At age sixteen, he decided to become a Catholic priest. "The idea of priesthood and celibacy was a solution to this whole thing: my loneliness on the one hand and my sexual shyness on the other." The insurmountable problem, however, "was how I was going to be a Catholic priest in a country like Syria when I'm supposed to be a Muslim." Although he had to give up the idea, for more than a decade he made it a habit to dress entirely in black, as if in priestly vestments, and to practice celibacy.

Ammar's flight from sexual indulgence was reinforced by his abhorrence of the looser moral standards he encountered abroad. When he finished high school in 1983, his mother urged him to go to England to study the language. Although the cosmopolitan sensibilities of his parental neighborhood of Al-Jisr al-Abyad were liberal by Syrian standards, they were nothing compared to those he found in London:

> I was on my own for the first time and of course surrounded by people my age and older. And the mores were completely different, especially sexual mores. I was just shocked. The drinking was too much. The idea of wanting to lose control to that extent I could never really understand. So I think that made me retreat more and more unto religion.

Even his months in London did not prepare him for his next venture: going to Moscow for higher education. This was not an unusual choice since the Soviet Union was Syria's superpower patron. Ammar won a fellowship from the Syrian-Russian Friendship Society to study astronomy at Moscow University. While he had no bent for the sciences, the idea of studying the heavens resonated with his spiritual longings.

What he found at Moscow U., however, was far from heavenly. He was crammed into a dorm room with four other Arab students, all Lebanese. The building was nearly new, having been constructed for the 1980 Moscow Olympics, just a few years before, yet he found it already in a rundown state.

> There were cockroaches everywhere. Behind every bed there was a small hole from which cockroaches came, and we tried to plug it, and they kept unplugging it. It was the most disgusting thing. And yet at some point we got used to them. We were brushing them off our clothes when getting dressed. And then there were a lot of ants so wherever we put sugar, ants invaded. We realized at one point when we were drinking tea that ants were probably in it. If we ate cheese it probably had ants in it. There was no way we could do anything about it. So we just became cavalier about it and we joked about it. And finally, we just stopped joking because we had grown so used to it.

This sordid situation also kindled questions. In addition to being strategic allies, the Syrian and Soviet regimes were ideological cousins. Baathism had drawn heavily on Communism and proclaimed similar goals. Ammar's father had been a Baathist, and although Ammar himself hated Bashar Al-Assad and his cronies, this stemmed from personal experience, not ideology. Now, however, he started to wonder: "What did socialism have to do with living like that, in such poor conditions? It was incomprehensible."

He also found himself appalled at consequences of the meanness of life under Communism: "Because of the poverty and restrictions at that time, you could buy Russian girls for a pair of jeans. They'd be your slaves for a month if you gave them a pair of jeans and bought them vodka. Russia, because of that socialist system, reduced its people to that level where they prostituted themselves for ludicrous things."

That was a temptation difficult for most college age men to resist, perhaps especially ones from cultures where sex was less readily available. Ammar, however, was repelled by it:

> OK, fine, you want to meet girls. I can understand and respect that even though I was too shy and awkward to do it myself. But it wasn't about having girlfriends, it was about having sex. Sometimes some of the Russian girls who were brought in and were too drunk ended up being, frankly, gang raped by three or four people at a time. This was not something I could stomach.

This was going on in Ammar's own room. But what could he do about it? Fortunately, one of his four Lebanese roommates was a Shiite Islamist, a member of Hizbullah, who shared Ammar's revulsion at dissolute behavior. They joined forces and

> established rules that no girls were allowed in our room. If people wanted to have "friends," then go somewhere else. That system allowed our little room to become an island so at least I could come back and not have to worry about people getting drunk or walking in on someone raping someone.

The pathetic abasement of young Russian women was not the only disquieting thing Ammar encountered in Moscow. Baathist Syria was a regimented society, but in the Soviet Union Ammar discovered degrees of government control that went further still.

> Why would people be so nosy about what you were doing in your own room? To control how you decorate or what pictures you put up, or whether it's tidy or untidy? When I was sick inspectors came in, and we'd already been warned to tidy up our rooms so we tidied up, and nevertheless they came and said, "why is this there? Why is that there?" What the hell? I

want to put things the way I like them. Why are you bothering me about it?

Likewise, the Syrian students at Moscow U. had little trouble identifying the *mukhabarat* agent sent to keep tabs on them: although posing as a fellow student, he was older, poorer, and an Alawite like President Assad. But Ammar learned that spotting Russian spies was more difficult. When he inquired about the procedures for withdrawing from the school, he was asked if his discontent "had anything to do with not liking their socialist system," which Ammar denied. Then, a woman teacher with whom he had developed rapport came to see him. "Why do you always wear black?" she asked. "Is there something wrong?" She assured him that he could confide in her. "I realized she was spying on me," Ammar recalls. "And it was really unfortunate to see this nice woman being forced to spy." Here was a society, he realized, where ordinary citizens informed on one another. This happened in Syria, too, but it was not common. Of course, "revolutionary" rule had come to Syria much more recently. Was Russia the image of Syria's future?

Ammar's burgeoning political consciousness crystallized around the Syrian "election" that was held while he was in Moscow in 1984. It was a referendum in which the populace could vote "yes" or "no" to another term for Hafez Al-Assad, but there was only one right answer.

Ammar was now 18 and eligible to vote. Indeed, more than eligible: he received a communication from the embassy requiring him to come there and vote. Doing as told, he found this scene: "They had a table with three security guards, and they take your passport, smile at you and give you the paper ballot to fill out in front of them. So, of course I voted yes. There was nothing I could do." He was far from alone. According to the official results, 99.97% of Syrian voters approved giving their president seven more years. It is anyone's guess how many may have felt as Ammar did: "I hated myself afterwards."

Within eight months of arriving in Moscow, Ammar returned to Damascus. "I came home: a) religious, and b) anti-regime," he says. "Of course everyone was anti-Hafez Assad. But now I was more committed."

Committed to what? There was no freedom for political opposition, so his political anger remained for the time being mostly dammed up inside. On the other hand, his religious feeling was easy to express. But nothing came easily to Ammar's restless soul.

His Hizbullah roommate had impressed him. In the midst of a large group of Arab students who seemed to live for the moment, this one "was the only person who knew what he wanted. He was focused on his studies and he didn't have that confusion that everyone else had." So Ammar, who in the course of his young life had flirted with Catholicism, Sunnism, and even Buddhism, now had a dalliance with Shiism. At least, he spent some months reading Shiism. But it left him cold. Unlike Sunnism, Shiism is hierarchical, and despite all his yearnings to belong, Ammar chafed under authority.

So at the end of this period of study, he declared himself reconfirmed in his Sunnism. Although he had gotten there by a circuitous path, he was ready to enter adulthood as a conventional member of his society, practicing his faith and, as he imagined it, perhaps making a living as a shopkeeper. His experiences in Moscow and London, not to mention his own high school, had been less than satisfying, and he felt no appetite for more schooling. His parents, however, would have nothing of the idea that Ammar would thus descend the social ladder, however "classless" Syrian's socialist society pretended to be. They proposed instead that he resume his education in America, an intriguing proposal to which Ammar acquiesced.

He landed at a small school in an out-of-the-way place, the University of Wisconsin at Stevens Point. "The first year was a shock," he recalls. "This time the problem was just coping with being on my own. Growing up problems. Transforming myself from a spoiled child into a person that can actually do his laundry, ironing, grocery shopping and the like. It took me a while to get used to it."

Ammar never fit in easily even at home, so it was no surprise that he had difficulties finding his niche in Stevens Point. But there were things about America that he liked, starting with the friendliness. The school assigned him a "host family," an elderly couple who invited him and some other Arab students to their home for holidays and took them out boating on the lake nearby. Ammar discovered that "in America teachers have office hours, and you can go ahead and talk to them. So I struck up friendships with teachers," something unthinkable in Syria where, despite the official socialist ideology, professors have a sense of rank that makes it rare for them to devote time to students individually. Ammar had always yearned to be mentored, and in Wisconsin the people regarded that as their responsibility, even their calling.

Battening on these relationships, he flourished, but only briefly. He was still fragile, and a poor performance in math and a plunging Grade Point Average led him to drop out in the second semester of his sophomore year. "I didn't have enough guts to stick it out," he says.

He had one Syrian friend, and when he moved to Madison, taking a job in a restaurant, Ammar moved in with him. There was a mosque in Madison where he worshipped, and it had a small library where he indulged in reading "Qutb, Muslim Brotherhood manuals, the Qur'an commentaries, the Hadith, whatever."

A guest preacher from Jordan fired Ammar with the idea of joining the Afghan mujahideen fighting against Soviet occupiers. Here was a clear and noble purpose in which to invest his life. Ammar handed his passport and airfare to a local recruiter who would arrange his passage.

But before he could depart, his mother came to visit him. "She was like, 'you're going where?'" he recalls. Ammar by now was in his twenties, so rather than trying to defeat his plan head-on, she tried a stratagem. She persuaded him to join her in visiting some friends who lived in Los Angeles before he left the country. He recalls:

> One of the people my mom knew worked on a TV program called *Islam*. He met me and introduced me to a Pakistani fellow who ran the show and who had been in Pakistan not too long before and had gone to the Afghan camps in Pakistan. And he said: "what are you doing? They're going to put you on the frontline so they can kill you, especially since you're [mother is] known, so they can use your name as a martyr. Right now there is a civil war and they are killing each other; the Russians have pulled out and now they are fighting among tribes in provinces, among individual leaders. Why do you want to go? If you stay and become part of the community here, there are so many things you can do."

Ammar allowed himself to be dissuaded. He retrieved his passport and money from the recruiter, and relocated in Los Angeles as imam of the Islamic Center of South Bay-L.A., a mosque in Lomita. He led prayers, sometimes delivered the Friday sermon, cleaned up after services, and even performed a few conversions. There was no regular pay, but he was allowed to live in the mosque. For spending money, he took odd jobs: the night shift at a nearby filling station; construction work for a Syrian-American builder; free-lance research.

Immersing himself in Islamic theology, he composed a polemic against Shiism. He decided in the end not to publish it, but he had spoken of it, and rumors of its existence embroiled him in some controversy.

In February 1989, the publication of Salman Rushdie's novel, *The Satanic Verses,* sparked demonstrations and riots in Muslim countries. Iran's ruler, the Ayatollah Ruhollah Khomeini, issued a *fatwa* calling for Rushdie's murder. The *Los Angeles Times* sought comment from Ammar as a prominent local Muslim. At first, he sounded very much the angry young man. Publication of the book, he said was "a new step taken by the Western media to attack our religion."[6] But then he criticized Khomeini, as well: "To say that [Rushdie] should be killed is ridiculous. That is stretching the matter too far."

The next day pro-Khomeini demonstrators appeared at the mosque demanding Ammar's ouster. Pressure against him was reinforced by those who had gotten wind of his unpublished anti-Shiite screed. Within a month he left the mosque for a job with the Islamic television program where his mother's friends worked. But his forced departure had planted a seed of doubt in him. The religious certainty that had taken him so long to achieve began to give way to his old spiritual restlessness.

He did not abandon faith or resume the religious quest that had already taken him to so many destinations. Instead his curiosity focused on America. "I bought dozens of books on American history," he recalls. "I read everything: the communist point of view, Charles Beard on the economic interpretation of the constitution; the Federalist Papers; the [Henry Steele] Commager books; Barbara Tuchman, Daniel Boorstin, Bill Moyers, Paul Johnson, all the major works of American history."

As he read, the idea grew within him to return to college to study history. The University of Wisconsin was ready to have him back, and this time he was a more mature and assured student. He earned A's, made the Dean's List, and became president of the United Muslim Association on campus. He arranged to do an independent study, writing a paper on the early life of the Prophet.

From all appearances, he had finally gotten his life on-track. But this proved to be only the lull before the storm. He wanted to go on to graduate school, but his parents could no longer pay the tuition that was astronomical to Syrians, and he failed to get a fellowship. This was distressing, but soon something more profound began to bother him. It stemmed from the seed of doubt that had been planted by his ouster from the Lomita mosque and flowered when he gave a talk about Islam at a conference on comparative religion:

> There were Christians, New Agers, and whatever, and I found myself agreeing more and more with the atheist point of view. And I realized when I went back home, "Oh My God! I'm an atheist!" I remember I looked at the clock and it was December 21, 4:23 p.m. And that was when I lost my center.

He had not been chafing against the rigors of Islam. His crisis was purely spiritual. "I kept my conservative lifestyle. I was still shy and conservative and still said no to alcohol. But I was an atheist." He lapsed into a depression that lasted for a year, doing little productive except working in a restaurant to pay his bills. "I was just lost," he says. He began to think of suicide:

> I had lost my faith. I'm an atheist, and the world is not going to accept me. I realized I had become so different—whether I was in the East or West—that my loneliness felt so supreme at that time. So I decided to die with style and be romantic about it. I chose a knife. I chose a location, which was a nice spot by the Century Insurance Company building where they had a wonderful artificial lake, a very serene location. And I chose a date, which was the last day of my summer work, August 31st. So I continued working until then.

He found comfort in writing. He began by keeping a diary. "It was a crazy diary, I called it mindscapes," he recalls. "It was a diary not of events but of my thoughts, and they were really terrible. I felt I was going mad. So at one point I said to myself: 'If you are losing your mind, lose it on paper. Write.'"

The diary was filled with fantasies, mostly about religion, some about sex. Others were about his torments and his grandiose dreams of saving the world. From the diary he branched out to poetry, bits of novels, fantasy. In one, he imagined himself

> walking through the city of Damascus at night and meeting
> the winged horse, Buraq, that took the Prophet to Heaven.
> And Buraq comes, and I sit on his back and instead of going
> up I go down into a netherworld and over there all the
> prophets exist and all the mythical figures that play a role in
> the monotheistic religions and Middle Eastern legend....
> Every time I meet someone like Jesus or Gilgamesh, they give
> me a monologue of their life that's different from the legend or
> history that we know.

Looking back, he says: "I don't know what the point of that was except to be blasphemous." Perhaps he was trying out his atheist wings, but he seemed still to be wrestling with the same religious questions that had haunted him since his Muslim grandmother rescued him from the clutches of the nursery school nuns.

Having made the decision that "instead of dying by the knife, I might as well die by the pen," Ammar decided it was time to return home. "I began to take myself seriously as a writer," he says. And in case he could not make a living at it, he could live with his parents. "I had not saved any money, since I was planning to die," he recalls. So he called home to ask them to wire the cost of a ticket. "And two weeks later, I was back in Damascus."

For the next year, he enjoyed the luxury of working little, reading and resting. Back in his mother's orbit, he worked on translating a book on American film critics, *Criticism of*

Criticism, into Arabic. But when he was done, the Syrian Ministry of Culture, the only available publisher, refused to issue it on the grounds that it was "too American."

After a year, his mother wanted him to go to work, so she used her connections with the chief of Syrian public television. The starting salary was 3,600 Syrian Pounds per month, the equivalent of about $70 or $75. This was scarcely generous even by Syrian standards, but the point, so he was told, was that this was the first rung on the ladder into the establishment. "Don't worry about the salary; there will be other things in the future," Ammar remembers his new boss telling him. "I want you to work with me. I want to introduce you to the doctor," by which he meant Bashar Al-Assad, an optometrist before he became dictator.

The man did not know that Ammar had already been introduced to "the doctor" in junior high school, an experience that had left a lasting distaste. Thus, Ammar had little interest in joining the ruling elite which meant toadying to the Assads. Instead he found a job teaching social studies to grades 5 through 8 at the Pakistani International School.

He had little patience for the teaching materials he found available:

> When I looked at the books it was the lousiest form of history you could imagine. "This person was born on this date. He conquered whatever on this date. He was great." This was history. So I think I finished the book within a month and then I told them I don't ever want to see those books again.

Ammar threw himself into devising his own curriculum. For his teaching methodology, he turned to his thespian roots.

> I talked about the ancient Egyptians, pharaohs, the Sumerians, the Babylonians. I told them legends, mythology, and I acted them out. I always enjoyed that part. I acted out the different roles, and they were fascinated by that. It's like having

to prepare for a stage play. You have the script and you're reading and practicing to be actors. And we were reading the different parts and the myths, and I'd tell them the meaning of the mythologies: the underlying themes of mortality, achievement, recognition and so on.

The female teachers paid him a lot of attention. As his painful shyness toward women ebbed, he grew aware that he was considered highly eligible. "I was such an idiot, socially speaking," he recalls, "that I did not realize being the son of Muna Wassef, single, and having a good job, and being the age I was, all meant that I constituted 'a catch.'"

He began to spend time with one of the other teachers, a divorcée who had just returned from living in Canada and shared his more modern teaching methods. To Ammar she appeared to be a soul mate: "I thought of her as a Bohemian girl, raising two kids on her own. She's tough: she stood up to her husband who was abusive and she came here and stood up against tradition." They dated for some months and the progress of their romance became a hot topic among their adolescent charges. After 4 or 5 months they became engaged.

But soon thereafter, Ammar began to note another side to her:

> The more we went out the more I realized she was very traditional underneath the surface of that openness of hers. If you wanted to get married, you had to go talk to her parents or uncles in this case, since her parents had died. The family has to go to the family. In other words, we have to follow tradition. We have to speak about the early dowry; in Islam we call it the *mahar*.

The realization that he would have to conceal his atheism from her family in order to secure their permission grated on Ammar. Conversely, she was growing uneasy over his extreme liberalism. They cancelled the engagement.

A year or two later, he became involved with a Christian girl, but her parents put their foot down against the match. In their own right, they were tolerant, but as they told him, "It's the society we're worried about because our daughter will be shunned if she marries a Muslim and you will be shunned" for marrying a Christian.

It was around this time that Ammar took some early steps of political dissidence. He expressed some of his rebellious thoughts in poems. In one he ridiculed the official media for attributing all important events in the country to the beneficence of the ruler, writing sardonically, "under the patronage of the president, my mother gave birth to me."

More daring was his response to the 1999 referendum awarding Hafez Al-Assad a fifth term of office. "I remembered the referendum I had to vote in 1985 in Moscow, and I decided that now it is time to redeem myself," he recalls. He went to vote with his mother at the Ministry of Culture. The paper ballots contained two circles, green for yes and black for no. When you mark one of the circles "they look at you. You do it publicly: there is no booth." His mother went first and checked "yes." Then Ammar took his ballot and checked "no." As he reached to drop it in the ballot box, "A person comes from behind me, a security guy, and says, 'Wait a minute, you put No to the president.'" The security man, assuming that Ammar had acted by accident, took the ballot and gave Ammar a new one. Ammar took pen in hand and asked, "You mean if I check the black box, I'll be saying No to the president?" And when the reply came in the affirmative, he said, "That's what I am trying to say," checked No and dropped it in the ballot box.

A commotion ensued. "The security guy was more afraid than I was," recalls Ammar. "My mom was having a heart attack; she still hates me for it." There were, however, no repercussions. When the government announced the official tally, it said that nine million people had voted, and that all had voted Yes to another term for Assad, except, as Ammar recalls, "there were 917 empty ballots and 219 that said No. I was one of the No's, and I wrote a poem about it."

After his successive disappointments in romance with his fellow teachers, Ammar resigned himself to a life of bachelorhood. "It's nice to live the bohemian lifestyle," he said. Also, in the late nineties he was becoming more involved in Syria's small and fragile dissident community, and he signed a contract for publication of his first novel, *Menstruation*.

Saqi, a London publisher specializing in Middle Eastern subjects, published it in English in 2001, and it was soon translated into several other languages. Not surprisingly, Ammar visited the Saqi exhibit at that year's Damascus Book Fair, in the company of his friend Ma'an. A pretty young woman was manning it. Her easy manner gave Ammar the impression that she must have been a daughter of the elite, working just for the pleasure of books, not for need. Afterwards, he regretted not having made some effort to get acquainted.

A year later, at the 2002 Book Fair, he and Ma'an visited the Saqi exhibit again, and the same woman was there. This time, Ammar was determined to meet her. Her name was Khawla, and when the fair closed for the day, he and Ma'an went to dinner with her and a co-worker. Ammar found her "fascinating. She was definitely non-traditional and a woman who stood up for herself, in addition to being charming and witty." She also told them that she had children, an unusually bold thing for an unattached Syrian woman to reveal, since it would make her less desirable.

Khawla's mother, Nahla Qazak, was a doctor, a Palestinian woman whose family had fled Haifa in 1948 when she was six, in what Israelis call their War of Independence and Palestinians call the Naqba, or Catastrophe. Khawla's father was Abdul Wadud Yusuf, a well-known Islamist from the city of Homs who churned out novels and doctrinal books with titles like *The Believers' Explanation of the Koran* and *The Woman Revolution* and *They Were Barbarians*. His method was as modern and inventive as his point of view was reactionary. Several of his novels were in the style of science fiction, picturing future life after the restoration of the caliphate.

His interpretations were strongly traditional stressing the duty of *jihad* and the proper role of women. He permitted his wife to practice medicine, but her clinic was attached to their house, so she was not really working outside of the home, where he exercised unchallenged authority.

They had three sons and two daughters to whom he was generous and attentive. But he had a terrible temper and would beat them brutally, especially Khawla, the eldest, and Hammam, the oldest of the boys. Nahla was passive, lest he turn his fury on her. Although she had been raised in a religiously liberal home, as was common among Palestinians, she had donned the veil and adopted his orthodox lifestyle.

One day in 1980, amidst a wave of harsh repression of Islamists and other dissidents, Khawla returned from school to find both her parents missing and her house filled with *mukhabarat*. She was 12 and her siblings were 10, 7, 4, and 9 months. About a dozen security men stayed in the house apparently waiting to arrest any of her father's associates who might show up. Khawla expected that a grandmother or aunt would appear to take care of them, but the other family members had also been swept up in the security service's net.

Too innocent of politics to figure this out, she felt abandoned but did not allow herself to be immobilized. She realized that the care of her brothers and sisters was entirely on her own narrow shoulders. She cooked for them, and gave her baby brother his bottles and changed his diapers. Sometimes she had to do extra cooking, when the *mukhabarat* men, who remained at the house to arrest callers, demanded to be fed.

After a week, when Khawla went to the bathroom one night to get a diaper for 9-month-old Obaida, a *mukhabarat* man followed and grabbed her. She knew little of sex but understood that he aimed to have his way with her. She screamed, and one of the other *mukhabarat* pulled his colleague off her.

A few days later, Nahla was released, and the maternal duties that Khawla had borne so stoically reverted to her mother. But the family still awaited the release of Abdul Wadud whom they learned was being held in a detention camp called Sheikh Hassan. After six months they received good news: Abdul Wadud had been transferred to a prison in Damascus called the Citadel, a lower security facility where prisoners were often held prior to release.

For the first time visits were permitted, so Nahla went to see him, bringing Khawla. When Khawla and her mother caught sight of Abdul Wadud across the double row of fencing separating inmates from visitors, their joy quickly dissolved into horror. His fingernails were missing, and he bore other obvious signs of torture.

On one of their subsequent visits, they could not find Abdul Wadud. Nahla recognized a friend of his and asked where her husband was. The friend replied that Abdul Wadud had been taken back to the interrogation camp. Khawla asked her mother what it all implied, and although she cannot recall the exact words, her mother conveyed at once the bleak conviction that Abdul Wadud was lost to them forever.

And so it was. Despite her grim pessimism, Nahla asked after him for years and indeed decades. Some former inmates or prison employees told her that Abdul Wadud had died under torture, but the information was never definitive. Once, the family received a telegram from the *mukhabarat* instructing them to collect Abdul Wadud's body from *Muassa* hospital. But when they arrived, they were told there was no such person in the morgue. Sometimes security employees would offer to deliver packages to Abdul Wadud, but it became clear that they were keeping whatever goods she would entrust to them.

The loss of her father, the lack of knowledge of his fate, and her own ambivalence about his absence would have been more than enough for any adolescent to bear. But Khawla's travails did not end there.

The brutal suppression of the Islamists was accompanied by a fierce propaganda campaign exhorting the citizenry to look upon them as a mortal threat to the nation. Like Communism and Nazism, Baathism created a party state in which advancement in virtually any institution depended on membership and loyalty to the party "line."

School principals would have to be party members, and teachers ambitious in their careers would want to be, as well. There were also student party clubs for those eager to steal a march on their classmates. The daughter of a notorious renegade made a natural target for all of these upward-strivers. In her secondary school, the Baathist students shunned and harassed Khawla, often pulling off the *hijab* she wore as a girl from a religious home, while the adults took pains to avoid offering any approval of her classroom performance or allowing any fault of hers to go unpunished lest they be accused of giving comfort to the enemy. In one particularly egregious example, an art teacher became alarmed that an oil painting of Khawla's might win first prize in a contest. To avoid criticism for succoring the daughter of an undesirable, the teacher blotted out Khawla's signature and replaced it with the name of a student from a Baathist family.

All of this ill-treatment succeeded in making Khawla quite miserable, but then, suddenly, she was offered a way out. A marriage proposal arrived by mail from Saudi Arabia. The author had been a neighbor of Khawla's, but he had taken refuge in the ultra-devout kingdom because he was an Islamist activist and did not want to meet the same fate as her father. His name was Muhammad Al-Nashar Al-Rifay, and he was 24. Khawla was fifteen.

Muhammad's proposal threw Khawla into confusion. She wanted desperately to escape her life as a high school pariah. But, a ninth-grader, she did not feel ready for marriage and scarcely knew Muhammad. Her family said that the decision was hers, but uncles, aunts and grandparents joined in urging her to take this proffered way out and after more than a year she succumbed to their consensus.

Khawla was seventeen when they wed, and she moved to Dammam, in eastern Saudi Arabia, to be with her husband, free at last from all the abuse she had suffered since the arrest of her father. Sadly, it was not long before she concluded that she had escaped the frying pan for the fire. Muhammad, ardent in courtship, proved to be indifferent in matrimony. He left for work at seven each morning and returned at seven in the evening, and even then took little interest in his wife. During the long days Khawla was alone in the house without friends, relatives or even servants. Under the laws of Saudi Arabia, she could not go out without her husband. Muhammad had promised her that she could go to school. But he reneged, apparently averse to the burden of transporting her. To pass the time, Khawla cooked, kept house, read, sewed, and wrote five letters a day home to her family.

What remedied her awful loneliness was the birth of a daughter, whom they named Oula, which means, "glory." Four years later she bore a son and named him Mouhanad, a kind of sword. Then, Khawla's Saudi sojourn was brought to an abrupt end in a way she would never have chosen despite her unhappiness. Near the end of 1991, Muhammad learned he had advanced cancer. He entered the hospital, and twenty days later, he was dead.

So, with a mixed heart, Khawla made ready to return to the country of her birth. It held many painful memories for her, and it was soon to bring her new travails. In Islamic law, children belong to the father. If he dies, guardianship passes to his family rather than to the mother. As soon as she arrived back in Damascus, Khawla found herself in a war with Muhammad's family over Oula and Mouhanad. The root of it seemed to be money.

As is commonly done in the kingdom, where life insurance is regarded as contrary to *Sharia*, Muhammad's friends had donated to a kitty for Khawla and the children, amassing twenty thousand dollars. When Muhammad's family, which had already laid claim to his estate, learned of this fund, greed got the best of them. Custody of the children, to whom most of the treasure legally belonged, would convey claim to the money. Hoping to divert the family from this path, Khawla handed the twenty thousand to Muhammad's brother to manage. Legally, he dared not pocket it, since the money belonged to the children, so he invested it in rental property in their names and kept the proceeds for himself.

Even delivering up the cash to Muhammad's brother, however, did not end her struggles with his family. For reasons of pride, or to get a free hand with the funds that were in the children's names, or perhaps just out of his sense of the right order of things, Muhammad's father still wanted the children. Islamic law recognizes the mother's role as nurturer, but holds that children revert to the father's family at age eleven for a girl, nine for a boy.

When Oula turned 11, Khawla received a legal order from a *Sharia* court—which held authority over family and social matters even under secular Baathist rule—awarding custody to the grandfather. Shocked that she had received no notice of the hearing, Khawla deduced that her father-in-law had bribed the judge.

She felt desperate, not only for herself but also for the children who she knew did not feel loved by Mohammed's family. As Oula puts it: "I didn't like them. After my father's death they didn't act with us the way they did with other kids in the family, my cousins. They didn't care about us."[7] So Khawla packed up Oula and Mouhanad and disappeared.

When he realized what she'd done, her father-in-law went back to the judge and got a criminal judgment against her. For six months she remained on the lam with her two youngsters, 11 and 7, staying with various friends, all in all a pretty brazen feat in a totalitarian state. But what does a seven-year-old know of politics? Mouhanad recalls it as a wonderful adventure:

> I remember every single detail but I'm not going to say I felt bad or something, because we were having fun at the same time. We were traveling from city to city, place to place, and meeting new people all the time. That my mom was running away from the police, I didn't think much about.[8]

While Khawla and the children were hiding out, her family hired a lawyer who moved to overturn the custody decision. An honest and sympathetic judge delivered a Solomonic decision: custody was granted neither to Khawla nor her in-laws but to Khawla's mother. And he postponed Khawla's sentencing for running off with the children until the time came for one of the sweeping amnesties that the president would grant periodically to demonstrate his majesty.

That Khawla fought so tenaciously to keep her children was perhaps a natural expression of maternal instinct. More remarkable was the verve with which she strove, unbowed by the tragedies that had befallen her, to make a gratifying life for herself. She discovered a milieu of intellectually curious young adults who had lost parents to the regime's purges and persecutions. The group included both males and females, which in itself was a departure from society's norms. They invited thinkers with unorthodox opinions to lecture to them in the relative safety of private homes. "We were trying to come to terms with what had happened to us and why," says Khawla.[9]

Khawla also joined a hiking group run by a Jesuit priest from Holland, Père Francis, who also practiced psychoanalysis. When the regime forced Père Francis to move to Homs in order to remove his subversive presence from Damascus, Khawla entered therapy with one of his Syrian acolytes, *Pere Rami*. "I wanted to get rid of the pain inside me," she says.

For all her gratitude to the Jesuit priests who helped her, she was not drawn to Christianity even as she pulled back from Islam. "There is something very masculine in all the religious structures that have been imposed on us," she notes disapprovingly. Then she adds: "I don't know if there is God as he is usually thought of, but there is something good on my side." She had come a long way from her upbringing by Abdul Wadud.

The intellectual curiosity that was stimulated by this milieu prompted Khawla to volunteer to work at the Damascus Book Fair where she had her chance encounter with the handsome, longhaired author who wrote novels with such strange titles as *Menstruation*. Their first encounter, at the 2001 book fair came to naught. But when they met again, at the next year's book fair, they went to dinner with a group of friends, and during the meal Ammar declared: "Now that we've found you, we'll never let you go."

Khawla was surprised by the feelings welling inside her because she had reached a point of despair about finding love. "I felt hopeless about having a real relationship," she recalls. "I had had very bad experiences with my first husband and with various boyfriends. I felt that it would be better to have no man in my life again."

Ammar, however, seemed different. From that first group dinner, she was "interested in his thinking, his mind, his ideas about life. So I thought, 'why not?'" What attracted her was that he seemed,

> Both American and Syrian. His mind is very Western and at the same time he speaks Arabic and can feel what I feel, and

we can communicate. I have friends from Europe, but I cannot make very deep conversation or relationships with them. And I saw my sister with her husband from Prague, and there is difficulty in the relationship. So I figured I need a Syrian man or Arab man but with a Western mind, Western in relating to women and to my kids and everything.

Day by day, her attraction deepened, and one night she wrote in her diary that he was the man who made her "feel like I was waiting for him my entire life." Then, a couple of days later, she showed him this entry. Ammar didn't know how exactly to react, but it seems to have made a deep impact, at least subconsciously, when he called her the next evening. He recalls:

> I was supposed to call her and I was going through some ground rules in my head: "remember, she used to be married, she has kids, she's probably looking for a commitment, so just keep it simple." Then I picked up the phone and we started talking. And at one point I don't know what we said but then I referred to myself as "the person you're about to *marry*." And at once I thought: "what the hell am I saying?" And she said: "excuse me, did you say something about marriage?" And I didn't know what to do and we laughed about it. Then I said, "What I'm trying to say is that I like you."

Khawla, however, did not let it drop; she dared him to repeat those words to her face the next day, which he did. Three days later she moved in with him together with her children. Oula was 15 and Mouhanad, 11. It took them three months to be sure that they loved each other, and at the same time Ammar fell in love with the children. "If I needed a family and kids then that's the family and kids I've always wanted; it's perfect. They're a wonderful package deal."

Ammar and Khawla were sufficiently nonconformist that they might have lived together unwed, but the children,

Ammar says, needed "a chance at feeling settled so they're not wondering all the time." In addition they reasoned that marriage would shield them from anyone "putting fear in our lives or bothering us because we are breaking the rules and the laws." So in January 2003, they were wed.

Ammar was now making a living by writing summaries of the Syrian press for the Canadian embassy, doing translations, and aiding Western journalists as a fixer and translator. Through his widening circle of contacts among foreign diplomats, he learned of the Syrian European Business Center, an EU-funded program intended to boost the private sector. It had languished under Baathist socialism, but the regime now want to revive it to stimulate growth. As a demonstration of its reform-mindedness, it supported a special initiative to encourage female entrepreneurs, with no less a figure than the vivacious, British-born and raised first lady, Asma Assad, as its official patron.

Under the aegis of this project, Khawla secured office space for a marketing clinic that she and Ammar ran. Out of this office they launched the Tharwa Project. Taking advantage of the brief relaxation that followed Hafez Al-Assad's death in 2000 and his succession by his son, Bashar, Tharwa propounded a range of liberal goals. Its statement of purpose declared that it aimed "to provide a free platform for the discussion and dissemination of ideas that can contribute to raising the standards of civic awareness" in the region, with the hope of "supporting ongoing processes of democratization … [and] peace-building … . Helping in bringing greater understanding to gender-related issues … . [And] helping promote … basic principles of human rights."[10]

The activities of Tharwa were carried out mostly in cyberspace. Even in its most lenient moment the Assad regime rarely allowed private groups to discuss issues in person. In addition to Ammar's own output, the Tharwa website published writings by mostly young Syrians whom Ammar recruited, and it also carried reprints and translations from other sites and organizations. For example, the site, "bitter-lemons.org," run jointly by Israelis and Palestinians, publishes weekly exchanges on various aspects of the Israel-Palestinian conflict. Tharwa translated each of these into Arabic, and did the same with the debates on the sister site, "bitterlemons—international," which covers the gamut of regional issues. The presentation of such an evenhanded debate between Israelis and Arabs was almost unheard of in the Arab world, especially in a country like Syria where the state-controlled press addresses such issues in hyperbolic and propagandistic terms.

Ammar, himself, views the Arab-Israel conflict through the prism of the struggle for accountable government in the Arab world. He explains:

> On one hand the whole concept of building a homeland for the Jews in the midst of an Arab land had a problematic aspect to it when it came down to the rights of the people who actually lived there. But ... the people who sold their lands to Jewish organizations, they knew what they were doing and they were Arab, mostly Syrian and Lebanese. In other words there is something in our way of life, our feudal structure at that time that played into the hands of the Zionist project. I realized that the best thing is to cut our losses and to try to reach a compromise so that we can end the conflict because the conflict is always going to be used by our own leaders to rob us blind. It is another instrument of oppression, even in the hands of the Palestinian leaders. After the establishment of the Palestinian authority, the "peace process" was used by Arafat and others to divert attention from their corruption, and they established a police state while the Palestinians were aspiring to a democratic state.

However, Tharwa's primary focus was not this issue, but rather the status of minorities in the region, a subject that may have resonated with Ammar due to his own mongrel Arab-Kurd, Christian-Muslim background. The word, *tharwa*, means wealth, and the Tharwa Project's slogan is "Difference is Wealth."

Ammar, however, was more a loner than a joiner, and he participated little in the activities of other dissidents. Even more than through Tharwa he made his mark through the articles he wrote in foreign newspapers, his defiant statements on-the-record to Western reporters, and his path-breaking willingness to speak to the Israeli press.

His essays were relentlessly critical of the regime. In the spring of 2003, he wrote, "The Syrian regime is painting itself into a dark and dreary corner that could mean a showdown with the United States."[11]

The next year he grew bolder. In an op ed in the *Daily Star*, he wrote:

> The Syrian regime ... faces a serious existential crisis, that of potential international isolation as a prelude to potential regime change. Still, it does not seem capable of delivering much-needed reform to help avoid this. Its ... human resources ... are obviously not enough, and its hesitant reaching out to the opposition is insufficient.[12]

A week later, following riots by Syrian Kurds, Ammar was back on the *Star*'s op ed page warning, "The ruling Syrian regime is faced with a new challenge that it can only win if it is ready to adopt drastic changes in its style and internal composition."[13] In April 2004, at a conference in Istanbul, a reporter for *Jerusalem Report* asked Ammar for an interview and was stunned when he accepted. "Abdulhamid, 38, readily agrees to sit down for an interview with an Israeli-based magazine," said the *Report*. "He's not sure what the consequences might be, Abdulhamid says, but he's willing to take his chances."[14]

Taking chances was rapidly becoming Ammar's trademark.

In his next newspaper essay he commented disdainfully that the Syrian government's "decision-making process is hopelessly flawed, if not nonexistent."[15] A month later, he protested that, "Four years after ... Bashar Assad ... clearly promised change ... no major change has taken place in the country."[16]

In July 2004, Ammar left Syria to accept a six-month visiting fellowship at the Brookings Institution in Washington, DC, whence he continued his assault on the regime. About Syria's ambassador to the United States, he wrote:

> Most politicians who met with [Imad] Mustafa tend to come away with the impression that the man, though capable and well intentioned, represents mostly himself rather than his regime or any power center within it. ... Syrian policy these days is becoming increasingly hard to explain to American audiences, no matter how eloquent the person attempting to do so.[17]

He allowed himself to be quoted in the *Washington Post*, calling his government an "obscurantist regime."[18] And in subsequent op eds, he tackled the extremely sensitive issue to Damascus of its "continued and shameless dabbling in Lebanese affairs."[19] He called for full compliance with Security Council resolution 1559, requiring withdrawal of all Syrian troops from Lebanon.[20]

As if it weren't enough to beard his government in this way, Ammar also gave free vent to liberal opinions that were iconoclastic in the Arab and Muslim worlds. Although he remained a citizen of a police state, he seems to have decided to speak whatever was on his mind. He told one interviewer, "Muslims feel humiliated [because] we are supposed to be at the center of the universe, and here we are at the margins of it. For 500 years, we have not contributed to human progress."[21] He told another that "moderate Muslims" needed to take "a more brave ... and ... clear stand" on terrorism and on "the reformation of the Islamic idea itself."[22] He sharpened the point about terrorism in an op ed in Lebanon calling for an end to efforts "to differentiate between what they call 'freedom fighters' and those described as terrorists." He addressed this in particular to Palestinians. "The passing of Arafat," he wrote, "whose attitude toward suicide bombings was always pragmatic (and amoral) anyway, should be taken advantage of to permanently mark the end of the violence option."[23]

As his half-year at Brookings drew to a close, and Ammar prepared to return to Syria, he brazenly told an interviewer that he was going home with hopes of a "velvet transformation," a play on the so-called "velvet revolution" that brought down Communism in Czechoslovakia. "I think the regime is internally weak, and we can actually do it," he added.[24]

To Khawla, Ammar's bravado was terrifying. Having seen her father disappear into the torture chambers of the regime for political apostasy, she knew the risks only too well. Although she spoke little English and was attached to her mother and siblings in Syria, she wanted to keep her husband in the safety of America.

She shared her feelings with the wife of Syria's ambassador in Washington, Imad Mustafa. A few weeks later, Mrs. Mustafa called Khawla with a surprising message. She said that she had just heard from her husband who was in Damascus for consultations. He told her that he had discussed Ammar with Bashar Assad directly, and that the president had told him to pass along the word that it was okay for Ammar to return to Syria.

This reassurance only had the effect of intensifying Khawla's fears. She suspected it was a trap. She begged Ammar not to return. But he was deaf to her pleas. "For the only time in our marriage, I thought of divorce," she says.

Instead she clung to Ammar fiercely, accompanying him almost everywhere he went once they got back to Syria, even to interrogation by the *mukhabarat*. Despite the regime's assurances that he was welcome to return, Ammar was met at the Damascus airport in January 2005 with a message to report to security. The relatives who were there to greet them were thrown into a panic, but Ammar acted nonchalant. "It took me some time to find out exactly which security apparatus wanted to speak to me," he noted dryly to the *New York Times,* "but then I met with them for two days in a row. I was very up front about my activities and even talked about things they didn't know yet, like an article I had co-written with an Israeli. One of my interrogators told me that what I was doing would have been unthinkable a few years ago, and he's right."[25]

How much had things changed in Syria? Ammar seemed intent on finding out. In addition to energizing the work of Tharwa, which he had continued while in Washington, Ammar looked forward to executing the ambitious agenda he had thought up for DarEmar, the publishing house he had founded.

At first he envisioned it as a place to publish his own works and those of other young writers. But then his vision grew, and he conceived the mission of bringing the seminal works of the European enlightenment to Arab audiences. "Take the Federalist Papers, the works of Descartes, Hume, Kant, Locke," he told an interviewer. "As far as I know, only some of Kant's work has been translated into Arabic, and many of these other philosophers and writers haven't been translated at all. It's really ridiculous."[26] By making these books available, he could nurture the current of liberalism in his nation's political discourse.

No less important than his formal projects was the place that Ammar carved out for himself as a public intellectual, an unprecedented role in Baathist Syria. He conducted himself as if he were in a free country, much to the distress of Khawla. "Every single moment in my very bad experience with the *mukhabarat* when I was a child filled my dreams and my daytime thoughts," she recalls. "It was real fear."

From Damascus, he continued to contribute scathing op eds to the Lebanon *Daily Star.* He published in Lebanon because, as he put it in one essay, "Syria's media sector is one of the most tightly controlled in the Arab world."[27] In another he repeated that "the Syrian regime ... has painted itself into a corner."[28] In a third, he wrote that the political elite's "inability to grasp" the need for deep reform "poses an existential threat to both regime and country."[29]

His daring was unmatched, and it did not stop at generalized complaints. Some dictators have been known to tolerate a certain amount of criticism of the status quo as a pressure valve for discontent so long as blame is cast upon their subordinates rather than themselves. Had Ammar been thinking tactically he might have toed this fine line. But he was determined to speak his mind, and he took aim directly at the top man. About the state of Syria's economy he quipped that "Assad suffers from the Versailles syndrome,"[30] an allusion to Marie Antoinette's comment, "Let them eat cake." In an interview with London's *Guardian,* he likened the Assad regime to the mafia: "The capo di tutti capi [Hafez Al-Assad] has died but Michael Corleone [the tough son in *The Godfather*] is missing and Fredo [the weak son] is in charge."[31] This had such nice bite; he repeated it on other occasions, referring to Bashar as "not Michael Corleone but his hapless brother Fredo."[32]

Others watched Ammar's performance, incredulous. One paper reported that journalists wondered "how it is that [Ammar] is not dead."[33] While quoting him, the *Guardian* noted that "Abdulhamid ... has avoided prison so far."[34] Ammar treated the issue jocularly, saying that he was "courting death by media."[35]

But this game was no joke. An American academic stationed in Damascus suggested the broader stakes:

> A lot of people are waiting to see if Ammar is going to get into trouble. Some want to see if this means they can advance

their own agendas and stick their necks out. But there's a lot of resentment as well. People here have spent their careers observing all the red lines and playing by the rules, and if Ammar gets away with it, they're going to feel like fools.[36]

In other words, if Ammar survived, then the gates of free speech would be flung open in Syria.

The regime was not going to let this happen. This probably would have been the case under any circumstances, but Ammar's one-man campaign of defiance came at a particularly sensitive time. Less than a month after he and Khawla returned to Damascus, a mighty car bomb in Beirut claimed the life of Rafik Hariri, a former prime minister and leader of Lebanon's nationalist forces, as well as many bystanders. All suspicion in this brutal crime pointed to the Syrian government. Although the former ruler, Hafez Al-Assad, had allied with the Soviet Union and kept Syria in the ranks of the region's radicals, he had also always kept a door slightly open to the United States. In this way, he preserved maneuvering room. His less adroit son had now steered straight into a cul de sac: Washington was not prepared to give Damascus a pass on the Hariri assassination; neither were several other governments with ties to Lebanon. Bashar had blocked his own escape route from diplomatic isolation.

The regime's reflex reaction to mounting international pressure was to clamp down harder domestically. Some political prisoners who had been released were rearrested. A couple of members of the rubber stamp parliament who had spoken out independently were imprisoned or fled abroad. Discussion groups that had been tolerated for a short time were forced to close. The last of these was also the most well known, the eponymous Atassi forum, whose forced closure in 2005 was protested by Ammar in Lebanon's *Daily Star.*

During Ammar's first two months back in Damascus, he was summoned for questioning several times. Khawla always insisted on accompanying him. In March, a month after the Hariri killing, the confrontation rose to a higher level. Ammar received a phone call from Assef Shawkat, chief of military intelligence and the man many believed to be the mastermind of Hariri's death, asking him politely to come in for a chat. Shawkat had already tried to get his mother, the film star, to silence Amar, only to be warned that she would fight like a banshee if he were harmed.

Shawkat extended his large paw, and Ammar mustered his strength to match the other man's grip to show he was not intimidated. Because of the pretense that this was a friendly meeting, Shawkat could not easily object to Khawla's presence. Instead, he said to her soothingly, "Don't worry, Ammar is among family here," which reassured her not one whit.

Within minutes, Shawkat had kindled Ammar's wrath by accusing him of working for foreign enemies. Shawkat pointed out that the Middle East department of the Brookings Institution which had recently hosted Ammar—the Saban Center—was bankrolled by a "Zionist." As Ammar's temper flared, Khawla intervened to keep the meeting calm, glossing each man's words to the other with mild interpretations. Shawkat suggested that it would be better for Ammar to seek funding for his projects from the Syrian government than overseas sources, and he asked how much was needed to run Tharwa. Ammar understood Shawkat's new-found charitable streak as an attempt to buy his loyalty and services, so he tossed out a low number to signal that he needed no assistance and was not for sale. There the meeting ended.

In the ensuing weeks, Ammar received a couple of other calls from Shawkat, purportedly just to keep in touch; of course the real meaning was to let Ammar know that the regime had him in its sites. But Ammar did not cease tossing rhetorical darts. In June, Shawkat called and asked Ammar to come see him, complaining as if he were a neglected friend, that Ammar had been too distant. This time, Ammar told Khawla that he did not want her to come.

Shawkat sent a car for Ammar, who recalls:

> We go to the office, entering the security compound through a gate. I go inside and they take me through a back door to a different car. And we go out again, through a different gate. This time, they took my cell phone away. And I said to myself nervously, "What's happening here?" But then they end up taking me to a place that is ten minutes away called the Officers' Club. Apparently the general's regular office was being renovated.

There it was, in the rich leather chairs of Shawkat's temporary office at the Officers' Club that, over tea, Shawkat delivered his veiled death threat and Ammar experienced the epiphany that he would rather live to fight another day than to embrace martyrdom and devastate his wife and mother and newly adopted children.

After Shawkat wrapped Ammar in a bear hug to seal their agreement that Ammar would depart the country, a car delivered him back to his home. As soon as he entered he told Khawla, "we have to leave," and without missing a beat, she began to pack their things.

Eventually she would feel relief to have her family safe, despite the colossal challenge of starting over in a new country where she knew almost no one and did not speak the language. But for the moment, she felt nothing except intense focus on the tasks of their departure.

The family settled in Silver Spring, Maryland, a suburb of Washington, DC, and Ammar, with Khawla at his side, threw himself into dissident activism with greater energy than before. He joined the Syrian National Council, perhaps the broadest ideologically of the various exile groups. In short order the SNC nominated him to the executive of the National Salvation Front. The latter coalition was founded when Abdul Halim Khaddam resigned as Vice President of Syria and took refuge in France. He joined with Ali Sadreddin Al Bayanouni, another exile who headed the Syrian Muslim Brotherhood, perhaps the most moderate of the various national branches of that group. The Brotherhood's grassroots base in Syria, together with Khaddam's connections among the Baathist elite, gave the NSF a potential for greater political clout than other exile groups.

For Ammar—poet, idealist, nonbeliever—Khaddam and Bayanouni made strange bed fellows. Nonetheless, he decided that liberals like himself should join this coalition because of the possibility that it could shake the Syrian power structure. He tried to influence the NSF, persuading it to adopt a "bill of rights." He also urged the selection of a leader younger and bearing less baggage than Khaddam and Bayanouni to be the public face of the NSF. This proposal went nowhere, and some accused Ammar of having himself in mind for the position. But Ammar says he is well aware that his own views on politics and religion are too liberal for the Syrian mainstream.

His presence in the leadership, however, made the NSF more approachable for the U.S. government, which used Ammar as a liaison to forge loose ties with the group. Nonetheless, after a year, Ammar decided to withdraw from the NSF. The main reason was that the work of Tharwa was expanding, and the two roles did not mesh well. A small cadre of Tharwa activists continued to work inside Syria. Some of them disagreed with Ammar's decision to work with the NSF; and all of them were in danger of being compromised by the regime's ability to link Tharwa to the NSF on the grounds of Ammar's leadership in both organizations.

With grants from U.S. agencies, Ammar and Khawla opened a small but modern headquarters for Tharwa in the Washington suburbs. Much of its activity continued to be cybernetic, through a bilingual website replete with reprints and translations as well as original content, much of it from Tharwa members still in Syria. In addition, Tharwa offered an online institute, teaching courses about democratic ideas in which dozens of Syrians enrolled. And it carried out weeklong training programs in democratic ideas and dissident methods for young Syrians who slipped away to a foreign country. In addition, Tharwa began to produce television programs for transmission into Syria via a satellite network set up by Syrian dissidents with U.S. support.

Tharwa broke new ground by monitoring Syria's 2007 elections, the April balloting for members of the parliament and the May referendum awarding Bashar Al-Assad another seven years as president. Both exercises were, of course, farcical. Government officials, for example, announced that the president had received fifty percent more affirmative votes than the total number of registered voters it had announced only a month before. Tharwa managed to get ten of its members to circulate among polling places, gathering evidence of the fraud.

All of it was posted on a special section of the Tharwa website called "the Syrian Elector," which received 40,000 visits. Here, Tharwa's observers reported that in the parliamentary election, many voters were handed ballots on which the name of a candidate had already been inscribed; and while the government announced that 63 percent of eligible voters had voted, Tharwa offered its own estimate that the true number was around 7 percent.

In the presidential referendum, Tharwa's monitors told of university students who said they had been warned they could not take final exams if they did not vote; government employees who said their workplaces had been marched to the polling stations *en groupe*; shopkeepers and taxi and microbus drivers who said they were fined for not posting portraits of the president in their stores or vehicles; and army recruits who said they were forced to give their voting cards to their officers to vote on their behalf. All of this, as it was also reported, took place in a context in which no ballot was secret, all voting occurring in the view of officials. The Syrian Elector also reported on other regime shenanigans to maximize the vote of approval for President Assad, for example:

> In Homs, one of our team members there reported having witnessed a ten-year-old boy being allowed to cast a yes ballot for the president to the cheers of the crowd, all legal norms aside. No, this was not his father's ballot, this was a ballot *especially* given to him by the "nice" security people at the polling center. Such is the Assad democracy.[37]

In December 2007, 156 Syrians, signers of a manifesto demanding liberal reform, met at the home of Riad Seif, a former Member of Parliament and senior dissident, to form the Damascus Declaration Council. More than 100 others who could not attend phoned in. By open ballot, they elected a "shadow government." This unprecedented step signaled the birth of "a serious, organized opposition movement," commented Ammar. "Their part was to give us an alternative we can point to. Now our part is to publicize and support them." Since then, Tharwa has been in the forefront of bringing the Damascus Declaration to Capitol Hill and the international news media.

During this time, Ammar and two other Syrians opposed to the regime were invited to the White House for an hour-long tête-à-tête with President Bush. They succeeded in persuading the president to include human rights as one of the criteria for improvement in Washington's relations with Damascus.

The Syrian authorities felt relieved of a headache when Ammar agreed to leave the country. But his exile activities have become a thorn in Assad's side, and the regime gives signs of regretting that it let him out of its grip. Trying to rein him in from afar, security officials paid a menacing visit to Muna. Although she is hard to intimidate, the officers warned darkly: "Khawla has brothers here. She should be concerned about their safety."

Ammar remains optimistic that "Assad democracy" will not last much longer. But he is less hopeful that the true liberal democracy that he yearns for will soon replace it. He explains:

> From the first moment, what the Syrian system does to young people is beat them down into submission to the established order, whether it is the political order, the social order, the sectarian order, whatever. Free thinking is not something that exists in the culture, basically. This is something that goes far deeper than Ba'athism. It is a cultural ethos, and it has been with us for centuries.[38]

As for his own future, Ammar speculated on what would happen if an opposition alliance like the National Salvation Front came to power. "They will try to be democratic, but I will definitely be in the opposition. I will still be making noise, still working with young people and complaining about the injustice of the system."

Conclusion

Models for a Rising Generation

In 2005, when a million Lebanese filled the streets to demand the restoration of their nation's independence and President Hosni Mubarak announced that Egyptians would choose their own ruler for the first time in five thousand years, observers proclaimed the dawning of an "Arab spring." But by the end of 2008, much of this excitement had turned to ashes. The man who had had the temerity to run against Mubarak languished in jail while assassins hunted down Lebanese patriots. "Hopes for democratic change fade in the Middle East," lamented the *Washington Post*.[1]

Yet, like the crash after a high, the gloom that enveloped Middle Eastern liberals and their Western sympathizers was as overdrawn as the earlier euphoric hopes. It took 21 years for the flowers of the 1968 "Prague spring" to blossom in the "Velvet Revolution" of 1989. Next door in Poland, nine years of martial law, mass arrests and even killings passed from the birth of Solidarity in 1980 to its triumph and the resurrection of democracy.

Each grasp for freedom leaves a legacy on which future efforts build. The possibilities that people imagine are dampened but not extinguished by disappointment. There is no way to know whether the Arab spring will need another nine or twenty-one years to achieve its fulfillment, or fewer or more. What we do know, as I argued in the Introduction, is that it will depend on human choices more than on socioeconomic "determinants."

The seven dynamic individuals I have profiled here are not alone. In selecting each, I passed over several countrymen (or women) who would also have made worthy subjects. But to say there are others is not to say there are nearly enough. Confusingly, overwhelming majorities of Middle Easterners say they favor democracy, but it is not clear what they mean by this because many of the same respondents also say that they want *sharia* to constitute the law or that they do not consider elections or press freedom important.[2] There is no algebra that can tell us how many citizens must desire and understand democracy or be willing to fight and sacrifice for it before they will be able to achieve that goal. But it is safe to say that the critical mass has not been reached in the countries of the Muslim Middle East.

We can be confident, however, that reinforcements are on the way. My seven subjects were born in the 1950s or 1960s; they are each in middle age. In the generation behind them, the number of democrats is far larger. How do I know? Because the Internet is humming with their voices. There are 60,000 bloggers in Iran alone.[3] Estimates of the number in the Arab countries range from 25,000 to 100,000. They seem to have more in common with their non-Middle Eastern peers in the blogosphere than with the traditions of their forebears. In the main, they are free in spirit and critical of what they find around them. It is hard to doubt that most want to live in freedom.

Here, for example, is the Bahraini, Mahmood, of *Mahmood's Den,* one of the oldest and most popular of the region's blogs:

> A great majority of the students I talk to mention how their classrooms echo with their teachers' shouting and instilling fear in them rather than a love of learning. Schools, for decades now, have been void of any challenge, creativity, warmth, empathy and individuality . . . . [W]e definitely do not need nor want societies that are illiterate, empty, uncreative and passive acceptors of any substandard ideologies and ways of life.

Oh, the "three R's?" Read—Remember—Regurgitate! That's the tenet of the education system we currently have in the Arab and Islamic world.

Here is *Saudi Eve,* who blogs from her home country and scandalizes it with religious irreverence and tales of love and romance:

I have a persisting daydream.

I walk a Saudi street. I'm wearing an abbaya. Every type of harassment I've ever been subjected to on a Saudi street (staring, terrifying religious advice, explicit sexual advances, etc.) are instead represented by one action: people pulling on my abbaya.

I carry this futuristic beam weapon. I shoot them. They vaporize.

I become larger with each hit I make, and the abbaya gets torn a bit each time. After a couple of hits, I'm very large (tall as a two story house) and almost naked. I'm left with a two piece ensemble that looks like a belly dancers' costume but black. Yet no one comes near me now. They are afraid.

After that, I just walk the streets of Saudi, feminine and undisturbed.

Another feminist daydream was posted by *Freedom for Egyptians:*

Once upon a time
in a land far away,
a beautiful, independent,
self-assured princess
happened upon a frog as she sat
contemplating ecological issues
on the shores of an unpolluted pond
in a verdant meadow near her castle.
The frog hopped into the princess' lap

and said: "Elegant Lady,
I was once a handsome prince,
until an evil witch cast a spell upon me.
One kiss from you, however,
and I will turn back
into the dapper, young prince that I am
and then, my sweet, we can marry
and set up housekeeping in your castle
with my mother,
where you can prepare my meals,
clean my clothes, bear my children,
and forever feel
grateful and happy doing so."
That night,
as the princess dined sumptuously
on lightly sauteed frog legs
seasoned in a white wine
and onion cream sauce,
she chuckled and thought to herself:
I don't freakin think so.

Then there is the Egyptian iconoclast who blogs under the moniker, *Sandmonkey*, whose site sports a placard, "Buy Danish," as well as this mocking appeal for donations: "Support the Neo-con American Right-wing Zionist Christian Imperialist Conspiracy in the Middle-east!" In April 2008 when Egyptian Prime Minister Ahmed Nazif visited his alma mater and was confronted by a tough questioner, *Sandmonkey* commented: "Things have changed. A Cairo University student faces off PM Nazif and gets arrested for only half an hour after doing that. He didn't go to jail, didn't get anally raped and nor was his entire family rounded up and sent to jail. Life's little victories."

During Israel's 2006 war with Hizbullah that drove many on both sides from their homes, *Sandmonkey* posted:

> I was speaking with Lisa [an Israeli blogger] and she was telling me how depressed she was after seeing an Israeli refugee camp for people escaping the North. I decided to check her flickr account to see the pictures of how an Israeli refugee camp looks, ... and it depressed the hell out of me, although the cause of our depressions wasn't the same. The Arab readers will know exactly what I mean.

Beneath this *Sandmonkey* posted half a dozen photos of a tidy Israeli tent city near the sea, replete with bustling mess hall, and then he added this gloss: "That's their refugee camps. I swear to god I could sell this as a tourist destination and Egyptian tourists would go. The first two weeks would get fully booked ... in 5 minutes."

A "twenty-something" Saudi-raised Jordanian woman who blogs as *And Far Away,* describes herself as "liberal" and a "feminist." She posted this take on the Arab condition:

> I am not a self-hating Arab, in fact, I am extremely proud of my Arab heritage .... Yet, I am not particularly fond of look-ing at the past and saying, "Oh! Once upon a time, we ruled most of the civilized world."
>
> Keyword: Once upon a time.
>
> As a wise friend once said, Andalus Shmandalus, we now officially *suck.* Sadly, many centuries after the fall of the Abbassid state, we keep insisting that this terrible situation is a result of how we do not properly apply Islam ... and how the entire world is in a conspiracy against us.
>
> Religion is not the answer. Conspiracy theories will only grow more self-pitying "helpless" generations.
>
> Instead, we need a hundred years and shitloads of *educa-tion* to pull ourselves out of this endless black pit we have dug with our own hands.

Jadi, who identifies himself as a twenty-seven-year resi-dent of Tehran, explains that his Farsi blog was blocked so he started a new one in English, which "IS NOT my native language. I'm not good at it. But I think writing in poor english is much more BETTER THAN not writing at all." This is his thumbnail sketch of Iran's foreign policy:

> Enemy is a VERY famous concept in my country. Have you
> read Orwell's 1984? They also have to have an Enemy
> because they have to have someone to bear the burden of all
> the problems. Here, we also have an Enemy. It used to be
> "East and West" ... but now it is limited to USA and Israel
> .... But our regime needs an Enemy to survive.

In addition to these, there is *Iraq the Model,* produced by three Sunni Baghdadi brothers, a site so supportive of the U.S. overthrow of Saddam Hussein that until the authors identified themselves some American anti-war bloggers speculated that it was actually put up by the CIA; and *Saudi Girl,* a relentless voice for women's rights who eventually revealed "herself" to be an empathic young man; and the consortium of blogs that is waging the "take off the veil" campaign; and thousands of others.

The quotes above are from sites written in English, as are about half of the Arab blogs (and in the Maghreb, there are many in French).[4] The blogs written in Arabic are, on average, somewhat less liberal, but these too often give voice to rebellious ideas and feelings. Alaa of the highly influential *Manal and Alaa's Bit Bucket,* posted this taunting reaction to an Egyptian court's reaffirmation of the state's refusal to recognize the religion of Bahai in their official identity papers:

> After depriving Baha'is of their right to have official docu-
> ments ..., infidels such as Baha'is ... are now forced to act
> hypocritically. Forced to pretend that they are Muslims....
> One day a man might propose to your sister.... This person
> might be an infidel (God forbid), and you would not be able to
> tell, because when you check his ID card it will state that he
> is a Muslim ... then infidels will f*** your sister.[5]

Also in Arabic are the alternately sad and defiant, introspective and angry musings posted on the *Diary of a Homosexual Woman*.

Of course, many bloggers do not address political topics, and among those who do not all are democrats. There are sites that advocate contrary points of view, even violent jihadism. Surprisingly, a recent study of Iranian blogs found that "religious/conservative" bloggers were less likely to use their real names than "secular/reformist" bloggers, which raises the possibility that many of these anti-liberal voices are concocted by the regime.

The region's dictators and theocrats have tried to rein in the blogosphere by blocking sites and arresting bloggers. The Saudi regime has blocked many but arrested few. One notable exception was Fouad al-Farhan, a thirty-two-year-old father who was locked up for four months in 2008 apparently because he had denounced the incarceration of a group of Saudi dissidents on a tenuous claim that they supported terrorism. The Egyptian government has not done much site-blocking, but it has imprisoned a handful of bloggers. Karim Amer, then 22, was sentenced to four years in 2007 for insulting President Mubarak and Islam. While Amer was punished for irreverence toward Islam, a couple of the other jailed bloggers have been Islamists. According to one reputable study, the Iranian government blocks 11 to 21 percent of secular and reformist blogs and a smaller number of others.[6]

On the whole, however, the bloggers seem to be getting the better of their duels with the regimes. Not only have they succeeded in circulating a vast trove of heterodox and subversive material, they have also won most of the direct confrontations, at least in the Arab world. They have waged publicity campaigns on the Internet in defense of blocked sites or jailed bloggers, and in most cases, the sites have been unblocked or the prisoners released.

The cyber community has also won some victories that go beyond defending its own. When someone slipped Egyptian blogger, Wael Abbas, a video captured on a cell phone in an Egyptian police station, showing an arrested minibus driver being sodomized by officers, Abbas posted it on his site. As a result, the policemen were tried and sentenced to prison, an exceedingly rare occurrence in Egypt. In the spring of 2008, with Egypt seething over bread shortages, two strikes were organized, largely by means of notices on Facebook, and tens of thousands participated.

Facebook, thus, is being used to create networks of dissidents where they have not had the freedom to form legal organizations. In addition, there are at least a dozen high quality web sites or "portals" that aggregate Middle East-related material with a liberal twist. Activists are also making increasing use of YouTube. When Wajeha Al-Huwaider posted a brief video of herself driving in Saudi Arabia on International Women's Day 2008, the response was so strong that it inspired another idea. She and a few colleagues announced a campaign called "No to the Oppression of Women." It aims to:

> give every Saudi woman or resident ... the opportunity to
> speak before the camera about the oppression or violence she
> has been subjected to, with complete assurance of confiden-
> tiality. The cases will, provisionally, be broadcast on YouTube.
> Each victim will describe her situation and how the official
> agencies ignored her plight.

The campaign was launched in April 2008 with one woman's filmed account of being forced to marry against her will. Her anonymity was protected by the black full-face veil that most Saudi women are required to wear. When women were excluded (as always) from the Saudi team for the 2008 Olympics, Wajeha produced another brief video on YouTube, featuring a team of young women players posing in shackles and abbayas.

It is hard to see how the forces of stasis can suppress this rising tide. Having backed down in most of the early skirmishes over the arrest of a blogger here or there, could the regimes possibly jail thousands? It seems inconceivable, not to mention the possibility that bloggers could develop cybernetic methods to prevent their identities from being detected. As for site-blocking, the technological trend toward wireless reception directly from satellites will make that increasingly difficult if not impossible.

Blogging, which began in the United States in the early to mid 1990s, was imitated in the Middle East, starting only in 2003. Its growth is bound to increase multifold within a few years. According to the country-by-country data assembled by InternetWorld Stats, only two-thirds of one percent of the population of the Muslim Middle East used the Internet as of December 2000.[7] By 2007, that had risen to twelve percent. This means that the proportion was more than doubling every two years and it implies that within a few years, Internet usage will be ubiquitous in the region. Hisham Kassem plans for the new daily that he will launch in 2009 to have a full Internet version. For all practical purposes, therefore, the time-honored authoritarian practice of denying free speech will be rendered impracticable. It also means that the people of the Middle East, most of whom are young, will communicate freely not only with each other but with the rest of the world, as was never done before. Is it possible to imagine that they will rest content under the thumbs of autocrats, colonels, and mullahs while they watch the majority in every other region on earth select its own rulers?

If the auguries for democratization are as hopeful as I am suggesting, then why should we lift a finger? Why not let things take their course? The answer is that nothing is certain, and that even though democracy is bound to come to the

Middle East sooner or later, sooner will be better than later, for their sake and for ours. And, too, the more momentum behind the democracy movement, the more likely it will triumph peacefully.

Do we outsiders have the power to do anything about this? Certainly, the record of the Bush administration invites skepticism. The war in Iraq has been a debacle, and the peaceful programs to promote democracy have been fumbling and uncertain. Billions have been spent, but the effect is hard to see.

Without volunteering detailed suggestions for doing them better, I offer two points. One is that we need to fling open our gates to visitors, especially students, from the Middle East. Not all, but most, of the figures I have written about in this book were profoundly influenced by the experience of study in the U.S. So were some of the bloggers I have mentioned and many other of the region's liberals. The best way we have to help produce more like them is to enable Middle Eastern youngsters to spend time living here and especially to receive education here.

This bumps up against concerns about security. Our system of controlling our borders is still broken. Something that should be a sensitive instrument, sorting visa-seekers intelligently, appears to function only as an on/off switch. Before 9/11, the light was stuck on green. Our border guards would let anyone in, including some of the 9/11 bombers and some of their comrades who bombed the World Trade Center eight years earlier, although there was reason to know of the terrorist connections of a few of those admitted in both groups. Since 9/11, with egg on their faces, our border guards have switched to red: they are reluctant to let anyone pass, even proven friends of our country, at least without humiliating them.

Surely we can do better, whether it requires more money, improved training, new technology, or better leadership. We need a consular system that is sophisticated enough to weed out—or at least to tag for surveillance—individuals who might harm us, while making it easy and inexpensive for others to study or visit here.

Second we should provide consistent and vocal moral support to indigenous democrats like the people portrayed in this book who will be far more numerous in the rising generations, and we should raise holy hell when they are persecuted. Too often our government has swallowed its words for fear of irritating the powers that be. And we should offer greater material support to these struggling democrats. This does not mean putting individuals on stipends as the CIA used to do (or perhaps still does) to favored friends. Rather it means to offer grants to organizations, publications, and projects, as is done most effectively although on a small scale by the National Endowment for Democracy. To be sure, sometimes they will not want our support lest it validate the charge that they are our agents—a charge they face anyway. But this must be up to them to decide. We should stand ready to assist them if they want our help. And we should seek ways to mitigate the stigma, perhaps, for example, by melding ours with funds from other democracies. Although several new bureaucratic constructs have been created since 9/11 for the purpose of promoting Middle East democracy, little of the money spent has reached the people described in this book, or their like.

The seven people I have portrayed in this book will, *inshallah* (God willing), play large parts in bringing democracy to their region. It will be to our credit and our benefit if we do what we can to assist them and those who are already following in their footsteps.

Endnotes

The Protester: Wajeha Al-Huwaider of Saudi Arabia

[1] Mark Mackinnon and Alan Freeman, "Saudi Rift Feared with Death of King," *Toronto Globe and Mail*, August 03, 2005.

[2] Al-Huwaider to author, e-mail, March 10, 2008.

[3] This and all other quotes from Wajeha Al-Huwaider are from interviews conducted October 2007 in Manama, Bahrain.

[4] Sandra Mackey, *The Saudis: Inside the Desert Kingdom (New York: Norton, 2002), p. 95.*

[5] Wajeha Al-Huwaider, "Unfetter My Hands, Give Me My Freedom!" *Arab News*, July 30, 2002.

[6] Wajeha Al-Huwaider, "Banishing Love," *Arab News*, July 22, 2002.

[7] Wajeha Al-Huwaider, "Proof of Identity in Judicial Matters," *Arab News*, August 1, 2003.

[8] Wajeha Al-Huwaider, "Looking at Expatriate Women With Suspicion is Not Doing Us Any Good," *Arab News*, June 20, 2003.

[9] Wajeha Al-Huwaider, "A Woman and her Many Worries," http://arabview.com/articles.asp?article=183.

[10] Wajeha Al-Huwaider, "No Medicine Man Can Cure What Time Has Spoiled," *Arab News*, August 13, 2002.

[11] Wajeha Al-Huwaider, "You Can Stand the Heat and Still Prepare Unwholesome Food," *Arab News*, June 13, 2003.

[12]Wajeha Al-Huwaider, "Why Don't We Read?" *Arab News,* August 26, 2002.

[13]Wajeha Al-Huwaider, "The Road to Arab renaissance," http://arabview.com/articles.asp?article=201.

[14]Wajeha Al-Huwaider, "An Honest Dialogue With an American Colleague," *Arab News,* May 16, 2003.

[15]Wajeha Al-Huwaider, "Why Some of Us Look Elsewhere for Security," *Arab News,* May 30, 2003.

[16]"Alonousa," *metatransparent.com,* May 1, 2004, quoted in A. Dankowitz, "Saudi Writer and Journalist Wajeha Al-Huwaider Fights for Women's Rights," Middle East Media Research Institute, Inquiry and Analysis, No. 312, December 28, 2006.

[17]http://www.elaph.com/ElaphWriter/2005/3/45862.htm.

[18]Lawrence Wright, *The Looming Tower: Al Qaeda and the Road to 9/11* (New York: Knopf, 2006), p. 87.

[19]Abdulrahman Munif, *Cities of Salt* (New York: Vintage International, 1987), p.168.

[20]Mackinnon and Freeman, "Saudi Rift."

[21]Elpah.com, Febraury 5, 2006, Translated by Middle East Media Research Institute at http://memri.org/bin/articles. cgi?Page=archives&Area=ia&ID=IA31206/

[22]Rezgar.com, May 25, 2006. Translated by Middle East Media Research Institute at http://memri.org/bin/articles. cgi?Page=archives&Area=ia&ID=IA31206.

[23]Elham Manea, "'Give Saudi Women Their Rights'!" *Middle East Transparent,* 09 August 2006.

[24]Al-Hurra, May 26, 2007, trans. by Middle East Media Research Institute, Special Dispatch-Saudi Arabia/Reform Project, June 1, 2007, No. 1604.

[25]http://www.aafaq.org/english/pysk.aspx?id_alri=14

[26]Wajeha Al-Huwaider, "Help Women in Saudi Arabia to Buy Your Cars!" February 7, 2008.

[27]Samir al-Saadi, "Women Driving is Not in Conflict with Religion: Scholars," *Arab News,* Feb. 21, 2008.

28"Saudi Women's Rights Activist Wajiha Al-Huweidar Drives Her Car, Calling upon Authorities to Allow Women to Drive," Middle East Media Research Institute, clip no. 1712, March 8, 2008, transcript.

29"Saudi Shura Council Recommends Allowing Saudi Women to Drive with Limitations," Middle East Media Research Institute, Special Dispatch, No. 1875, March 18, 2008.

The Politician: Mithal al-Alusi of Iraq

1 This and other quotes from Alusi, except as otherwise noted, are from interviews in Baghdad, September 26–30, 2007.

2 Marion Farouk-Sluglett and Peter Sluglett, *Iraq Since 1958: From Revolution to Dictatorship* (London: I. B. Tauris, 2003), p. 160. The quote within is from Majid Khadduri, *Socialist Iraq: A Study in Iraqi Politics Since 1968* (Washington, DC: Middle East Institute, 1978), pp. 63–64.

3 Ibid., pp. 161–162.

4 In the end this did not spare him. In 1979, once the Saddam Hussein/al-Bakr alliance had crushed all competitors, Saddam turned on al-Bakr who saved his own neck by capitulating abjectly. The transition was heralded by official declarations that another "coup" had been foiled. Amid a fresh round of "democratic executions," al-Samarai was taken from his cell and killed. Just as this foiled "coup" was imaginary, Mithal believes that the story of Kazzar's earlier coup was a fiction of Saddam's. Either way, its effects on Iraq and on Mithal were the same.

5 Mithal knew his man. Seventeen years later, Saddam's two sons-in-law, who had defected, accepted a similar deal only to be butchered almost as soon as they arrived home.

6 Steven Erlanger, "Threats and Responses: Germany; Hamburg Police Raid 2 Import-Export Firms," *New York Times*, September 11, 2002.

[7] Douglas Franta and Desmond Butler, "The 9/11 Inquest: Now Americans Say Germans Bungled," *New York Times,* July 11, 2002. This was one of the few publicized cases of U.S.-Syrian anti-terror cooperation, and, given Syria's notorious handling of prisoners, it was cited by civil libertarians in their arguments against "rendition" of terror suspects to other governments.

[8] Farouk Nassar, "Libya First Arab State to Offer Public Support for Iran," *Associated Press,* October 10, 1980.

[9] Pranay B. Gupte, "Iraq's Foreign Minister Warns Against U.S. Renewing Close Tie to Iran," *New York Times,* October 26, 1980.

[10] Interview with Ali al-Furaji, Baghdad, September 29, 2007.

[11] Steven Erlanger, "Anti-Hussein Iraqis Briefly Seize Embassy in Berlin," *New York Times,* August 21, 2002.

[12] Fabien Novial, "Iraqi opposition members in Berlin hostage drama face court," *Agence France Presse—English,* March 26, 2003.

[13] Lucian Kim, "Raid Ends Seizure of Iraqi Embassy; German Officials Capture Activists Opposing Hussein," *Boston Globe,* August 21, 2002.

[14] "Former Baath Party officials in Iraq are beginning a course in de-Baathification," *National Public Radio,* March 29, 2004.

[15] Scheherezade Faramarzi, "Official in charge of de-Baathification program wanted by Germany in 2002 embassy takeover," *Associated Press,* June 7, 2004.

[16] Mikhail Gorbachev, *Perestroika: New Thinking for Our Country and the World* (New York: Harper & Row, 1987), p. 32.

[17] Francis Fukuyama, *The End of History and the Last Man* (New York, The Free Press, 1992).

[18] James J. Na, "Honoring a true martyr for freedom in Iraq," *Seattle Times,* March 9, 2005, http://seattletimes.nwsource.com/html/opinion/2002201059_na09.html.

[19]Erik Echholm, "Iraqi Indicted for Proposal to Open Talks With Israel," *New York Times,* October 6, 2004.

[20]This and all quotes or paraphrases from Jaboory are from interviews in Baghdad, September 26–30, 2007.

[21]James J. Na, "Profile of an Iraqui Politician," *Real Clear Politics,* January 28, 2005, http://realclearpolitics.com/ Commentary/com-1_28_05_JN.html.

[22]Quoted in Kerry Dupont, "Hero of the People," *National Review Online,* November 4, 2005. (www.nationalreview. com/script/printpage.p?ref=/comment/dupont200511040836. asp).

[23]Barry Schweid, "Head of secular party, under death threat, warns that Iran and Syria oppose democracy in Iraq," *Associated Press Worldstream,* March 4, 2005.

[24]www.instituteforcounterterrorism.org/apage/2786.php.

[25]Bobby Ghosh, "After Maliki, Few Good Alternatives," *Time,* Aug. 22, 2007.

[26]Bushra Juhi, "Iraqi legislator accuses U.S. Embassy staff of giving shelter to wanted minister," *Associated Press Worldstream,* June 28, 2007.

[27]Richard A. Oppel, "Iraqi forces try to arrest government minister," *International Herald Tribune,* June 27, 2007.

[28]Eli Lake, "Appeal to Bush Pressed by Alusi Over the Murder of His Two Sons," *New York Sun,* June 29, 2007.

[29]Ibid.

[30]Ibid.

[31]Eli Lake, "Iraqi Political Crisis Near End as Tawafuq Chief Quits," *New York Sun,* July 6, 2007.

[32]Sameer N. Yacoub, "Court: Iraq lawmaker can't be prosecuted for trip," *Associated Press,* November 26, 2008.

The Revolutionist: Mohsen Sazegara of Iran

[1]All quotes and paraphrases from Mohsen are from a series of interviews conducted with him in Washington, DC from February 12 through April 22, 2008.

[2] Jalal Al-e Ahmad, *Gharbzadegi [Weststruckness],* transl. by John Green and Ahmad Alizadeh (Costa Mesa: Mazda Publishers, 1997), p. 15.

[3] Mohammad Bagher Sadr, founder of the Dawa Party, had been executed by Saddam Hussein, who elevated a more docile and less accomplished clergyman to replace him as Grand Ayatollah. This replacement, also named Sadr although not closely related, eventually fell out with Saddam and was executed in his turn. It is his son, Muqtada, who emerged as a leading figure in Iraq after the 2003 U.S. invasion.

[4] Lajevardi, as we shall see, retained considerable power, but his chickens came home to roost in 1998 when he was assassinated by the MEK on the tenth anniversary of an infamous slaughter of some four thousand of their members in his prisons.

[5] Hajjarian was to emerge in the 1990s as a key figure in Iran's reform movement and a top adviser to President Mohammad Khatami. Amidst a wave of assassinations of reformers, Hajjarian was shot and left paralyzed.

[6] Elaine Sciolino, "Iran Protests Spread to 18 Cities; Police Crack Down at University," *New York Times,* July 13, 1999.

[7] Two years later, a former staff physician in Iran's Defense Ministry defected. He said he had examined Kazemi in the hospital, four days after her arrest and that she showed obvious signs of torture, including: evidence of a very brutal rape, a skull fracture, two broken fingers, missing fingernails, a crushed big toe and a broken nose, severe abdominal bruising, swelling behind the head and a bruised shoulder, deep scratches on the neck and evidence of flogging on the legs. ("Zahra Kazemi: Iran's Changing story," *CBC News,* www.cbc.ca/news/background/kazemi.)

The Publisher: Hisham Kassem of Egypt

[1] Roland Trafford-Roberts to Joshua Muravchik, e-mail, April 26, 2006.

[2] This and all subsequent quotes from Hisham Kassem, unless otherwise noted, come from a series of interview I did with him in Cairo, April 4–14, 2005 and March 26–31, 2006.

[3] Trafford-Roberts to Muravchik.

[4] Hamied Ansari, *Egypt: the Stalled Society* (Albany: SUNY, 1986), p. 89.

[5] Trafford-Roberts to Muravchik, May 3, 2006.

[6] Fatma El-Zanaty and Ann A. Way, *Egypt Demographic and Health Survey 2000* (National Population Council, Ministry of Health and Population, January 2001), table 14.1, p. 192. Table 14.2, p. 193. A different broad survey in 1997 found a median age of 10.9. See Omaima El-Gibaly, Barbara Ibrahim, Barbara S. Mensch, and Wesley H. Clark, "The Decline of Female Circumcision in Egypt: Evidence and Interpretation," *Social Science & Medicine*, No. 54 (2002), p. 210. For the 1995 data see Fatma El-Zanaty, Enas M. Hussein, Gihan A. Shawky, Ann A. Way, and Sunita Kishor, *Egypt Demographic and Health Survey 1995* (National Population Council, Cairo and Macro International, Inc., Calverton, MD, September 1996), p. 171, table 13.1. It shows a total incidence of 97 percent as compared to 97.3 percent in the 2000 survey.

[7] Omaima El-Gibaly, Barbara Ibrahim, Barbara S. Mensch, and Wesley H. Clark, "The Decline of Female Circumcision in Egypt: Evidence and Interpretation," *Social Science & Medicine*, No. 54 (2002), p. 205.

[8] Hisham Kassem to Joshua Muravchik, e-mail, April 27, 2006.

[9] CNN, "Beyond the Numbers—Part 2—Female Circumcision," News 3:47 PM ET, September 7, 1994, Transcript #381–2.

[10] Ibid.

[11] Charles M. Sennott, "A Struggle Against Intolerance; Embattled Coptic Christians are Fleeing Egypt," *Boston Globe*, January 18, 1999, p. A1.

[12]Christina Lamb, "Egyptian Police 'Crucify' and Rape Christians," *Electronic Telegraph* No. 1248, Oct. 25, 1998.

[13]"At Least 20 Killed in Kosheh Clashes," *Cairo Times*, 13–19 January 2000. See also "Egypts Copts After Kosheh," *The Estimate*, 28 January 2000, www.theestimate.com/public/01282000a.html.

[14]Hisham Kassem, "Wake-Up Call: The Country has Nothing to Lose and Everything to Gain from an Open and Sober Discussion." *Cairo Times*, vol. 2 issue 25 (4–17 February 1999).

[15]Diana Digges, "Strongholds of Orthodoxy: Whatever the Copts' Place in Society at Large, the Heart of Their Religious and Community Life Remains Intact," *Cairo Times*, vol. 2 no. 25 (4–17 February 1999).

[16]Ibid.

[17]"The Copts: A Question for Egypt," *Le Monde Diplomatique*, English edition, May 11, 2001.

[18]"Was it Worth it?" *Time*, vol. 167 no. 13 (March 27, 2006), p. 26.

[19]Samia Serageldin, *The Cairo House* (Syracuse: Syracuse University Press, 2000), p. 188.

[20]English translation published in "Referendum of May 25: Great Forgery Day," Freedomforegyptians.blogspot.com, July 25, 2005.

[21]Ibid.

[22]Quoted in Michael Slackman, "Mubarak Foe, Bravado Gone, Feels Victimized by Smears After Second-Place Finish," *New York Times*, October 19, 2005, p. A10.

[23]Slackman, "Mubarak Foe."

[24]Noha El-Zeini, "Rigging Elections Under the Supervision of the Judiciary," *Al-Masry Al Youm*, November 25, 2005. This translation was posted, apparently by an Egyptian, on the day the article appeared on the website of Zogby International. The English was poor, and I have corrected elementary errors of grammar and usage where there was no question of the meaning.

[25]Mustafa al-Bakry, "The American Decision to Communicate with the Muslim Brotherhood and Decline the Egyptian Regime's Demands," *al-Usboa,* September 26, 2007.

[26]Quotes in the paragraph from an interview with Hisham Kassem, Paris, March 22, 2008.

[27]Jackson Diehl, "Forsaking the Egyptian Free Press," *Washington Post,* Sept. 24, 2007, p. A19.

[28]Hisham Kassem to Joshua Muravchik, e-mail, April 27, 2006.

[29]Ibid.

The Activist: Bassem Eid of Palestine

[1]This and all other quotes from Bassem Eid, except of otherwise noted, is from a series of interviews with him in East Jerusalem and Ramallah, June 24–28, 2007.

[2]Larry Derfner, "Both Sides Now," *Jerusalem Post,* November 3, 1995.

[3]"The *B'Tselem* Storm," February 11, 1993.

[4]Interview with Hagai Tsoref, Jerusalem, June 28, 2007.

[5]Derfner, "Both Sides."

[6]Derfner, "Both Sides."

[7]B'Tselem, *Collaborators in the Occupied Territories: Human Rights Violations and Abuses,* Jerusalem, January, 1994, p. 205.

[8]Ibid., p. 206.

[9]Isabel Kershner, "The PLO Twilight Zone," *Jerusalem Report,* Feb. 23, 1995, p. 26.

[10]B'Tselem, *Neither Law nor Justice: Extra-Judicial Punishment, Abduction, Unlawful Arrest, and Torture of Palestinian Residents of the West Bank by the Palestinian Preventive Security Service.* Jerusalem, August 1995, p. 29.

[11]Ibid, p. 49.

[12]*Human Rights Watch World Report 199 6,* www.hrw.org/reports/1996/WR96/MIDEAST-06.htm.

[13]Derfner, "Both Sides."

[14]Ibid.

[15]Ibid.

[16]Barton Gellman, "American Dies in Custody of Palestinians," *Washington Post,* Sept. 30, 1995.

[17]Ibid.

[18]John Donnelly, "Furor Erupts Over Reports of Torture by Palestinians: Investigator Catches Fire from Both Sides," *Miami Herald,* Oct. 16, 1995.

[19]Barton Gellman, "Palestinian Rights Group Accuses Arafat's Authority of 'Large-Scale' Torture, *Washington Post,* May 27, 1997, p. A12.

[20]Bassem Eid, "A Change in the Attitude of the Palestinian Authority Towards Human Rights: Proof that Pressure Works," reprinted by Palestinian Human Rights Monitoring Group, April 15, 1998. (Original date and place of publication unknown.)

[21]Uri Avnery, "The New Collaborators," *Ma'ariv,* Sept. 16, 1998.

[22]Bassem Eid, "Blind Support for Arafat," *Ma'ariv,* Sept. 28, 1998.

[23]Bassem Eid, "Internal and External Obstacles Preventing Development in the Field of Human Rights," reprinted by Palestinian Human Rights Monitoring Group, October 1, 1999. (Original date and place of publication unknown.)

[24]Edward A. Gargan, "The Youngest Casualties: Palestinian Teens, Among Stone-Throwers, Face Bullets," *Newsday,* Oct. 16, 2000.

[25]*Child Fatalities in the recent Clashes,* PHRMG Reports on the Conflict, Oct. 4, 2000.

[26]PHRMG, "Closing of Gaza Airport," Oct. 4, 2000.

[27]*Inhumane Actions Against Humanity: A PHRMG report on the al-Aqsa Uprising,* PHRMG, Dec. 12, 2000.

[28]Raymond Whitaker, "Middle East: Tanzim Chief Barghouti Leads 'Peaceful intifada': As Fighting Continues Between Arabs and Jewish Settlers, Attention Focuses on the Man

Masterminding the Uprising Against Israel," *The Independent (London),*Oct. 20, 2000.

[29]Nor was it only Israelis and Palestinians whose reportage Bassem faulted. In 2001, the *Guardian*'s renowned Middle East expert, Robert Fisk, visited the PHRMG offices to collect statistics on the toll of the intifada. Bassem recalls what ensued: "I told him that 750 Palestinians had been killed by Israelis. He made it 1,050 in the newspaper. I was shocked! Such a respected journalist! How could it be? I called him and I said, 'I gave you the statistics in writing so as to avoid mistakes. And you added another 300 Palestinians killed to the number.' He started laughing, and I asked why, and he said, 'Because the number I wrote today will be accurate next month.'"

[30]Bassem Eid, "Media War Helps No One," *Ha'aretz,* November 22, 2000.

[31]Bassem Eid, "A Better intifada," *New York Times,* Feb. 1, 2001.

[32]Bassem Eid, "A Plea for Realism," *Common Ground News Service,* June 7, 2002.

[33]Bassem Eid, "Time for the Palestinians to Choose Life," *Haaretz,* June 4, 2003.

[34]PHRMG, "The Intra'Fada: The Chaos of the Weapons," April, 2004.

[35]Bassem Eid, "The reign of the Thugs," *Haaretz,* Jan. 28, 2004.

[36]Eric Silver and Sa'id Ghazali, "Arafat Sacks Top Officers to Quell Unrest," *Independent (London),* July 18, 2004.

[37]Ibid.

[38]Eid, "Our Bloodletting."

[39]This and all quotes from Hatem Abdel Qader Eid are from an interview in East Jerusalem, July 4, 2007.

The Feminist: Rola Dashti of Kuwait

[1]Kuwaiti TV, Nov. 11, 2007; clip available at www.memritv.org/clip/en/1633.htm

[2] This and all other quotes from Helal Mahmoud Al-Bezri are from an interview in Kuwait City, November 16, 2007.

[3] This and all other quotes from Rola Dashti, except as otherwise sourced, are from interviews in Kuwait City, November 14–18, 2007.

[4] Anh Nga Longva, "Kuwaiti Women at a Crossroads: Privileged Development and the Constraints of Ethnic Stratification," *International Journal of Middle East Studies*, vol. 25, no. 3 (August 1993), p. 444.

[5] John M. Levins, "The Kuwaiti Resistance," *Middle East Quarterly*, vol. II, no. 1 (March 1995).

[6] Brian Katulis, *Women's Rights in Focus: Kuwait*, Findings from Focus Groups with Kuwaitis on Women's Rights, Freedom House, March 8, 2005, p. 9.

[7] Ewen MacAskill, "Kuwait Breakthrough on Votes for Women," *The Guardian (London)*, May 17, 2004.

[8] "A Bridge Across the Gender Gulf," *Irish Times*, June 23, 2007.

[9] This an all subsequent quotes from Khawla are from interviews conducted with her in September and October 2006 in Silver Spring, MD.

[10] Challiss McDonough, "Kuwaiti Women Appear on Political Landscape This Election," *Voice of America News*, VOA English Service, June 28, 2006.

[11] Steve Coll, "In the gulf, Dissidence Goes Digital; Test Messaging Is New Tool Of Political Underground," *Washington Post*, March 29, 2005.

[12] Rola Dashti, "Can There Be Democracy Without Marginalization?", *Bitterlemons-international.org*, edition 28 vol. 3 (July 28, 2005).

The Dissident: Ammar Abdulhamid of Syria

[1] Anthony Shadid, "Syria Heralds Reforms, But Many Have Doubts," *Washington Post*, May 18, 2005.

[2] Ammar Abdulhamid, "Syria: Mr. Assad, take down our wall," *Daily Star,* May 31, 2005.

[3] This account of the meeting between Abdulhamid and Shawkat is based on interviews with the former in Silver Spring, MD in September 2006. I was unable to get Shawkat's version because the Syrian government denied me a visa.

[4] If his father's surname was Chahine and his mother's Wassef, why was Ammar given an altogether different name? The canons of naming are not as fixed in the Arab world as in the West. One of Muhammad Chahine's brothers wanted a name sounding Arab rather than Kurdish. In the end, the brothers agreed to unify the family name, and to all go by Abdulhamid as their legal name. But by then, Muhammad's theater career was already established, so he continued to use Chahine professionally.

[5] This and all subsequent quotes from Ammar, except as otherwise noted, are from a series of interviews conducted with him during, September 2006 in Silver Spring.

[6] John Dart and Terry Pristin, "'The Satanic Verses'; Why Islam is Outraged Over Novel," *Los Angeles Times,* February 15, 1989, p. 1.

[7] Interview, October 17, 2006, Silver Spring, MD.

[8] Interview, October 17, 2006, Silver Spring, MD.

[9] Faiza Saleh Ambah, "For Women in Kuwait, a Landmark Election," *Washington Post,* June 29, 2006.

[10] *The Tharwa Project,* http://www.tharwaproject.com/node/1859.

[11] Ammar Abdulhamid, "Will Syria be Next?" *Korea Herald,* April 7, 2003.

[12] Ammar Abdulhamid, "Syria's Year of Living Dangerously," *Daily Star (Beirut, Lebanon),* March 27, 2004.

[13] Ammar Abdulhamid, "Out of the Dark: Syria's Kurdish Question Reborn," April 9, 2004.

[14] Yigal Schleifer, "The Young Syrian," *Jerusalem Report,* April 19, 2004, p. 24.

[15] Ammar Abdulhamid, "Misreading the Sanctions Message," *Daily Star*, May 18, 2004.

[16] Ammar Abdulhamid, "Prepare for When the Arab Bottle Breaks," *Daily Star*, June 30, 2004.

[17] Ammar Abdulhamid, "A Distrustful Washington Eyes Syria," *Daily Star*, July 13, 2004.

[18] Nora Boustany, "A Modernizer challenges Syria's Old Order," July 30, 2004, p. A14.

[19] Ammar Abdulhamid, "Will the Syrian Regime Take on the World?" *Daily Star*, September 3, 2004.

[20] Ammar Abdulhamid and Elias Aoun, "Syrian-Lebanese Relations: The Time for Sacrificing is Over," *Daily Star*, October 22, 2004.

[21] Frank Langfitt, "Scholar Criticizes Islamic World, War on Terror," *Baltimore Sun*, September 13, 2004, p. 2B.

[22] "Muslims Against Terrorism," Radio Scripts—On the Line 1-01570, *Voice of America News*, September 26, 2004.

[23] Ammar Abdulhamid, "Stop Splitting Hairs on 'Terrorism,'" *Daily Star*, December 11, 2004.

[24] Corine Hegland, "Is Syria in Washington's Gun Sights?" *National Journal*, vol. 36, no. 51 (December 18, 2004).

[25] Lee Smith, "A Liberal in Damascus," *New York Times*, February 13, 2005. Section 6., p. 18.

[26] Katherine Zoepf, "In Syria, Building a Civil Society Book by Book," *Chronicle of Higher Education*, January 14, 2005, p. 33.

[27] Ammar Abdulhamid, "Syrian Media Reform: A Glass Half Full or Half Empty?" *Daily Star*, February 5, 2005.

[28] Ammar Abdulhamid, "Reform Starts with Lebanon Withdrawal," *Daily Star*, February 22, 2005.

[29] Ammar Abdulhamid, "Syria's Salvation is Through Reform," *Daily Star*, February 12, 2005.

[30] "Syrian Leader Faces a Pivotal Moment," *Cox News Service*, March 10, 2005.

[31]Ewen Macaskill [earlier spelled MacAskill], "Assad Wins Street Victory but not the War," *Guardian (London)*, March 12, 2005, p. 19.

[32]"Exclusive: Jerusalem Post Correspondent Reports from Syria. How Syria's Web Hackers are Outsurfing the Mukhabarat," *Jerusalem Post*, March 17, 2005, p. 1.

[33]"Exclusive: Jerusalem Post Correspondent Reports from Syria. How Syria's Web Hackers are Outsurfing the Mukhabarat," *Jerusalem Post*, March 17, 2005, p. 1.

[34]Ewen Macaskill, "Assad Wins Street Victory but not the War," *Guardian (London)*, March 12, 2005, p. 19.

[35]"Exclusive: Jerusalem Post Correspondent Reports from Syria. How Syria's Web Hackers are Outsurfing the Mukhabarat," *Jerusalem Post*, March 17, 2005, p. 1.

[36]Lee Smith, "A Liberal in Damascus," *New York Times*, February 13, 2005. Section 6., p. 18.

[37]"Syrian Elector Provides Continuous Coverage of the Presidential Referendum." Syrian Elector. 27 May 2007. Tharwa Project. Accessed: 29 Aug. 2007. tharwacommunity.typepad.com/syrianelector_english/2007/05/syrian_elector_.html.

[38]Interview, Silver Spring, MD, July 18, 2007.

Conclusion: Models for a Rising Generation

[1]Ellen Knickmeyer, "Democracy Activists Disappointed in Bush," *Washington Post*, January 17, 2008.

[2]David Pollock, *Slippery Polls: Uses and Abuses of Opinion Surveys from Arab States*, Policy Focus #82, Washington Institute for Near East Policy, April 2008, pp. 39–42.

[3]John Kelly and Bruce Etling, *Mapping Iran's Online Public: Politics and Culture in the Persian Blogosphere*, The Berkman Center for Internet & Society at Harvard Law School, Research publication No. 2008-01, April 6, 2008. The estimate 60,000 "routinely updated blogs."

[4]Most Iranian sites are in Persian.

⁵*After Sentencing Abdul-Kareem and the Infidel Baha'is: They Will f*** Your Sister.* 8 May 2008. Manal and Alaa' Blog. 24 Feb. 2007 www.manalaa.net/the_heathen_and_your_sister.

⁶Kelly and Etling, *Mapping Iran's Online Public,* p. 38.

⁷"Middle East Internet Usage." *Internet World Stats.* Accessed: 30 April 2008. www.internetworldstats.com/stats5.htm.

Index

Photo Credits

The Protester: Wajeha Al-Huwaider of Saudi Arabia
Photo courtesy of Wajeha Al-Huwaider.

The Politician: Mithal al-Alusi of Iraq
Photo of Mithal al-Alusi, 2009 election campaign poster for the Iraqi Nation Party.

The Revolutionist: Mohsen Sazegara of Iran
Photo courtesy of Mohsen Sazegara.

The Publisher: Hisham Kassem of Egypt
Photo courtesy of the National Endowment for Democracy.

The Activist: Bassem Eid of Palestine
Photo courtesy of Bassem Eid.

The Feminist: Rola Dashti of Kuwait
Photo courtesy of Yasser Al-Zayyat/AFP/Getty Images.

The Dissident: Ammar Abdulhamid of Syria
Photo courtesy of Ammar Abdulhamid. Pictured with his wife, Khawla.